No Dig Organic Home & Garden

GROW, COOK, USE & STORE YOUR HARVEST

Charles Dowding &
Stephanie Hafferty

Permanent Publications

Published by
Permanent Publications
Hyden House Ltd
The Sustainability Centre
East Meon
Hampshire GU32 1HR
United Kingdom
Tel: 01730 823 311
          International code: +44 (0)
Email: enquiries@permaculture.co.uk
Web: www.permanentpublications.co.uk

Distributed in the North America by
Chelsea Green Publishing Company, PO Box 428, White River Junction, VT 05001
www.chelseagreen.com

All photographs by Stephanie Hafferty and Charles Dowding except page iv Heather Edwards,
13 Richard Collet-White, 28, 32, 207 Felix Hoffman, 31 Michael Denney, 32 Rosie Stott,
105 Darren McGrath

Designed by Two Plus George Limited, www.TwoPlusGeorge.co.uk

Printed in the UK by Bell & Bain, Thornliebank, Glasgow

All paper from FSC certified mixed sources.
The Forest Stewardship Council (FSC) is a non-profit
international organisation established to promote the
responsible management of the world's forests. Products
carrying the FSC label are independently certified to
assure consumers that they come from forests that are
managed to meet the social, economic and ecological
needs of present and future generations.

British Library Cataloguing-in-Publication Data
A catalogue record for this book is available from the British Library

ISBN 978 1 85623 301 9

Disclaimer
The information in this book has been compiled for general guidance and is not intended to replace the
advice and treatments of qualified herbal practitioners or trained health professionals.

Do not attempt to self-diagnose or self-prescribe for serious long-term problems. Heed the cautions
given and if pregnant or already taking prescribed medication, seek professional advice before using any
herbal remedies or cleaning preparations included in this book.

If you use any of the information given in this book or recommend it to others, the author and the
publisher assume no responsibility for your actions.

So far as the author and publisher are aware the information is correct and up to date at the time of
publishing.

Contents

"The judges were bowled over by the sheer volume of useful information in this comprehensive book. Written with obvious passion by people who practice what they preach, it's full of immensely logical and clear explanations ... A hugely practical book that is perfect for anyone interested in growing their own veg."

Judges' statement on *No Dig – Organic Home & Garden*,
winner of The Peter Seabrook Practical Book of the Year Award
at The Garden Media Guild Awards, 23rd November 2017

About the Authors

Charles Dowding is a pioneer of organic and no dig growing since 1983, creating and cropping four market gardens, the largest of seven acres. He has written nine books, including the best-selling *Organic Gardening – The Natural No-Dig Way*. He runs a busy YouTube channel and teaches extensively at home and abroad.

Stephanie Hafferty is an organic no dig kitchen gardener, writer and chef, specialising in seasonal plant based food. She is passionate about sharing her knowledge of growing and cooking to feed families and communities. Stephanie regularly writes for *Permaculture* magazine, gives talks, workshops and courses on food growing, seasonal cooking and making potions. Stephanie lives as self sufficiently as possible, growing on her allotment and in her smallish garden at her ex-council home.

Introduction
by Charles & Steph

If only they could talk, and yet, plants do tell us a lot. In this book we condense our observing and responding into key insights that help you reach the heart of the matter, those essential and simplest methods for achieving great harvests.

A beautiful method

Growing food is often presented as a list of procedures. Life is snuffed out of the process, rules are given, but the reasons not always explained, or not logically explained, and digging tops that list. The conventional method of learning by rote reduces connection and interest, yet you the gardener need to be and feel intimately involved.

Gardening is about learning and enhancing natural processes. Using the methods we explain, you will understand what you need to do, when to do it, and in the quickest way, whether it's preparing ground, sowing, weeding or harvesting. If you have time to be creative, even the difficult vegetables grow easily, and billions of lively organisms in the soil are smiling with you.

No dig is key to growing healthy plants while also saving time, and it's just the best method for building an empathy with nature's ways. The health and vigour of your plants show that they like this approach, and observing the details of how they grow is your best way of doing a 'soil test'. That is another complication which confuses many, and it may even be a barrier to the gardener's involvement. Use the first two chapters here to familiarise yourself with soil and site, in order to discover its potential.

Appropriate skills, empowering results

We want you to learn appropriate skills, the ones that make the most difference, for the least effort and time. We have much feedback to illustrate this:

- "I just finished my first no-dig bed. From grass to planted squash in a couple of hours. I highly recommend this approach. It saves time and I need to save time. Also I can grow as I'm developing the plot. No need to create a blank canvas." (Gary, Leicester)

- "My results speak for themselves as I apply what you say. I work full time and can only garden on weekends, however, from May through October I did not have to once go to a grocery store (living in the Midwest of the US). Few people can say that in the area where I live." (Christine Beauchamp)

- "I have a postage stamp plot but with your technique I was able to grow several hundred pounds of produce." (Linda, Philadelphia)

- "Barely a weed in sight anywhere! No dig rocks." (Leila, Bristol)

More time, fewer problems

No dig is a straightforward method. Clearing weeds by mulching is usually the first and sometimes most difficult part, so we cover that in detail. Cover is the appropriate word; mulching means that soil does not need to recover after digging.

In contrast, when you disturb soil, its organisms feel disturbed (those that survive), and one way they recover is through growth of weeds, which in this case serve as healing plants. The words reveal all: disturbed soil needs to recover.

The beauty of no dig is that weeds are not needed for healing, so they grow less. After a thorough mulch, your weeds have disappeared and soil organisms are busy in their role of making growth possible, without having been disturbed. You can be creative, especially when the soil is fed and protected with a compost mulch, creating a lovely dark soil surface.

Visitors to Homeacres sometimes ask, "But where is your mulch; the soil is bare?" In damp climates, where slugs are potentially a problem, compost is the mulch you need, rather than undecomposed materials such as hay and straw which harbour many slugs. So we have adapted the mulch material, the soil food, to the damp climate of southwest UK and its potential pests. Each climate has its appropriate mulch.

We give advice to help you design your own best approach, from observing and understanding the climate and soil where you are. Then you are adaptable and can work out the best methods for your conditions.

This all means that our advice is useful across a range of climates. We are in zone 8/9, so timings and dates suit those conditions. But the approach is widely adjustable, as shown by the comments above. You can be creative, and have more fun with your gardening.

No dig rocks

With this book you can experience growing and eating through all four seasons. All of them. We show you methods of growing year round, with great results from less effort. Enjoy preparing, storing and preserving the food that you grow so that you can enjoy the flavour and goodness of homegrown food for a healthy, varied diet even during the hungry gap in spring. In addition, we give ideas for selling and trading your surplus.

We show you ideas for making useful equipment for your home and garden using upcycled items, making more use of your stuff. Our recipes for the kitchen, home, garden and body use homegrown and foraged plants. We also help you find new ways of reducing waste to boost your budget, and skills which enable you to become more self reliant, even in small spaces.

We explore ways of making your garden a closed loop system and, through your growing, how you can become more involved in and benefit your community. Discover the pleasure, happiness, feeling of empowerment and connection with the environment from working with nature and letting her guide you. Creatively, enjoyably.

American cup measures

We have used American cups in many of the recipes. Where cups are mentioned, we are using a 236ml (8floz) measuring cup.

Chapter 1
Growing Skills

The straight path to success

Even more than you need land, tools, seeds and compost, you need skills to create a garden, and to keep the soil healthy and full of plants.

On the one hand it's true that plants want to grow and that "all we need to do is encourage them". On the other hand, there is an amazing amount we can do to help plants grow more healthily, productively and for longer.

This plot is super abundant during its second summer, 20 months after a first mulching to clear the grass and weeds

Increasing success

This book is about

- Growing more food in less space and time
- Storing it if needed
- Preparing it in simple yet exciting ways
- Other uses for garden plants.

Follow the advice to create wellbeing and beauty in your plants and in yourself. Create a loop of positive feedback between healthy microbes in soil and the same ones in your gut. Then you have good 'gut feelings' about how to live, work and eat better.

Climate zones

The cropping and timing details are based on a mild, oceanic climate of zone 8-9, with some advice specific to those temperatures and moisture levels. The growing principles are similar in most middle zones, but some details need adapting for different climates.

Charles learnt this in his first year of market gardening, when adopting Ruth Stout's recommendation of a hay mulch for undug soil. It worked so well in her dry climate with cold winters, but bred an epidemic of slugs in Somerset's damp conditions.

The basics

These skills and understandings are your passport to better results for less effort. Some of them are importantly different to what you may have read elsewhere, but advice on growing has been skewed by many factors. All the advice here is based on results, what has been proven to work, and work well, over decades of growing.

Feed soil to feed plants

Vegetables are hungry plants and have potential to reward us with abundant growth, in undug and well fed soil, without using any synthetic feeds or fertilisers. Mulch with organic matter to feed soil in general, rather than plants specifically. It's an important difference, unknown to salesmen of fertilisers.

Soil fed with organic matter holds nutrients in stable, water-insoluble form, like a well-stocked larder. Then, when growing conditions arrive and coincide with plant roots seeking the means to grow, soil organisms increase in vigour and help roots to access nutrients, and moisture too.

From top:

Starting point late November: overgrown edges including Gert's fence, weedy soil

Weeds cut down, roots left in soil, mulched with card, brush, compost

By late May there are pea shoots to pick with garlic and onions growing well

Onion harvest from the far end of this area, early August

These mechanisms of plant growth are busiest in undisturbed soil, where life both visible and invisible has not been damaged by mechanical interventions.

No dig

After digging and tilling you see chopped earthworms and fleeing spiders, but what you don't see is even worse: the damage to soil's invisible inhabitants. Fungi are probably the main victims of cultivation, in particular mycorrhizal fungi that are killed by contact with air, not to mention from being cut in pieces.

Some gardeners claim that no dig is lazy, but they are crazy; it's about directing effort to where it's most useful. For example, leave mycorrhizal fungi undisturbed and they grow into great allies for plant roots, helping them to find food and moisture. Feed them with organic matter, and they can then work to feed your plants.

Less interventions bring benefits such as fewer weeds and better moisture retention. It's unfortunate that many gardeners have been taught to believe the importance of loosening and aerating soil, and they are therefore puzzled by the success of a no dig approach.

Some gardeners and growers use forks or two-handled broadforks, with results that please them, and without inversion of soil.

At Homeacres, a three year trial of the same vegetables in forked and unforked soil shows lower yields on the forked strip. The forking is to a depth of 25cm (10in), and precedes each planting.

Strips 2 x 9m (6.5 x 29.5ft)	Forked, 5cm (2in) mulch of compost, kg (lb)	No dig, 5cm (2in) mulch of same compost
Harvests 2014	67.92 (149.7)	78.55 (173.2)
Harvests 2015	90.23 (198.9)	101.71 (224.2)
Harvests 2016	120.33 (265.3)	142.14 (313.4)
3 year total kg (lb) trimmed veg	**278.48 (613.9)**	**322.40 (710.8)**

In untilled soil, pathogens have reduced access to plant leaves and roots thanks to extra vigour imparted by the mycorrhizal, and other beneficial fungi. In July 2016, Charles noticed a trial bed of potatoes in forked soil suffered late blight, while those in adjacent beds of untilled soil stayed healthy.

Forking trial October, forked strip on left, no dig on right, same compost

forked | no dig

Where soil structure has been squashed and broken by machines, forking may be worthwhile, just once. Then mulch with organic matter and leave soil life to re-establish the structure.

Details of setting up a garden without disturbing soil, and maintaining soil in a super healthy state, are in Chapter 3.

Where to grow in relation to other plants

Maximise the chances for healthy growth, for example by choosing the most suitable part of your ground for the most demanding plants, which are vegetables and fruits. Site them as far as possible from tall, woody plants, whose roots travel horizontally over a long distance, taking food and moisture during their growing season, as well as casting shade.

No dig means that woody roots from nearby plants can be more interruptive than when soil is dug. Where there is an edge to woody growth beyond, you could use a sharp spade to cut a line through soil every year, to reduce loss of moisture and nutrients to bushes and trees.

If you create a forest garden, the same principle applies: there is compromised growth at lower levels. On the other hand, there is a wider range of food. The established roots of perennial vegetables cope better with the demands of nearby woody plants, so it's best to site them accordingly, and grow annual vegetables where there are few or no roots of trees and shrubs.

Compost and organic matter for food crops

It's your call whether to import organic matter to a vegetable plot from elsewhere, which some claim is 'robbing fertility from another area'. Nonetheless vegetables need high fertility to prosper, and there are enterprises which generate organic waste such as stables, municipal composting, mushroom farms, tree and hedge pruning, for which vegetable growing is a suitable beneficiary.

Some gardens grow enough organic matter (grass, prunings, leaves, wastes) to feed the soil of a food plot from their own garden, although this still involves exporting organic matter from one area of the garden to another!

Nonetheless at Homeacres, Charles has noticed an increasing abundance of grass from the edges he mows, despite taking all the grass for composting. The soil is benefiting from fertility dropping off gardeners' boots, and from twice-yearly spreading of tiny amounts of biodynamic horn manure (preparation 500); see Suppliers page 211.

An 'appropriate amount of mulch for growing food' will vary from place to place, based on the understanding that soil kept healthy and fertile with an annual feed of organic matter will repay you for the effort and/or cost, many times over. Plus it depends how high a yield of food you want, from a given area.

Sowing and planting skills

If you are used to sowing seeds into tilled soil, it can seem strange in no dig that one is sowing into a surface mulch. The composition of this mulch will vary according to climate in particular.

In Somerset we sow into compost only, with no unrotted organic matter nearby, in order that slug numbers do not reach a level where seedlings get eaten. In drier areas or where cold winters kill the slugs, you can sow into drills between less decomposed mulches. Even woody mulches can work, but avoid undecomposed wood in the ingredients for making beds.

Check which mulches are suitable for your climate, in order to enjoy that great feeling when you sow seeds and they pop up quickly and evenly. When they don't, you have not only lost

White mustard sown for green manure, and salad mustard Green in the Snow planted beyond, then salad rocket

Broad beans in soil with wood shavings still decomposing at root level, showing yellow especially on left, and the crop was poor

Raking the compost surface before planting, to level and disturb, and kill any tiny weed seedlings

time and seeds, but are also wasting the precious resource of healthy soil lying idle, and suitable weather for growing.

You can sow either directly in the ground, or into trays and pots undercover. Sowing in a protected environment involves some trouble and expense, but results in even germination, strong early growth and a full garden over a longer period.

There are skills to learn about setting plants into mulched soil, such as how big the plants are, how deep to set them, whether to water in or not, and how to protect after planting (or not) from weather and pests. Each of these little things add up to big differences in growth – see Chapter 4 for more on sowing and planting.

Stay ahead of weeds

Weeds have potential to smother food plants and to propagate so fast that subsequent cropping becomes difficult and time consuming. Fortunately, no dig is a huge asset for having less weeds, because of undisturbed soil's propensity to germinate fewer weed seedlings.

Being on top of weed growth is a key timesaver, and means more food to eat from a smaller area. In the vegetable plot, clean soil allows more creativity. For example you can easily interplant more vegetables to boost yields with double cropping, instead of having to keep removing weeds.

Away from your cropped areas, allow weeds to grow in a designated wild zone(s), where they attract beneficial insects.

Weeds are specific to soil and climate: learn about local weeds, how they grow and reproduce, and learn also to differ-

entiate between annuals and perennials. Mulch appropriately to clear perennial weeds, especially when clearing ground. Deal with seedlings of annual weeds when they are tiny, in a 'little and often' approach.

The first season of mulching weedy soil needs special care (see Chapter 3). Once soil is clean and left undisturbed, you discover the joy of having more time to grow and harvest, then resowing and replanting into always-clean soil.

Dealing with pests and diseases

As with weeds, these can appear 'out of nowhere', or so it seems at the time.

Yet the common pests and diseases follow seasonal cycles of increase and decline, so you need to know the timings and likelihood of these in your area. Sow at times that heighten the chance of avoiding problems, and sometimes you can prevent damage by using covers and deterrents.

Vegetables suffer pests and diseases according to their family; see the table on spacings, page 30 (Chapter 4). This is empowering knowledge, for example, it helps you decide how often to 'rotate' crops from one place to another, see page 29, Chapter 4.

Skills for harvesting

Good picking is one of the most useful skills of edible gardening. It keeps your plants healthy, and cropping continuously. Plus, while harvesting delicious food, you tidy plants by removing any damaged or rotting leaves, which otherwise provide habitat for slugs and other pests, and it's a chance to check whether plants need watering, staking or protection from pests.

When harvesting food we always have two buckets – one for the crops and the other for the compost bin. Into the latter go damaged leaves, the odd weed if we spot one, slugs, caterpillars etc. Be thorough when harvesting; so as to encourage new growth: search for hidden fruits of summer squash, beans and peas, often obscured by leaves.

Interplant of spring onion and celeriac: this would be difficult if weeds kept germinating. Both planted late spring, then spring onions are harvested before the celeriac leaves cover over.

Grenoble Red lettuce before and after picking the outer leaves, one of 14 weekly picks

Regularity of picking depends on the type of plant and season. In order to keep plants producing and in good condition, harvest when they are ready even if you do not need the crop – spare food can be preserved (see Chapter 10), traded and shared, fed to animals or composted. Some vegetables can quickly 'go over' if not harvested regularly, producing seed and thinking that their job is done, or growing to enormous proportions, so regular picking in summer months is a great habit to acquire.

Longer, fuller seasons of harvest

At both ends of the growing season, have your ground as full as possible of edible plants. In spring this will be only a few, suitable vegetables but in autumn, all areas can be growing a crop, or green manure. Skills include learning the best times to sow each vegetable, especially for the second sowings of summer and autumn, and quick methods of clearing ground after harvests, which is easy with undug soil.

Sow seeds in autumn of vegetables that have a chance in your climate of surviving winter as small plants. They grow more quickly to harvest the following spring, than when started from seed in spring.

Harvesting leeks in spring

Homeacres compost heaps in late summer; nearest heap is six weeks from starting

Same beds (see page 6) 10 months later with second crop of salads after broad beans and peas

You can also extend the harvest season by growing some perennial plants, many of which crop in the hungry gap of spring. At that time, most spring-sown vegetables have not grown enough to crop, until summer is underway.

Lastly, a protected space of glass or polythene offers possibilities for cropping throughout the year, depending on winter's severity. Undercover growing can be in large greenhouses, small cold frames and under fleece or cloches over beds of plants.

Transforming wastes

Making your own compost is enjoyable in many ways, especially because you are converting waste material into something of great value. We learn something every year in the quest to make better compost.

Homemade compost may not look as fine as what you can buy, but contains many more beneficial micro-organisms. Learn about it in Chapter 7.

Storing vegetables

Different groups of vegetables store in different conditions. Garlic and winter squash keep best in warm, dry air, while carrots, beetroot and cabbage prefer cool dampness. Potatoes store best in dry, cool air, but never frosty. Well stored vegetables make the most of your harvests.

In milder climates, the garden is a winter larder of leeks, parsnips, kale and salads, which reduces the amount of storage space needed, and offers fresh produce when you really appreciate it.

Food preparation is a valuable way to store summer gluts such as tomatoes, courgettes, peas and herbs. Dehydrating fruits and allowing beans to dry on plants are further options to help every bit of food to find a mouth, sooner or later.

Four seasons, each so different

When a garden and store are productive all year, you taste the seasonal differences. Some months are relatively barren, others are wildly rich of food that offers best nutrition for that time of the year. Root vegetables and squash give warming carbohydrates in winter, then tomato and cucumber offer cool juiciness in summer.

A fantastic aspect of eating seasonally is the anticipation and appreciation of new flavours in every month, especially in late spring to early summer. That time offers a progression of new harvests such as peas, beans, beetroot, carrots, calabrese and summer squashes.

Salad leaves can be harvested in almost every month. See Chapter 16 for easier ways of growing the most appropriate ones for each season, and efficient ways to pick them. Then you marvel at how the bowl of leaves changes its colours, textures and flavours throughout a year.

Chapter 2
Where to Grow, Size of Plot, Deciding Inputs

Evolve a design as you garden

Neither plans nor plants are static; they need to grow together. Start some groundwork like clearing and tidying, before deciding too much. For a food garden, imagine plants growing, how you will tend them and the frequency of your visits, often early or late in the day.

Siting a plot for growing

Proximity to dwelling

Since vegetables can give a high yield of food, and often require attention, it's worth giving them a favoured location near to home. Sometimes it makes all the difference to a crop's success that you notice and remedy some recent pest damage, or that harvests are ready and risk spoiling if not taken. The more frequently you can be there, if only for brief visits, the better it is.

Soil, slope, aspect

Soil cannot be changed, but we can improve it. Before starting it helps to know if the soil is sticky or crumbly, rich or thin, soggy or sandy, rocky or clear of stones. Dig a small hole to see.

Then look at the size and growth of all plants, beyond your area too. If they are generally large and of rich colour, soil fertility is already high and you need less additions of organic matter. Otherwise, for vegetables especially, you need extra mulches to build fertility from the top.

Dibbing holes in a new bed

Clockwise from top left:

A good site for a new bed

Bed filled and ready to plant or sow

All sown and planted, frost in mid May

Early July growth is strong, netted too

Winter salads planted August, early September

Salads by late
October, some
grew all winter

- If on a steep slope, you could make terraced beds with higher sides along their bottom edge. For a larger area, get a quote for a digger to scrape out a level terrace or two, which may seem a big job at the time but will repay you with extra crops and time saved.

- On gentle slopes and in temperate areas of no exceptional rainfall, it works best to have beds running up and down the slope, rather than across it. Charles has done this for many years, so that when both watering and spreading compost, any excess runs down a bed rather than into a path below.

In high latitudes an aspect towards the midday sun is best, but not vital. One of Charles' successful gardens was on an 8 degrees slope facing away from the midday sun, at 51 degrees latitude.

Homeacres grass, weeds and conifers, November 2012: I had the conifers cut down and planted apple trees

For a family of four, consider a total cropped area, including paths and edges, of around 46sq.m (500sq.ft). This could give 280kg (617lb) vegetables per year if you double crop and all grows as it should. In cooler climates and when growing lower-yielding vegetables, you could expect half this amount of produce.

Nearby trees and shrubs, edges

For most food crops, nearby trees and hedges will compete for moisture in summer and for light when in leaf. Woody plants send horizontal roots further than they are high; for example you see suckers growing from a blackthorn hedge at a distance of twice the hedge's height. Trees that root especially close to the surface are beech, ash, poplar, maple, sycamore and willow – and 90% of all tree roots are in the top 0.6m (2ft) of soil.*

Here are some options to lessen the effect:

- Site food plants away from woody ones

- Grow plants tolerant of shade, leafy vegetables in particular

- Prune the trees and hedges that are too close, for example by coppicing.

See the footnote for more on tree roots.

All in one place

Food growing in one, compact area saves time and makes it easier to protect from pests. Plus it reduces the amount of edges, which take time to maintain.

Structures with protective edges can stand in their own areas, such as polytunnels and greenhouses. Likewise established fruit trees other than on dwarfing rootstock, and some perennial vegetables.

* www.forestry.gov.uk/fr/infd-5w2le6

Size of plot

See how much food you can harvest off a small to medium area, before creating a large one. To give an idea, the average yield of Homeacres beds over a whole season is around 10kg/m² (2lb/ft²) and this figure allows for the width of a path beside each bed. Yields for vegetables such as carrots, lettuce and beetroot can be as high as this in just half a season, while Brussels sprouts yield less and they take a whole season to grow (see Chapters 14 and 15 for yield figures).

You can increase harvests over a whole season by re-sowing and planting in summer, as soon as or even before a first harvest is taken. For example carrots sown between spring lettuce give a combined yield of up to 12kg/m² (2.4lb/ft²) in autumn, adding to a similar yield of lettuce leaves in spring and early summer, from the same area.

Inputs needed

The first year of setting things up is demanding of time and resources; it's about investing in the plot. Get things right in the first year and life becomes more easily bountiful thereafter. Inputs of organic matter at this stage are the most worthwhile investment.

Importing less resources is worthwhile, but does require more time, for example that you learn extra skills such as seed saving. Self sufficiency is more viable in a community, where for example there can be a composting operation, tool sharing, and extra labour at key moments.

Time

Create time by avoiding unnecessary jobs such as digging and tilling. As well as the time you gain by not disturbing soil, you save even more time in the growing season because there is less need for weeding and watering. Likewise, you don't need to wash and sterilise pots before reuse, or to water plants every day, or to separate perennial weeds before filling the compost heap.

Gardening has been made more complicated than it needs to be, and myths have accumulated around jobs you are supposed to do. Be wary of 'advice' from those who want to sell more products or promote their methods. Gardening literature is full of much-repeated nonsense such as the supposed danger of watering plants in sunlight, and the supposed forking of carrots after spreading compost (they don't when compost is on the surface).

The main timesaver is to crop a smaller area more efficiently, with soil in peak health and plants growing throughout the season.

Organic matter

In some form or other you need this for vegetables in particular, because they respond so well, and more than repay the time and cost. Well fed soil grows less weeds, holds more moisture and crops for longer, so you need a smaller area to grow the same food.

A trial

To see what difference of growth there might be, following addition of a layer of compost, we set up two strips of ground in February 2013, both 2×9m (6.5×29.5ft). The soil is dense silt with a loamy surface, and was growing grass and perennial weeds at the time, so we laid 600 gauge (light-impermeable) polythene over the top to have almost no weeds by late spring. One strip received no addition of compost; the other received

From top:

After cutting ivy, brambles and nettles then digging out the main woody roots

Tree maidens planted, after laying cardboard with a membrane mulch to hold it in place

By August first year, steady growth, all M9 rootstock, but a badger has dug up the fabric

The fruit border one year after starting the clearing process, and mulching with compost

Vegetable	Undug no compost kg/lb	Undug with compost kg/lb
Beans Czar	0.83 (1.8)	0.75 (1.6)
Beans Borlotti	0.23 (0.5)	0.77 (1.7)
Squash Kabocha	2.74 (6.0)	7.75 (17.1)
Squash Kuri	3.07 (6.8)	8.95 (19.7)
Celeriac	1.14 (2.5)	2.82 (6.2)
Beetroot	20.86 (46.0)	25.96 (57.2)
Leek Zermatt	1.37 (3.0)	2.48 (5.5)
Leek Bandit	3.36 (7.3)	5.55 (12.3)
Cabbage Filderkraut	6.18 (13.7)	6.16 (13.6)
Cabbage Kalibos	0.85 (1.9)	1.14 (2.5)
TOTAL kg/lb	**40.63 (89.5)**	**62.33 (137.4)**

a 5cm (2in) layer on the surface, of aged and well decomposed (composted) cow manure.

The same vegetables were planted in each strip and harvests recorded, giving a total by late winter of 40.63kg (89.5lb) from the un-composted strip, and 62.33kg (137.3lb) from the composted strip (see table opposite).

The difference was so stark that we decided to discontinue the experiment of adding no compost, and added some to both strips.

Green manures

It sounds easy: for a small cost of seeds, grow fertility at home. However this often involves extra work and time to clear the green manure plants, also to remove any large weeds before they seed amongst the green manure. In damp climates, the leaf cover can increase slug numbers, while green manure plants with woody stems take nutrients from the soil, if they are incorporated (the normal recommendation), to aid their own decomposition.

Green manures need clean soil to establish in, so they are not a way to clear weedy ground. Here are some options:

- Fast growers, of which the easiest is white mustard, *Sinapis alba*. Sow in early autumn at 2×30cm (1×12in) spacing, or broadcast seed, to have plants as high as 1m (3ft) by winter. Frosts below -5°C (23°F) kill the mustard plants and result in a thin debris of white stems on the surface: no digging is needed and the soil now contains free organic matter from leaves and roots. Buckwheat can also be grown like this, or sown earlier in summer, and it's killed by frost.

- Sow grazing rye, phacelia and field beans in autumn (similar spacing to mustard) as an overwintering green manure: pull or cut off the bean stems in spring, while rye and phacelia need a light-excluding cover for four weeks, and in damp climates there is a residue of slugs.

- Longer term green manures are grasses and leguminous perennials, which include alfalfa, red and white clover, and there are leguminous annuals such as trefoil and vetch. These are suitable for larger areas where there is space for building fertility, while food crops are growing elsewhere.

Sowing mustard green manure in early autumn into pre-watered drills, after harvesting winter squash

Freshly cut wood chips can be used to mulch perennials

Another option comes in late summer. Sow empty spaces with fast growing salads such as mizuna, salad rocket or leaf radish, either for eating, or if you don't eat them all, for green manure.

Mulching materials

Polythene mulches are mainly to clear weeds. We use them only where weeds are rampant and particularly if there are perennials such as couch grass (*Elymus repens*) and bindweed (*Calystegia septum* and *Convolvulus arvensis*). You can reuse polythene mulches several times, but won't need to once soil is clean of perennial weeds.

Thick cardboard kills weeds and is a free resource, but the small pieces take longer than polythene to lay and to weight down. It needs careful overlapping, to prevent weed growth out of the sides, and after 10 weeks or so you may need to lay a second layer on top, until perennial weeds have died. On some paths at Homeacres it even needed a third layer in a few places, four months after the first mulching.

Woodchips are a free and useful mulch for bushes, trees and perennials. For vegetables, woodchips make sowing and planting difficult, plus it's slower to build fertility with wood than with compost.

Seeds and plants

For seeds that are difficult to save, it's worth buying good ones (see suppliers, page 211) because those little nuggets of growing information have more influence on harvests than any other input.

Sometimes rather than buying a packet of seed, it's cheaper to buy plants if you need just a few, especially of vegetables that are difficult to raise from seed, for example aubergines and peppers.

For more on seed saving see Chapter 11.

Water

In wet weather, water butts may be sufficient for your needs. However in dry weather, it's easy to empty a whole butt onto a couple of thirsty beds.

From experience of using a well and the costs of maintaining its pump, we think that investing in a water system is viable only in arid areas, for large plots, or where there is no mains water.

Tap water varies in quality but generally it is fine for back-up watering in climates where watering is not a major part of growing.

The June 2015 issue of *Which? Gardening* (UK) has a report on the growth of 40 pot plants watered with rainwater, and 40 of the same plants watered with tap water. The latter grew slightly larger, possibly because of minerals in the hard tap water and slight acidity of the rainwater.

Protected cropping

Investment in a polytunnel and/or a greenhouse will repay you over many years, because they:

- Extend the season both ends
- Allow you to grow exotic crops and of greater diversity
- Enable propagation of fine plants.

Polytunnels require re-cladding with new polythene every 5-7 years, but their ecological imprint is usually smaller than greenhouses, which usually need some sort of concrete base. Homeacres garden has many concrete foundations of greenhouses, from when the site was a nursery over 40 years ago. And there is glass in the soil.

As well as a financial input, protected areas need considerably more time spent on them because of the extra speed of growth, more picking, and extra watering compared to plants outside. In time and area terms, count protected areas as about quadruple the space they occupy. Hence they are a way of increasing the food growing area.

Cleaning a homemade greenhouse; the stone walls of its base hold some extra heat at night

Chapter 3
No Dig, Clearing Weeds & Ongoing Soil Care

Save time while enjoying bigger, healthier harvests

Preparing soil for growing is about clearing weeds, including the roots of perennials that may be invisible during winter. Vegetables in particular are hungry plants: they need soil to be free of weeds, and also well fed.

Mulches of compost feed the soil while clearing weeds, and allow you to grow food at the same time as weeds are expiring in darkness; other mulches such as polythene are useful for persistent weeds.

Weed free for food crops, especially vegetables

Weeds grow fast and multiply freely, until they have colonised all bare space. Yet to grow vegetables we need bare space, especially when sowing and planting.

Once vegetables are growing, you could let some weeds grow around them, but this creates future weed problems. Just one annual weed can quickly shed hundreds of seeds, or perennial weeds multiply through spreading roots underground. After which, it is considerably more difficult

Mulching of newly planted trees, both to feed soil and prevent weeds

First, we laid cardboard and overlapped its edges

Green waste compost on top in 5-7 cm (2-3in) layer

Landscape fabric rolled over and edges buried with a blunt spade

In August (main photo) with one plant of winter squash between each tree

and time consuming to make new sowings and plantings, compared to the minimal time needed to deal with small numbers of small weeds, when soil is maintained in a weed-free state.

Clearing weeds

The next five and a half pages are about starting with weedy soil. If your plot is almost weed free, just check the last two pages of this chapter which cover soil maintenance in no dig gardening.

Mulch materials lie on the surface and block light from weeds, whose roots then expire from using up their reserves in futile growth. New weed leaves grow, but cannot photosynthesise in the darkness under a mulch.

Annual weeds mostly die after two months without light, but it takes twice or three times as long for most perennial weeds to die. A few continue to grow for even longer, but even so a first year of mulching to starve them of light reduces their vigour considerably. Then in following years it's possible to remove the weak regrowth, either by pulling leaves or by levering some surface roots with a trowel.

Mulching options to clear ground

The tables give examples of how to use mulch materials, plus their good and bad aspects, which vary according to climate, soil and site. There is no one formula that fits all situations, so here are some options for starting out:

- If your soil is full of weeds but you want to sow and plant immediately, and have little compost, then digging is an option, to bury weeds and expose clean soil.

- If you can get hold of sufficient compost for a 10-15cm (4-6in) layer, spread it on the undisturbed weeds and (if it's the right season) you can sow/plant straight away, while weeds are dying. Money spent in buying compost is an investment that repays you for several years. In starting with a weedy plot, you need a thicker layer of compost, then in the following years you need less, as in the bottom table, below.

- Where perennial weeds are rampant and you can wait a year before sowing tender vegetables such as carrot and lettuce, polythene mulches are useful as in the top table, below. During the time that perennial

Non-biodegradable mulches for clearing weeds

Non-biodegradable mulches to clear weeds	Relative cost	Useful life	Effective at excluding light?	Advantages	Disadvantages
Black polythene	Low	3-5 years	Yes if thick – hold to light to check	Total darkness underneath	Allows no rain to pass through
Woven polypropylene e.g. mypex	High	10-15 years	1% light passes through	Allows rain through, durable	Expensive, shreds when cut
Non-woven polypropylene fabric	Low	1-2 years	20-30% light passes through	Cheap, looks nice. good with card under	Tears easily, short life
Biodegradable black polythene	Med	6-8 months	30% light passes through	Biodegradable, in decades	Admits light, degrades very slowly

> The quarter acre of beds and paths at Homeacres are clear of weeds all year round, through small but regular inputs of time, two hours per week in summer. In contrast, there are plenty of weeds and wildlife around the edge.

Biodegradable mulches for clearing weeds

Mulch material for clearing weed mass	Thickness to clear weeds	Repeat application if needed	Suitable for paths?	Advantages	Disadvantages
Compost of any kind, may be less rotted	10-15cm/4-6in	5cm/2in for fertility maintenance	Only if there are very few or no weeds	Feeds soil too; grow veg while weeds are dying	Possibly expensive; remove any perennial weed regrowth
Hay, grass	15cm/6in when compressed	If many weeds grow through	Yes, preferably where few slugs	Feeds soil, a use for spoiled hay	Cool in spring; weed seeds and slugs
Straw	20cm/8in when compressed	If many weeds grow through	Yes, preferably where few slugs	Often cheap, feeds soil	Cool in spring; weed seeds and slugs
Cardboard	Thick grades	Often 8-10 weeks	Good with shavings on top	Free resource	Remove tape, staples, needs time to secure
Woodchips, shavings, sawdust	15-20cm/6-8in	Possibly	Where few weeds or with card under	Often free, quick to spread	Slow to decompose; maybe wait a year to plant
Soil of the best quality possible	10-15cm/4-6in	n/a	Scrape topsoil from path to bed	Uses up any unwanted topsoil	Weed seeds, variable quality
Carpet, wool only	One carpet	n/a	Yes	Effective weed suppressant	Slug build-up, old wool carpets best
Newspaper	15-25 sheets	Often 8-10 weeks	Yes but difficult to anchor in wind	Free	Cool in spring, slugs, securing edges, overlaps

weeds are dying underneath polythene, you may still plant potatoes and cucurbits if you spread some compost too, as in the following example (overleaf). Also you could plant some perennial vegetables through polythene; see Chapter 13.

Mulching examples

At Homeacres the soil was totally covered by a thick, weedy mat of different grasses including couch, creeping buttercup, dandelion and bindweed (mostly *Convolvulus arvensis*, field bindweed). In a few places there were brambles and woody shrubs, whose main roots I dug out.

Otherwise, apart from two beds that were dug as part of comparative trials, none of the soil was moved or loosened in any way, rather we placed mulches on top to kill the grass and weeds. On different beds we trialled all of the mulches mentioned here, except for newspaper, for which there was too little time.

The main compost mulch on beds was 18-24-month-old cow manure, with just a few dark residues of straw bedding, and it was suitable for planting into. On one bed I compared growth in this compost with a neighbouring bed covered in home-made, 12-month-old compost, and there was little difference.

Another trial compared growth between two beds, one filled with composted cow and horse manure, the other with green waste compost. From a spring planting, the latter grew onions of half the size, before a second crop of beetroot grew equally well on both beds.

Soil/compost comparison

Using two beds of the same size, 1.2×2.4m (4×8ft), we filled one with Homeacres topsoil, the other with a mix of compost from animal manure and homemade heaps. Many more weeds grew in the bed filled with soil, while we compared growth and harvests of the same vegetables in each bed. Over four years, the results have been good in both, a little stronger in the bed filled with compost. The soil bed has been helped by a compost mulch since its second year.

In the first year, harvests were 19kg (42lb), compared with 20kg (44lb) from the compost bed. In the second year, there was twice the weight of parsnips in the compost bed, where also they suffered less canker. In the third year, three yacon plants in both beds gave 8.6kg (19lb) in compost and 6.8kg (15lb) in soil, while the oca harvest was similar at 2.7kg (5.8lb) in compost and 2.6kg (5.7lb) in soil.

Five photos to show any differences in growth between beds filled with soil or compost

Nearer bed filled with compost, further bed with soil, directly on weeds

By mid spring the growth is quite similar, same plantings on each bed

The beds in midsummer after many harvests, soil on right; the kale is vigorous

By the second autumn the compost bed is growing larger plants

In the third summer, with compost mulch on both beds, the soil bed on right gave slightly lower yields (main photo)

compost | soil

Area of grassy weeds and bindweed, first mulch of composted cow manure

Opposite:
Summer abundance; any weeds growing through holes are starved of light

1 Laying mulch of cardboard, then compost on top

2 Area almost finished with last compost mulch and cardboard to lay

3 By early spring some perennial weeds are pushing through the compost mulch, so...

4 Area now covered with polythene, worms busy underneath, fully moist

5 Courgettes planted in holes in polythene into compost overlying dying weeds

6 Mulched veg growing through holes in polythene

7 Courgettes growing while bindweed continues growing under the polythene

8 Harvest of Sarpo Kifli potatoes in late summer

9 From other end, winter squash in early autumn

A six step example

You can combine mulches to clear perennial weeds and grow vegetables at the same time. In winter and early spring Charles extended Homeacres' cropping area by mulching an area between two blocks of beds that were separated by grass and weeds.

Three factors suggested polythene as surface mulch, over the compost underneath:

- The weeds included large amounts of two vigorous perennials, couch grass (*Elymus repens*) and field bindweed (*Convolvulus arvensis*)

- There would be little time to keep removing regrowth of these weeds during the growing season

- There were enough beds elsewhere for tender, close-spaced vegetables such as salads and spinach, also for those with small seeds that need sowing directly, such as carrot and parsnip. You can't grow these through a polythene mulch.

1. Feeding soil: Charles compares options

On some of the area I spread a 4in (10cm) layer of less decomposed cow manure that contained some yellow straw. At this stage you can also use leaves and wood mulches that are partly but not fully decomposed.

On another area I spread the contents of a greenhouse hotbed, made 10 months earlier from horse manure. It was 50-70% wood shavings that looked similar to when the heap had been filled.

In one corner I also used up a compost heap which I had discovered to contain aminopyralid (see box) herbicide, an unfortunate result of adding my neighbour Jenny's horse manure to activate and bulk up my own compost.

Aminopyralid weedkiller is known to persist and any farmer using it in the UK signs an agreement with Dow Chemicals that they will not sell any harvests that were treated with it – but it seems that these are not legally binding agreements. Furthermore some gardeners use lawn weedkillers with clopyralid, as persistent as aminopyralid, so there is a risk of contamination in green waste/municipal composts if they were made with poisoned grass clippings.

This weedkiller, unbeknown to her or me, had been used on the hay she bought and when such hay is eaten, the aminopyralid passes through animals into their dung. Unlike most other poisons it does not break down in composting, but only in contact with soil organisms, over a year or more. I spread the compost 15cm (6in) thick to reduce its area of use, then grew a susceptible crop (potatoes) to learn how durable the effects might be.

I applied all these mulches in midwinter and by early spring many of the less vigorous grasses were dead or dying, while the couch grass, creeping buttercup and dandelion were starting to push their leaves through. I could have spent time removing them with a trowel, perhaps spreading another 5cm (2in) of finer compost on top, for planting into, but in this case I laid a light-excluding mulch on the surface.

2. Laying a weed-suppressing cover

I used different materials, mostly 600 gauge polythene which I had bought cheaply from a farmer after it had covered his lambing polytunnel for 11 years. The wind had caused some splits but there were still large pieces useful for mulching.

There was not quite enough polythene so in one area I laid cardboard and then landscape fabric on top. They combine well because the card stops weeds growing, as long as you overlap edges by 4-6in (10-15cm), while the membrane keeps it in place. This saves having to secure the cardboard's edges with weights such as stones, which cause decomposition underneath them, allowing weeds to find light and regrow.

3. Growing through the covers

What you can grow depends on the material, your climate, the weeds and any soil pests. We always have slugs underneath polythene and cardboard, so there is no point in planting salads, chard, brassicas or beans. Plus, these vegetables need close spacing that would mean a lot of holes in the polythene and cardboard, allowing perennial weeds to grow into the light.

So the best options are widely spaced vegetables that tolerate some slug damage. I enjoyed success with potatoes, courgettes (zucchini) and winter squash.

To plant potatoes in mid spring, I cut crosses in the covers at 45cm (18in) spacings, and used a trowel to slot tubers below the 10-15cm (4-6in) compost mulch, nestling at soil level. For the squash and courgette plants in late spring I cut round holes of 10cm (4in) diameter, 60cm (2ft) apart, and used a trowel to make holes for pot-grown plants.

4. While plants are growing through a weed-covering mulch

Remove any small weed leaves that appear through the planting holes, to ensure that weed roots underneath are not fed by photosynthesis. How often you need to do this depends on the weed roots but by autumn, most will be dead, except if there are bindweeds and marestail (*Equisetum arvense*).

The first potato stems may struggle to find their small slits or holes in polythene and need guiding through; after that they grow easily. Cucurbits quickly cover an area, provided you plant them in warmth, say a week after the last frost.

5. Harvests

Potatoes grown this way are best gathered as soon as their leaves are half yellow, before slugs damage the tubers. The date of harvest depends on type of potato, around mid-summer for second earlies and late summer for maincrops. Cut off the haulm to compost (even if it has some blight) and pull back the polythene cover, which can be reused. Potato tubers lie near the surface and you can gather them without digging, perhaps using a trowel for some that are more buried.

To harvest squashes, cut them carefully after most leaves have died in early autumn, when the fruits' skins and stems are turning dry and hard.

6. Clean soil

By late summer the couch grass and other weeds had all died, only some weak bindweed persisted, and we pulled out its surface roots to compost, after removing the covers. The surface was level, soft and weed free, ideal for a late summer planting of mustard salads, to crop through autumn and winter.

In December I created raised beds by scraping the top 5-7cm (2-3in) of compost and soil from what became 18in (45cm) pathways, onto what is now the 1.2m (4ft) raised beds. There is no need for wooden sides.

After weeds are cleared

When soil is clear or mostly clear of perennial weeds, growing is easier and you can be more creative with sowings and spacings. The most important thing is to maintain soil fertility, and to keep weeds in check. Surface mulches of organic matter achieve both of these.

A weed free surface for sowing and planting

Soil management is easy and vegetables grow healthily when you think 'feed soil' rather than 'feed plants'. Feeding soil with organic matter sustains a matrix of life, plants included. By contrast, most liquid or granular feeds, such as NPK fertiliser, do not necessarily give the balance of food needed by plants at all stages of growth, nor do they benefit the soil or its inhabitants. Instead, synthetic fertilisers risk leaching of soluble nutrients, and they poison some soil fungi.

Mulches of compost

A compost mulch is long-term soil food and allows easy growing:

- You can sow and plant straight into it
- Its dark surface warms readily in spring
- It harbours fewer pests than most undecomposed mulches.

Calabrese in July, planted through a mulch of broad bean stalks

October, on left after removing the last polythene, and on right we planted salad mustards after harvesting potatoes

During winter, I raised beds with topsoil first, then added compost on top

Composts for a soft surface to sow and plant in

Compost mulches annual dose 3-5cm (1-2in)	Best for	Likely weed growth	Advantages	Disadvantages
Own compost av. 8-12 months old	All areas	Often many weed seeds	Often healthy microorganisms	Weed seeds, woody pieces and lumps, variable quality
Animal manure av. 18-24 months	Vegetables	Variable, most in horse manure	High in nutrients	Beware wood bedding; lumps need breaking
Town/green waste compost	Trees, ornamentals and veg	None	Easy to spread, good as thin surface layer	Often devoid of life-organisms, quite low in nutrients
Mushroom compost	All areas	None	Easy to spread and fair nutrient levels	Slightly high pH
Leaf mould 18-24 months old	Trees and ornamentals	Few	Even texture, no lumps, many fungi	Low nutrient levels
Store compost in sacks	Vegetables	Few	Easy to spread	May be expensive, some synthetic nutrients

Other mulches to feed soil

Biodegradable mulches to feed soil	Thickness to apply (p.a.)	Suitable for paths?	Advantages	Disadvantages
Hay, grass	5-7.6cm/2-3in	Possibly, except for the weed seeds and slugs	May be cheap, feeds soil	Excludes warmth, harbours pests, sowing tricky
Cereal straw	5-10cm/2-4in	Yes but beware slugs	Often cheap	Excludes warmth, harbours pests, obstructs sowing
Woodchips, shavings, sawdust, chopped bark	2.5-5cm/1-2in	Yes, and over cardboard if weedy	Quick to lay, adds long-term fertility	Slow to feed soil, obstructs sowing
Seaweed	5-10cm/2-4in	No	Trace elements, healthier growth	Time to fetch and carry
Charcoal	2.5cm/1in	Possibly	Weed free, holds nutrients and moisture	Brings no nutrients, lumps obstruct sowings

Top:
30-month-old cow manure. Heaps with better aeration will compost more quickly

Bottom:
Homemade compost ready to spread, lumps broken with the manure fork

Furthermore, and depending which compost you spread:

- There are water-insoluble, slow release nutrients for most of the season, available to plants as they need them.

Many composts contain weed seeds, but you can deal with them easily. The quickest method is to run a rake or hoe horizontally through only the surface layer of compost, as soon as tiny weed seedlings are first visible. This will be either in early spring, or within 2-3 weeks of spreading compost if it's the growing season and the surface has been moist. Disturbed weed seedlings die in sun and wind, and there is no need to collect them: it's a quick job to be rid of hundreds or thousands, almost before you see them.

The top table has information on composts you can make or buy, for spreading once a year. Even a thin scatter on top is worthwhile, to stimulate fungi and other soil organisms. For higher vegetable yields and double cropping, an annual application of 3-5cm (1-2in) is worthwhile.

Mulches other than compost

In the growing season, any organic matter on the surface has food for soil organisms in a stable, water-insoluble form. In slug-free climates you can use undecomposed mulches to feed soil while growing vegetables. In damp climates with slugs present, compost is best. The bottom table gives some examples, and suggests which mulches are suitable for paths.

In dry conditions it's possible to 'chop and drop', leaving the remains of an earlier harvest on the surface, as a mulch to plant through. For example the photo (page 21) is a summer planting of calabrese, to crop in autumn, planted through the dry stalks and leaves of the previous planting of broad (fava) beans.

In forest gardens the parameters are different again. In the soil is a mass of living roots and on the surface are old leaves and stems, with a constant turnover of plants, some growing and some decaying, the latter being recycled into nutrients for new growth. Imported mulches are rarely needed; it's more a question of trimming and training plant growth at the level you want. See the work of Martin Crawford *et al.*

Chapter 4

Sow, Plant, Space, Water

Increase the chances of your seeds emerging and succeeding

A little seed goes a long way when you sow in the best place and time, and healthy seedlings are then more able to resist pest and disease.

Sowings in summer and autumn are more time-specific than in spring, so plan ahead with a diary of your future sowings through the year, and buy seed ahead of sowing time.

Troubleshooting

When buying seed you can't be certain how it will germinate in the garden, because industry germination tests are most commonly in laboratory conditions. An '84% germination' rating as claimed by the seed company will not be 84% in your soil, compost and temperatures.

In the UK, seed is legally viable when laboratory germination rates are above only 70%.

A solution for some vegetables is to save your own seed (see Chapter 11). Also check the table on page 26 of average times between sowing and emergence, so you have a better idea if it's worth waiting any longer for no-show seedlings.

When the temperature is correct but emergence is thin, weak, or not happening at all, it is probably because the seeds are too old. You need to buy more seed from a different place and sow again, and email the seed company too.

First sowings and plantings early spring before covering the bed with fleece. Also this was a trial of rockdust on half of each bed

Seed freshness: 22 days from sowing onion seeds of
two different companies, in trays on the hotbed

Intersowing radish
and parsnip together

Emergence and healthy growth are considerably more likely when you sow at the appropriate season for each plant. Check the 'best sowing months' column below, and modify them according to your zone.

Sowing

Sowing methods depend on the season, time available, cost of seeds, their temperature requirements and whether you have a facility for propagation. Some vegetables are difficult to germinate and grow as small plants, so it's sometimes worth buying small plug plants.*

Sowing depth

- Cover small seeds with a depth of soil or compost that is no thicker than the seeds' thickness. For example, lettuce seeds are slender and need almost no cover at all; if you can keep them moist, they germinate well when left on the surface. The tiny seeds of celeriac and celery require some light for germination, so are best left uncovered.
- Larger seeds such as beetroot and chard can be at 1cm (0.5in) depth, while peas and beans can be deeper again, 3-5cm (1-2in).

1. Direct sow

- Suitable for large seeds including garlic and potato, and for vegetables of which one eats the tap root – carrot, parsnip mainly.
- Unsuitable for slow growing seeds such as celery and celeriac, and warmth-demanding plants such as aubergine, or plants needing much space such as cucurbits.
- Advantages are speed of sowing, less materials needed, less forking of tap roots.

* www.organicplants.co.uk

- Disadvantages are pest damage to seedlings, the chance of irregular spacings with gaps, less opportunity to weed before spring sowings, more seed needed.
- Top tip in spring is to be patient, even for vegetables that resist cold. Place your bare wrist on the soil surface in daytime, and delay the first sowings if it feels sharply cold. The spring equinox is often a starting point for outdoor sowing.
- Next job is weeding 2-3 weeks after sowing and probably thinning after that.
- Special tips for no dig are 1) spread surface compost in autumn or winter so that the weather has made it softer before sowing, 2) break lumps lightly with a rake as soon as weather allows in late winter, 3) hoe before sowing in spring, if many weeds are emerging in the compost.

2. Sow in plug/cell/module/small pot

- Suitable for all plants including many root vegetables: beetroot, radish, turnip, kohlrabi and swede grow well from module sowings, but carrots and parsnips may grow a forked root.
- Advantages include the gain of growing time from starting seeds undercover, easier weeding than from direct sowing, healthier plants from starting in more ideal conditions, economical use of expensive seed, and more chance of having full beds.
- Disadvantages are the need for potting compost, trays and a bench, preferably undercover, regular watering and ventilation. It's more worthwhile to propagate many different vegetables than just one or two, since seedling care takes similar time whether you tend a few or many plants.
- Next job is weeding, 2-3 weeks after planting, and harvests of quick growing vegetables soon after that.

Compost comparison with basil, same sowing date, West Riding on left and Arthur Bower on right

3. Sow in seed tray

- Suitable for seeds of irregular germination especially brassicas, lettuce, basil, and for tiny seeds such as celery and celeriac.
- Unsuitable for large seeds such as peas, beans, chard and beetroot.
- Advantages are less space and compost needed to germinate many seedlings, no empty gaps in module trays from non-germinated seeds, and sturdier plants from being able to bury stems when pricking out seedlings.
- Disadvantages are that seedlings in trays sometimes damp off, so avoid sowing too thickly, do not overwater, and prick out while seedlings are still small, before they crowd each other.
- Next job is pricking out tiny seedlings, just four days from sowing for lettuce and brassicas in summer: pricking out small seedlings can be as quick as sowing seeds into modules because the latter needs care and often requires a thinning of seedlings.

4. Intersow, interplant

- Suitable for any vegetable whose growth profile does not compete with the companion, such as garlic between winter salads in autumn; carrots between garlic and leaf lettuce in early summer, sweet corn between winter squash in early summer; corn salad between Florence fennel in early autumn; broad beans between corn salad in late autumn.

DAMPING OFF

This fungus causes seedlings to wilt and die within a day, and results from overwatering: it is entirely avoidable by watering less. Do not water thick-sown seedlings in dull weather, as the resulting moisture stays on the leaves for enough time that fungi can breed. A further remedy is to sow less thickly, but timely and correct watering is the main one.

Late winter sowings in seed and module trays on windowsill: lettuce, spring onion, dill, coriander

Interplanting of lettuce between red cabbage and kale, 6th July

Same bed after penultimate pick of lettuce, 15th July

- Unsuitable for plants that need light and moisture at the same time, such as cabbage and beetroot.
- Advantages are savings of time and space, sometimes better growth all round, see spacings on page 30.
- Disadvantages may be that you want to keep one of the companions growing when there is no more room, resulting in competition.
- Next job is harvest the first sowing, which allows the second one to grow and mature in its turn.

Charles' experiments to compare vegetable growth from sowings on different dates, over many years, reveal striking but variable differences according to moon phases. The Maria Thun biodynamic moon calendar works well but some of its advice is different to other moon calendars that follow similar principles. We find it helpful to structure sowings with a moon calendar, as long as the favourable moon date is at the right time according to season, and occurs when you have time to make the sowing.

Sowing vegetables

Vegetable	Best sowing months*	Best place to sow	Days from sowing to first leaves	Tips, temperatures are for 0-3 weeks
Aubergine, capsicums	2-3	Undercover in modules/ seed tray in warmth	12-20	25-30°C first 3 weeks
Beans broad (fava)	11-4	Dibbed direct or in large modules	12-24	Slow to appear
Beans climbing and dwarf	5-6	Dibbed direct or in large modules	7-10	Wait for frost free nights before sowing, 20-25°C
Beetroot, chard, leaf beet, spinach	3-7	Undercover in modules, or direct	8-14	Easy seeds with many options
Broccoli, Brussels sprouts, cabbage, calabrese, cauliflower, kale, kohlrabi, radish, swede, turnip	2-8	Seed trays undercover, or outdoor seedbeds	6-12 in spring, 4 in summer	Outdoor sowings need pest protection
Carrot	3-7	Direct in soil	10-20	If dry, water drills only
Celery, celeriac	3 celeriac, 3-5 celery	Seed tray undercover and some warmth	15-20	Do not cover seeds, place glass over seed tray, 20°C
Chicory, endive	6-8	Any	5-9	Easy to germinate, summer sowing gives best harvests
Corn salad (lambs lettuce)	late 8-9	In drills outside or in modules	10-14	Wait until moist weather arrives in early autumn
Courgette, pumpkin, squash	4-6	Modules then potted on, or direct a month later	5-10	Give warmth to seeds, for best germination 25°C
Cucumber, melon	4-6	Modules/small pots undercover in warmth	5-7	In modules or small pots and 25-30°C for best results
Florence (bulb) fennel	6-8	Modules undercover or direct	7-12	Best results from summer sowing
Garlic	10-3	Direct is easiest, or in pots	14-28+	Possible large bulbs at close spacing
Leek and onion	2-3 onion, 4 leek	In modules multi-sown, or in outdoor seed drills	10-18, if cool 22	Easy but may be slow
Lettuce	2-9	Undercover esp. in summer (seed tray in shade) or direct	5-12	None or only light cover of compost; do not overwater seedlings
Oca, yacon	3-5	Pots undercover and frost free	14-20	From roots or buds
Oriental leaves, rockets	8-9	Any	4-5	Easy to germinate, in summer
Parsnip	3-6	Direct in soil	12-26	Can be pre-germinated before sowing
Peas	2-4	Modules, pots or direct	6-10	Germinate in warmth, grow on cooler
Potato	3-5	Direct in soil	15-30	Can regrow even if damaged by frost
Sweet corn	late 4-5	Dibbed into beds or in modules	8-12	Germinates best in warmth 20-25°C
Tomato	2-4	Undercover in warmth	7-12	Should emerge evenly if seed is good, 20-25°C

* both undercover and outside, 1 = January, 12 = December, zones 8-9. See Appendix.

sowing tech.

Planting

Plants grow best when set out small, which minimises root disturbance and makes them faster and easier to plant. Three to five true leaves is a good size for salads, brassicas and beets, which should reach this stage within four weeks of being sown undercover.

There are exceptions: fruiting vegetables, such as tomatoes and squash, are best planted when the roots have filled a 7.5cm (3in) pot, mostly before any flowers open.

1 Summer sowings of wild rocket and mustard in a seed tray

2 Using a pencil to lift seedlings from the tray with all their roots

3 Lettuce, with its roots coiled into a small hole and its stem buried too

4 Spring sowings, average three per module of leek, pea and spinach

5 Early spring celery and celeriac just pricked out

6 Sowing Czar and borlotti beans mid spring, one seed per 4cm (1.5in) module

7 Grenoble Red lettuce seedlings in early autumn, 22 days after sowing, were pricked out 5 days after sowing

Ready to plant, early summer leeks, sown 3-4 per module eight weeks earlier

Long tools: homemade dibber, dibbing for broad beans

Making holes

Use fingers, trowel or a dibber to make holes for planting. Wooden dibbers of 90cm (3ft) length are quick to use, and you can make a cheap, long-handled dibber out of a wooden spade handle: saw then chisel the end to make it rounded. The point of a dibber leaves a gap under module transplants, but this does not affect growth.

Planting depth

Make holes a little wider and deeper than the surface level of compost in modules or pots, so that plants are buried 1cm (0.5in) below the module compost's surface, up to their first true leaves. This anchors floppy stems in the ground and gives stability to plants, which then grow more sturdily than plants from direct-sown seeds.

After planting push the surface soil or compost firmly downward onto the new plants' rootballs, so that roots are well cushioned on all sides. Hang on to any unused plants for a week or two, in case you need to fill gaps later.

Watering

This is worthwhile for newly-placed plants, both to give the moisture they require and to help roots settle into contact with soil/compost all round. Save water by giving only a little, directly onto the rootball of each plant.

You can water plants at any time of day, because the main volume of water is going below the surface, to where evaporation is minimal. It's not a problem to water leaves in bright sunlight, because water droplets evaporate before they can magnify sunlight enough to scorch leaves (see page 32 of *Gardening Myths and Misconceptions* in Bibliography).

If the weather stays dry and warm, water each plant again after two days, and even again two days later if it's hot, after which you can usually leave roots to explore for themselves. They will soon team up with mycorrhizal fungae, which forage tiny droplets of moisture for them, out of soil that is impenetrable to larger root hairs. At Homeacres, new plantings in the no dig trial beds settle faster than the same plantings in dug beds.

Next job

In wet weather be vigilant for slugs, and generally for any other pests that are common to your area (see Chapter 5) because new plants are more tender and vulnerable than established ones.

A fortnight after planting, remove or hoe any small weeds, which in untilled soil is a quick and satisfying job, one to look forward to rather than dread. Weeding gives a chance to check how your little plants are growing and if there are any gaps, to fill them with seedlings left over from planting time.

> The maturity of certain vegetables like garlic and radicchios is governed by day length, so they give best harvest when sown at a specific time of year. A further group of vegetables mature at any time of year, but give notably better harvests in one particular season, for example peas and broad beans which crop much more in early summer than in autumn, so it's preferable to sow them in early spring rather than early summer: the latter is possible, but is barely worthwhile.

Summer – clear and resow/replant

A fantastic part of no dig is the easy and rapid clearance of finished crops in summer, to make way for successional plantings and sowings.* Because you have few weeds, the main task is to twist out stumps of cabbage, lettuce, spinach, etc., leaving most of their roots in the soil, where they become food for soil organisms as they decompose.

- If any clearance or harvest disturbs the soil, press it down again with your foot.

Legumes

These can be cut at or just below soil level to leave roots and the few remaining nodules of nitrogen, for use by the next planting. Peas and beans which pass beyond flowering stage will have used most of the nitrogen modules for their cropping (see page 49 of *Gardening Myths and Misconceptions*), so there is little increase in soil nitrogen after a legume harvest. Whereas nitrogen is increased by the residues of legume green manures, when you cut or mulch the plants before or during flowering.

Watering

Watering is minimal for summer plantings in untilled soil, even in dry conditions. Often in summer, after we have struggled to push a dibber into the hard, dry surface, plants get away quickly in the undisturbed soil.

Weeding is minimal after summer sowings and plantings, because most weeds' seeds have already germinated and been dealt with in the spring. No dig results in few annual weeds during summer and autumn.

Rotation

Rotation is good practice, but is an over-repeated mantra. Healthy soil can easily support two consecutive plantings of vegetables in the same family, such as broad (fava) then French beans, cabbage then mustards, and carrots then fennel. All are half-year crops, so in terms of time in the ground they are not much different to planting Brussels sprouts in the spring, for harvests up to a year later.

A gap of one to two years between vegetables of the same family, when soil is healthy, is a reasonable baseline, but not a rule. Japanese natural agriculture succeeds without rotation, and they advise the opposite, called 'continuous cropping'. Plant health is increased by saving seed each year so that a soil and climate 'understanding' can build between successive plantings of the same crop, in the same place.

Write a timeline

You need knowledge about each vegetable's requirements of warmth and day length, and local knowledge, to create your timeline for summer and autumn sowing. In many climates, vegetables mature in half a season: in zones 9 or above, carrots, beetroot, potatoes, many brassicas, spinach and salads can be sown in both spring and summer. See Charles' website† for a timeline suited to zones 8/9 and check his diary‡ for seasonal advice on sowing, planting and harvesting too.

---

* www.youtube.com/watch?v=PdjtNPKd6ro video on summer clearing and replanting
† www.charlesdowding.co.uk/wp-content/uploads/2014/12/Sowing-timeline.pdf
‡ www.charlesdowding.co.uk/product/charles-dowdings-vegetable-garden-diary

Autumn from summer sowing: module-sown beetroot 14 weeks after sowing four seeds per module

July new plantings of fennel and beetroot watered in – they followed spring lettuce

Vegetable spacings (not including perennial veg, unusual veg, and most herbs; see Chapters 13-15)

Vegetables, singles unless stated	Family*	Quick, smaller harvests, cm/in	For larger plants, longer cropping, cm/in	Related tips
Aubergine	S	40×40 / 16×16	50×60 / 20×24	Check variety; some are naturally smaller plants to space closer
Basil	M	5×15 / 2×6	22×22 / 9×9	Regularly pick new stem shoots and larger leaves, this prevents flowers
Beans broad (fava)	F	10×38 / 4×15	15×50 / 6×20	The wide spacing is for longer cropping
Beans climbing	F	n/a	30×50 /12×20 double row	91cm / 36in between double rows; don't overcrowd
Beans dwarf, French	F	30×30 / 12×12	38×38 / 15×15	1 or 2 seeds per station; picking is easier on wide spacing
Beetroot singles	G	5×25 / 2×10	7×38 / 3×15	Eat thinnings
Beetroot clumps 4/5 plants	G	25×25 / 10×10	33×33 / 13×13	Carefully twist the largest of each clump for first harvest; repeat after 1-2 weeks
Brussels sprouts	B	45×45 / 18×18	60×60 / 24×24	Healthier harvests at the wide spacings
Cabbage for hearts	B	30×30 / 12×12	45×45 / 18×18 or more	For early harvests use the close spacings
Cabbage for leaves	B	22×22 / 9×9	30×30 / 12×12	Cut plants to thin, as first harvest
Calabrese, broccoli	B	30×30 / 12×12	60×60 / 24×24	For overwintered broccoli 60×60 / 24×24
Capsicum chilli, pepper	S	35×35 / 14×14	60×60 / 20×20	Space closer in cool climates, for earlier harvest before season ends
Carrot	U	1.5×15 / 0.5×6	2.5×30 / 1×12	Thin larger roots as needed, to keep a row/bed in full growth for longer
Cauliflower	B	40×40 / 16×16	60×60 / 24×24	The closer spacing is for smaller, earlier curds
Celeriac	U	35×35 / 14×14	45×45 / 18×18	35×35 / 14×14 is for rich soil or later planting
Celery	U	25×25 / 10×10	30×30 / 12×12	Closer is good for self-blanching and late plantings
Chard and leaf beet	G	10×20 / 4×8	25×25 / 10×10	Can be singles or grow in clumps of 2/3
Chervil, coriander, dill, parsley	U	5×15 / 2×6	22×22 / 9×9	Pick larger leaves and almost-flowering shoots for longer cropping
Chicory, endive hearts	A	20×20 / 8×8 and thin	38×38 / 15×15	Remove each plant after harvest to make space and reduce pest habitat
Chinese cabbage	B	27×27 / 11×11	35×35 / 14×14	Fast growing; remove as hearts mature
Corn salad (lambs lettuce)	V	7×7 / 3×3	12×12 / 5×5	Cut main head when side shoots are first visible
Cucumber greenhouse	C	45×45 / 18×18	60×60 / 24×24	Longer lived plants from wider spacing
Cucumber ridge	C	38×60 / 15×24	45×76 / 18×30	Can cover a lot of ground, or a trellis
Florence fennel (bulb)	U	20×20 / 8×8	30×30 / 12×12	Closer spacing gives thinnings first

Spacings

Plants are sociable, especially when young. Wide spacing is for plants that grow large, but they don't always like the empty space when small; plus it's an inefficient way to use precious space, and interplants/companions/multisowing solve this problem. Use the table for a start-out guide, then you can vary spacings a little according to your needs, soil and climate.

Sow extra seeds and thin, or interplant fast-maturing, companion vegetables to help widely spaced plants to establish. For example plant lettuce or herbs such as coriander and dill between Brussels sprouts and other wide-spaced brassicas: you gain a harvest, and the brassicas establish better.

Salad leaves have more options than most vegetables

For cutting small leaves, sow direct in rows 10-15cm/4-6in apart, and after 2-3 weeks thin plants to 2cm (1in) within each row. Thinning saves space and time, because any crowding increases the risk of yellowing and mildew-covered lower leaves.

Cutting is quick, but you need to remove old and diseased leaves from the harvest, and plants are more weakened by cutting than by picking. You need to resow 3-5 weeks after the previous sowing.

For larger leaves, stronger flavours and to make less sowings, space salad plants wider apart and equidistantly at 22cm (9in), or closer for spinach, chard and beets, so they have space and moisture to produce over a long period, 10 weeks or more. After each pick, plants have bare space and better circulation of air all around, resulting in less slugs and mildewed leaves. Resow 10-15 weeks after the previous sowing.

SISTERS

The oft mentioned three sisters of squash, sweet corn and climbing beans require a hot climate to succeed together, and in zone 8 or colder, it's unlikely that sweet corn grows tall enough to support a decent crop of climbing beans, before summer ends. We like two sisters in zone 8/9, a sweet corn between each squash plant at 1m (3ft) spacing. Their needs for light, warmth and root space are complementary.

Vegetables, singles unless stated	Family*	Quick, smaller harvests, cm/in	For larger plants, longer cropping, cm/in	Related tips
Garlic	L	5×30 / 2×12	10×35 / 4×14	It's possible to have large bulbs at close spacing
Kale	B	10×20 / 4×8	35×35 / 14×14	Many options; the closer spacing is for salad leaves
Kohlrabi	B	15×15 / 6×6	25×25 / 10×10	Thin 15×15 / 6×6 progressively when harvesting
Leek singles	L	5×25 / 2×10	15×30 / 6×12	Singles are easier to dib deeply, if you want pure white stems
Leek clumps ¾ plants	L	20×20 / 8×8	35×35 / 14×14	Higher yields, shallower planting, easier
Lettuce for hearts	A	15×15 / 6×6 for Little Gem	25×25 / 10×10	Up to 12×12 for icebergs and romaine
Lettuce for leaves	A	2.5×15 / 1×6 sown direct	22×22 / 9×9 planted	22×22 / 9×9 can give 10-12 weeks of harvest
Melon	C	50×50 / 20×20	60×60 / 24×24	Can be grown upwards, undercover
Onion for green salad	L	1×15 / 0.5×6	2.5×20 / 1×8	Or plant 20×20 / 8×8 as clumps of 6-10 onions
Onion for bulbs singles	L	5×22 / 2×9	7×30 / 3×12	With wider spacing you can interplant beetroot in summer
Onion for bulbs clumps 4/6	L	25×25 / 10×10	35×35 / 15×15	Less chance of mildew at wider spacing
Oriental leaves	B	15×15 / 6×6	25×25 / 10×10	Mustards, pak choi, mizuna, leaf radish – wider spacing for stir-fry leaves
Parsnip	U	2.5×30 / 1×12	10×40 / 4×16	Wide is for early sowings and larger roots
Peas dwarf and shoots	F	5×20 / 2×8	22×22 / 9×9	Option to plant clumps of 2/3 at 22×22 / 9×9
Peas tall (6ft)	F	n/a	10×121 / 4×48	One row along or across bed, needs supports
Potato first early	S	30×30 / 12×12	n/a	Grow as a catch crop since short time needed
Potato second early, main	S	135×35 / 4×14	60×60 / 24×24	45cm / 18in is a good average for most potatoes
Pumpkin	C	60×60 / 24×24	121×121 / 48×48 or more	Widen spacing to win competitions
Radish	B	2.5×15 / 1×6 sown direct	2.5×25 / 1×10 or 15×25 / 6×10 planted	4-5 seeds per module for planting as a clump
Salad leaves, many	-	2.5×15 / 1×6 sown direct	22×22 / 9×9 planted	Inc. rocket (both types), land cress, purslane
Spinach	G	7×20 / 3×8	25×25 / 10×10	Large leaves from 22×22 / 10×10 and longer lived plants
Squash inc. courgette	C	50×50 / 20×20	60×60-91×91 / 24×24-36×36	Wider spacing for winter squash
Swede	B	33×33 / 13×13	40×40 / 16×16	40×40 / 16×16 for large roots to store over winter
Sweet corn	P	27×27 / 11×11	35×35 / 14×14	Chance of 2 cobs/plant at the wider spacing
Tomato bush	S	40×40 / 16×16	50×50 / 20×20	Wider space means easier picking
Tomato cordon	S	38×60 / 15×24	50×60 / 20×24	Less blight on wider spaced plants
Turnip	B	5×20 / 2×8	7×30 / 3×12	Closer spacing in spring and for leaves too

* Plant family abbreviations: **A** *Asteraceae*, sunflower, daisy, composite family; **B** *Brassicaceae*, *Cruciferae* (brassicas, cabbage); **C** *Cucurbitaceae*, cucumber and squash; **F** *Fabaceae*, legumes; **G** *Chenopodiaceae*, goosefoot genus; **L** *Liliaceae* (sometimes given as *amaryllidaceae*), allium genus; **M** *Lamiaceae*, mint genus; **P** *Poaceae*, grass family; **S** *Solanaceae*, tomato and nightshades; **U** *Apiaceae*, umbellifer family (flowers are umbels); **V** *Caprifoliaceae*, Valerianella genus

Sowing broad bean seeds into dibbed holes in late autumn

Make more of the space: interplant of coriander and dill in summer as catch crops between purple sprouting broccoli

Spring, just planted small peas, cabbage, beetroot, shallots

Same plantings two months later in late spring – peas, cabbage, beetroot

vegetable spacings

Watering

In dry conditions, giving water at sowing and planting times is important. The rest of the time, you can water less in no dig, compared to when soil has been disturbed and its fungal threads broken, and moisture is evaporating from exposed lumps of soil.

Plants in undug soil have better access to soil moisture at depth, thanks to capillarity at low levels remaining intact, and also thanks to surface mulches of all kinds.

Follow these five steps for a water-conserving method of sowing:

- Draw drills as normal, in the compost mulch or between any less-decomposed mulch materials
- Run a line of water, from can or hose, along the bottom of each drill, until the bottom is well wetted, but not the top or areas between
- Sow seed along the wet lines
- Draw dry soil over the top and firm with a rake or by treading with your foot
- Do not water again until after seedling leaves appear.

The dry soil on top serves as a capillary break and slows any rise of moisture from below, resulting in less evaporation.

Likewise at planting time it's best to water the new plants' roots only, not the soil in general; see page 28. This requires less water and encourages roots to go down rather than horizontally.

Other times to water are when fruiting vegetables are flowering and have swelling pods, cobs or fruits.

Vegetables that need watering the most are fast growing salad leaves, and surface rooting plants such as celery, celeriac and leeks.

Watering drills for carrot between new kale

Summer sowing in dry weather, treading in after sowing

Chapter 5
Prevent, Deal with Pests & Diseases

Learn potential problems and their timings, to reduce the impact

Problems come and go each month in a mostly predictable timetable, with variations caused by different weather. You can reduce damage by knowing when and which pests and diseases are probable, and what conditions they like. Sow when damage is less likely, make companion plantings and have defences in place, before damage escalates.

Chinese cabbage under mesh for protection from butterflies mostly, 1st October

Seasonal aspects

There are two sides to this, for both pest and disease.

- **Healthy plants in season resist pest and disease**. Discover when each vegetable is fully in season, attuned to prevailing temperatures, humidity and day lengths, and therefore able to grow most strongly. Sow seeds at best times, in relation to this knowledge: for example lettuce leaves are most in season and healthiest in spring, but suffer root aphids and more mildew from late summer. Therefore summer sowings of endive and chicory are more worthwhile than lettuce, for autumn harvests (see page 26 for 'best sowing months' table).

- **Pest and disease have their seasons of main prevalence**. Know these and it's sometimes possible to change sowing dates to avoid them. For example, in Britain sowing peas in spring gives healthy and abundant harvests in early summer, which is their natural time to crop. Then both mildew and pea moth arrive in midsummer, so that although you can sow peas in early summer for picking in autumn, the harvests of healthy pods are much smaller.

Companion plants

Many flowers are attractive to beneficial insects, as well as pleasing us. For a range of butterflies, bees, hoverflies and other insects, grow marigold (*Calendula*), scabious (*Knautia*), verbenas such as bonariensis, cornflowers (*Centaurea*), flax (*Linum*), and mallows (*Malva*). Try other flowers that are native to your climate, and see what insects they attract.

Vegetable flowers pull insects too, such as the small white flowers of coriander. But some combinations are perhaps less reliable than claimed, for example we have not had success with onions deterring carrot fly. See below for other ideas on that pest.

Pest knowledge

These examples are of some common pests and ways of dealing with them, or avoiding them altogether. If you are troubled by other pests as well, research their life cycle and eating habits, then work out how to minimise their impact on your plants.

Aphids (*Aphididae* family)

Of many colours – green, white, black and grey – they live mostly on the underside of leaves or on stems, eating plant sap, which may infect it with viruses from their saliva. Damage is curled and twisted leaves, stunted growth, wilting plants, sticky secretions and black moulds.

Aphids are the most common plant pest of temperate regions and may be damaging your plants without you realising, especially in a dry spring. They lay eggs only in autumn and these hatch to winged females in spring, whereafter new generations are born pregnant.

Aphid numbers increase when they are farmed by 'dairying ants', which even look after aphid eggs overwinter and take them to new plants in the spring. Ants feed off aphids' honeydew secretions, and leaves coated with honeydew often suffer black moulds.

A variation is lettuce root aphid, light grey in colour, whose numbers peak in late summer, causing lettuce suddenly to wilt and die, especially in dry years. They overwinter on nearby poplar trees and fly to plants in late spring, then accumulate through the growing season.

Reducing damage

- Spring is the season of general aphid damage: watering leaves and soil gives best help to plants, while other options are garlic sprays, and to introduce predators on undercover plants.

Aphids are attracted to weak plants, so healthy and moist soil is a key deterrent, especially in spring before predators establish – the predators need enough aphids that they

No pest/caterpillar damage on cabbages, sown late summer to heart up in spring, with an interplanting of maca

Aphids on the parsley in early summer have brought a virus

Lettuce root aphid damage happens quickly

can feast and breed themselves. Thereafter aphids are less problematic through summer and autumn. Predators include ladybirds, hoverflies, midges and lacewings, which are all killed by synthetic aphicides, so natural approaches are best.

Water reduces aphid numbers by direct contact; even spray the undersides of leaves for bad infections. Watering plants in dry weather, when aphids are prevalent, enables stronger growth that is less attractive to aphids. These include blackfly on broad (fava) beans, greenfly on lettuce and whitefly on tomatoes.

Tunnel on 11th April: healthy growth from careful picks, sown in winter salads' best sowing time for our climate, September

Some fly damage but Oxhella carrots are very dense, they were sown between garlic interplant

You can make or buy a weak garlic potion (see page 55) to spray weekly, in spring, onto leaves and stems of vulnerable plants. Aphids do not like the taste of sap with taints of garlic, and plant growth is unaffected.

Introducing predators is viable only undercover where they remain to breed and establish; for example in spring when seeing the first aphids, you may be able to buy parasitic wasps (*Aphidius colemani* or *A. ervi*) which then establish a population balance.

Carrot fly (*Psila rosae*)

These small flies, mostly unnoticed, lay eggs on soil close to developing umbellifer roots. Then the larvae or maggots, 5mm long (0.25in), burrow around celeriac, parsnips, parsley and most damagingly carrots. Their tunnelling starts on the surface then goes deeper, especially in autumn and during mild winters.

The flies have phases of emergence, with two peaks in late spring and early to mid autumn, depending on climate, and every year sees a different pattern of damage. Some years there is almost none, which can lead to false claims of success for the methods of protection in use at that time. Other years the whole crop may be rendered almost inedible.

Reducing damage

It's difficult to keep flies out altogether, especially in autumn. In spring sow early, to harvest carrots before the first emergence, and then for autumn/winter cropping sow in early summer, plus minimise fly access with covers, barriers and companions.

Covers of fleece and mesh offer some protection; also it's claimed that flies keep to ground level, so a 60cm (2ft) barrier around a carrot bed, of clear polythene, should keep

them out. However we have suffered damage when using fleece, mesh and barriers and find that in a bad autumn it is extremely difficult to keep flies out of carrots.

There are supposedly-resistant varieties of carrot but they suffer damage too, and are often of no special flavour either. By contrast Oxhella grows fat and develops a firm yet tasty core: you can trim off any damaged exterior and still have plenty to eat. It's the same with large roots of parsnips and celeriac damage is limited in extent.

Companion planting of onions, leeks, chives, garlic, radish and aromatic herbs is reckoned to deter or confuse flies by reducing/hiding the smell of carrot foliage, but damage still occurs in bad years, when pest-free carrots are unlikely.

Flea beetles (*Alticini* tribe)

These small, dark beetles, with stripes of varying colour, can fly or hop. Main damage is to leaves of young brassica plants in spring and early summer, especially in dry and sunny weather. When not feeding, beetles hide in the soil and some of their larvae eat plant roots.

If the weather is fine and there are enough flea beetles around, they can kill young seedlings. Most problems are at that stage, whereas established plants have tougher leaves, allowing them to survive and continue growing when conditions improve.

Flea beetle numbers depend also on what agricultural crops are growing nearby and if you are close to fields of oilseed rape (canola, a brassica) then you can expect extra damage, even in late summer.

Reducing damage

- Protect seedlings with covers, or by raising plants undercover; sow less in spring and more in late summer; water; plant companion flowers.

Grow brassica seedlings undercover, especially in spring, so that they are pest free during their most vulnerable phase of small, tender leaves. Flea beetles are not adventurous in terms of entering greenhouses and polytunnels, so any undercover space affords protection.

Spring sowings are more affected than later sowings so where possible, wait until mid to late summer before sowing turnips, rocket, mustards, pak choi and mizuna. These crop better in autumn because it's naturally their time to grow leaves rather than to flower, which they do quite quickly when sown in spring.

Water young brassicas in dry, spring weather to help them grow away from damage. In damp weather there is less flea beetle activity.

Covers can help (see below) but often there are flea beetles already in the soil when covers go on, so damage continues underneath.

Having some nearby plants of pot marigold, California poppy and coriander can attract wasp predators, while companion planting of smelly herbs can deter flea beetles, but this makes only a small difference.

Moth and butterfly caterpillars (larvae)

Most plants host one or two types of caterpillar but when you are sowing in season and have healthy soil, the damage should not be severe. However there are exceptions, regional variations and differences year on year according to weather.

Butterflies fly by day and moths by night, and the latter often cause more damage. For example the leek moth whose larvae burrow invisibly into the heart of leeks, and sometimes even kill them by eating all the new leaves. Cabbage moths (*Mamestra brassica*) have brown wings and large, brown caterpillars that burrow into hearts, as do the green caterpillars of small cabbage white butterflies (*Pieris rapae*). They often cause more damage than the more numerous, yellow/black and highly visible caterpillars of large cabbage white butterflies (*Pieris brassicae*).

Some moths also lay eggs in the soil during summer and autumn, which develop into cutworms; they can eat plant stems, an outright kill. Cutworm populations are usually kept low by parasite wasps, encouraged by mixed flowers, wildflowers and no dig, healthy soil.

Reducing damage

- In zones of mild winters, grow more winter brassicas to avoid summer insects, sow kale-broccoli-Chinese cabbage in mid summer, and spring cabbage in late summer.

Pinching or collecting caterpillars is feasible if you have only a few plants. Have a good search under leaves.

Sometimes doing nothing is effective because once a few caterpillars appear, the parasitic wasp, *Cotesia glomerata*, can start its cycle of laying eggs inside them, so the caterpillars are eaten from inside: this wasp is attracted to coriander flowers. Other predators are normal wasps and some birds, which gobble them up.

Another option is to spray *Bacillus thuringiensis*, made from soil bacteria. Buy it as powder, which keeps for several years, mix with water and spray on leaves every 2-3 weeks, to give fatal indigestion to caterpillars and without harming other insects or mammals. Neem oil is another possibility.

Covers

Using covers for crop protection helps to protect plants from extremes of weather and pests and also helps to extend the growing season, allowing for earlier and later plantings. There is far too much emphasis on using chemicals for pest control and sadly disbelief in some horticultural societies that one can grow abundant food using organic methods. Prevention, observation and maintenance is better than cure – protecting plants to reduce problems is more effective than treating problems if they arise.

Most of our beds are 1.2m (4ft) wide and are straight sided, which makes them very easy to cover securely with cloche hoops, fleece and other crop protection. Curvy beds can look lovely but they are more difficult to cover and you can end up in a tangle trying to harvest and care for your veg (we know this from experience).

Protective covers are manufactured using different plastics and last for many years with care. It is more cost effective to buy large rolls and cut to size; you can share the purchase with other gardeners in your community to spread the cost. Always make sure that birds and small mammals can not get trapped in your crop protection.

Supple, bendy bamboo pushed into old metal tent poles and covered with netting to protect brassicas from birds; the flowers attract beneficial predators to the allotment

Fleece in April over new plantings at Homeacres; seedlings push the fleece up as they grow

Plastic clip and bulldog clip used to hold fleece in place, both fastened down with tent pegs

Fleece

Fleece comes into its own in the early spring, when it protects first plantings from the extremes of frost and winds, offering enough protection to help the young plants establish and provide earlier harvests. It offers some protection from wind, late frosts, cold summer spells, pests and birds whilst allowing air to circulate and around 70% of light to get through.

It is worthwhile buying a roll of the best quality; 30 gsm (0.88oz/sq. yd) is ideal. It is thicker, lasts longer and is less likely to shred, unlike cheap fleece that disintegrates too quickly. Fleece is light, easy to cut, spread and remove. Store it rolled up so that it is easier to unroll and reuse.

Fleece spread across young plants should be reasonably taut to stop the wind flapping it about and damaging the plants, but it also needs to be easy to remove for weeding and harvesting. Hold in place with large stones or buy special clips that are held in place with tent pegs. Bulldog clips with tent pegs work well too with the advantage that they are completely recyclable: fasten the bulldog clip to the cover and slide the tent peg through the curved handles of the clip.

Fleece can be quickly spread across potatoes and other sensitive crops in an emergency, if unexpected frost is forecast. Some frost damage may occur where it touches leaves, but warmth is held below so there is less damage.

Above right:
Cloche hoops made from MDPE water pipe over lettuce in front, against rabbits, and mesh over wild rocket at back against flea beetle

Right:
Covering Chinese cabbage prone to butterfly larvae, with enviromesh spread across cloche hoops made from 5mm (0.2in) wire

Netting

We use 20mm × 20mm 'bird' netting and 7mm × 7mm 'butterfly' netting to protect plants, secured with large stones or tent pegs, pushed through the holes. Netting protects against cats, birds, squirrels, chickens, deer, rabbits and badgers (to a certain extent as they can dig under it).

Butterfly netting protects brassicas very effectively. It needs to be spread across cloche hoops or frames tall enough so that the brassicas are not touching the netting – a determined butterfly can sit on the netting and lay her eggs through the hole if there is a leaf touching it. It does the same job as enviromesh but looks more attractive. The holes are too small for most insects though, so do not use it to cover anything that requires insect pollination. The difference between veg protected with butterfly netting and that left uncovered is significant, with much less damage and loss of crops.

After the butterfly season is over, bird netting is fine over the winter for brassicas. Usually small birds find a way in and out, useful for controlling pests.

The larger holes of the bird netting allow bees and other beneficial insects to gain access. It is invaluable as a way of protecting crops from hungry pigeons and can mean the difference between abundant winter harvests and shredded plants. At the allotment, during the winter of 2015/16 Steph covered all of her annual brassicas with cloches and bird netting but neglected to protect the perennial White Star broccoli: it was totally stripped by pigeons and although it slowly recovered once protected, harvests were small that year.

Bird netting is excellent to use on fruit cages to protect soft fruit. Place the netting shortly before the fruit ripens and remove when the harvest has finished, to enable birds to eat pests. Holes in the netting are easy to repair; sew them up using string.

Twigs

We found out by chance that very twiggy hazel that still had leaves on it not only supports growing peas but also protects them from pigeons. The hungry birds stripped peas growing up leafless twigs, destroying the whole crop in a weekend.

Mesh

This white, woven netting can protect against cabbage white butterfly, aphids, leek moth, carrot root fly and flea beetle, although it cannot guarantee total protection from the very small insects. Spread across the bed or over cloche frames and use stones or clips with tent pegs to fasten: don't make holes as opportunistic insects may seize the opportunity to go inside the cover. A disadvantage is that it reduces light by around 10% which reduces growth a little.

It makes a good temporary cover for young brassica plants to keep butterflies off. Use it on top of module trays in the

Tip...

Recycle old wire coat hangers or similar strong wire, cut into 15cm (6in) lengths carefully, using wire cutters. Bend over at the top and use instead of tent pegs.

Protecting a small cherry tree from birds; the enviromesh is put on just as the fruit start to ripen and removed when all have been harvested; laundry pegs hold the mesh in place, and it is also weighed down with stones on the ground

greenhouse during times of intense butterfly activity to protect young brassicas. Cabbage white butterflies will fly through open doors and windows and their caterpillars can devour whole trays of seedlings.

Mesh works well as a temporary cover to keep birds off cherries and soft fruit. It looks rather ghost-like but is effective and there is no risk of the birds getting tangled up.

Plastic seed tray lids

Plastic tray lids add extra protection in an unheated greenhouse and on young plants outside as mini cloches – from the cold, from rodents, slugs, snails, woodlice. We noticed that seeds covered with this extra layer, even those on heat mats, germinated sooner than those without it. We also use them outside on trays for protection from birds until the seeds germinate.

The bought ones have adjustable ventilation in the lid, stack easily for storage and are long lasting. You can use homemade plastic covers too – cut down plastic bottles or clear plastic trays from shops.

Glass jars are a possibility too but need removing during the day if it is sunny, otherwise the plants can be frazzled.

Polythene

Polythene is usually easy to obtain for free – offcuts from a polytunnel are the most durable but you could also try sourcing it from the packaging of large goods such as mattresses and builder's polythene that is often discarded after one use. It is always worth asking around. However this type of polythene is not UV treated and becomes brittle after one summer.

Stretch over a homemade frame to make cloches and small greenhouses.

Bubblewrap is a useful resource. Save large sheets of bubble-wrap to use in the winter as extra insulation in the greenhouse.

From top:

Two lengths of timber are screwed to the wall and the pallet is positioned up to it, not attached

The sides' base and front are screwed to pallet, the wall supports and each other; the frame is hinged to the top of the wall supports

The plywood sides are added and wooden supports screwed to the wall, for holding the top open

Coldframe

You can make one on top of an old pallet, as long as you can source a large panel of glass, or make a panel of polythene for the top. This one (below left) used a pallet against a brick wall.

1. Wall supports: cut 10×5cm (4×2in) timber into two lengths of around 84cm (33in), saw the tops at an angle to match your desired frame slope, and drill holes top-middle-bottom for screwing into pre-drilled rawl plugs in the wall.

2. Base edges for each side at right angles to the wall: cut 23×5cm (9×2in) timber for sides, screw to wall supports and pallet.

3. Screw a front board to the pallet. The photos show two lengths of 15×5cm (6×2in) timber, one on top of the other to give more height for plants, or use 23×5cm (9×2in) as for the sides.

4. Screw metal braces of 90 degree angle to anchor the sides and front to each other and to the pallet.

5. Have help to hold the panel of glass or wood-framed polythene against the wall, and attach it to wall supports with 7.5cm (3in) hinges.

6. With the frame in its closed position, measure and cut some 12mm (½in) plywood to fill the side angles, and screw this to wall supports, and to the front.

Slugs

Whether small or large, slugs and snails ('slug in a shell') mostly perform a useful task of recycling plant waste, with high populations in areas of damp climate. However large summer slugs eat so much that precautions are vital in moist, warm weather. They emerge on damp nights, after which there is nothing more disappointing than finding damaged or disappeared plants in the morning.

Reduce slug numbers by having less habitats in and close to beds of vegetables. Slug populations are lessened by regular removal of vegetables' decaying outer leaves. Where stone walls and dense bushes are close to vegetable beds, and in wet summers, active control is needed.

Reduce slug habitats near to sensitive plants

This is vital for salads and almost any new planting or sowing. Cut or mow nearby grass short, maintain cropped areas clear of any weeds, especially in the month prior to sowing and planting, and use compost as a mulch for vegetable growing, rather than mulches of undecomposed organic matter.

- In temperate climates and if your garden is shady, and/or the only site for growing vegetables is close to walls and/or leafy plants with damp areas underneath them, the chances of slug damage are

Making cloche hoops: MDPE water pipe cut to size and fixed to the ground using short pieces of bamboo

Cloche hoops are easy to use and very effective. They can be bought ready made but are simple to make from recycled parts. Here are four options:

1   Cut to size with a hacksaw a 25mm (1in) MDPE water pipe. Place on top of stakes (bamboo, wood, metal). Use crossbeams made from hazel or bamboo for extra strength.

2   Or young hazel, birch or 'bendy' bamboo, bent into a C shape, and push each end in the ground.

3   Or 4 or 5mm (0.15 or 0.2in) wire, bent into a C shape, and push each end in the ground.

4   Or old pop up tent poles cut to size using a hacksaw. These are strong, easy to bend and push in the ground.

N.B. Always be careful when removing bendy cloche hoops. Keep hold of the end as you are pulling it out so that it does not move up quickly, to avoid injury.

Foraged hazel, twisted around each other to create unique and beautiful plant supports, these made by Josh Rogers; this technique can also be used to make cloche hoops and taller structures for beans, peas, climbing flowers and over soft fruit bushes

Pushing netting back to harvest salad leaves over cloche hoops made from 5mm (0.2in) wire; leeks under enviromesh to protect from leek moth

Cloche made from recycled pop up tent poles, over brassicas at the allotment in January, to protect from deer and pigeons

Old gazebo frames make excellent fruit cages and protection for taller plants. They are easy to access, dismantle and store if you want to in the winter.

slugs

Slug damage is on outer leaves, leaving the heart clean

These slugs were under a cardboard mulch, and bindweed too!

Even with charcoal mulch and with slugged leaves removed, these cabbage are damaged high because of the nearby population. You will have more success with plants that are less interesting to slugs, such as alliums and most perennial vegetables. Consider taking an allotment, where the open nature of sites means slugs are less numerous and easier to keep in check.

Sow, plant to reduce slug damage

Sow each vegetable in its best season so that you have stronger plants.

- Plants are most vulnerable at seedling stage, so where possible use month-old plants rather than sowing direct. Module-raised (plug) plants with well-established roots can grow away from slug damage after planting, whereas small seedlings may not. We find that four-week-old lettuce resist a fair amount of nibbling.
- In damp conditions, do a quick check of new plantings daily, for example at dusk with torch and knife, or bucket. Barriers may help (copper, wool) but in wet summers it may also be necessary to use a few pellets as described below.
- After sowing carrots and salads especially, be prepared to resow after two weeks if no seedlings appear (they were probably eaten; check for tiny stems), and use a few pellets if it is still raining; see below. Or apply nematodes before sowing and planting.

Water less often and in the morning

Water less frequently and more thoroughly, so that the surface around plants is dry for longer; in dry weather the interval between watering can be up to four or five days on average. For salads it may be just three days in summer heat but in a winter polytunnel, you can leave three to four weeks between

REDUCING SLUG HABITAT

1. When harvesting salads and brassicas, have a bucket for compost ingredients too, where you put all yellow leaves and weeds (and slugs!), so as to leave no slug habitat around plants.

2. Reduce slugs in and around brassicas such as swedes, kale, Brussels sprouts and cabbages, by weekly removal of yellow and older leaves at their base, because slugs often hide under them by day.

3. Straight away after the last harvest of any plants, clear all the debris and weeds in order to have the surface bare (though still mulched with residual compost) and with no slug habitat before planting again.

watering from December to February, as long as the soil is fully moist to start with.

- Water in the morning so that the ground surface and leaves are dry and less slug-friendly by evening, when slugs start moving around.
- Soil enriched with compost holds moisture for longer, so less watering is needed: spread an inch or so every year to keep soil healthy and water retentive.

Products to control slugs

- Use in extreme conditions only, for example water with nematodes before sowing and planting, and their effect lasts for six weeks. It's an expensive method, a last resort in wet weather only.
- 'Organic' slug pellets with an active ingredient of ferric (iron) phosphate, also contain chelating agents – these are toxic to worms: see research by Dr. Kathy Lewis, head of the Agriculture and Environment Research unit at the University of Hertfordshire.* They are less poisonous than metaldehyde pellets, but use them sparingly, only one or two beside sensitive plants.

Moles and voles

No dig encourages moles by providing worms to eat, but more significantly it reduces damage caused by them. Because of soil stability, they make fewer new tunnels, resulting in fewer uplifted plants. We find that once a run (tunnel) is made, they continue to use it and do not lift or disturb more soil. As far as you can, avoid damaging their runs so that they do not need to make new ones. However should you have a particularly

---

* www.gardenforum.co.uk/news/company/are-ferric-phosphate-slug-pellets-really-safer/

pests

Clockwise from top left:

Rabbit grazing of outer leaves of carrots; stalks remain

Lettuce and endive netted against rabbits and birds

Woodlice damage to bean leaves, serrations on the edges, mostly lower leaves

Winter parsnips gnawed by rats and rotting from canker, but there is still plenty to eat

Badger damage, looking for slugs in endive

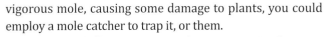

vigorous mole, causing some damage to plants, you could employ a mole catcher to trap it, or them.

Voles are a different matter and more worrying because they eat root vegetables. For example, you may see carrots wilting after voles have eaten their bottoms. Voles rarely venture to the surface so trapping them is difficult, but some peanut butter should lure them to a mousetrap. It needs to be under the shelter of leaves, otherwise voles shun it because they are wary of raptor birds.

Examples of damage by other pests

Rabbits like young heart leaves and any sign of damage tells you to cover plants with net or mesh; often this is simpler than attempting to fence a whole plot.

Woodlice chew leaf margins, mostly of young leaves and sometimes stems too: if your plants are much damaged, look to use mulches with less wood content, and remove any decaying wood nearby.

Rats cause most problems in autumn and winter to sweet and root vegetables; if you see signs of their gnawing, best harvest and keep the crop somewhere safe.

Badgers are destructive when they dig holes for worms and slugs; if present, it's best not to grow sweet corn or strawberries, and any fence needs to be very strong.

Diseases

Plants sown at the correct time and grown in healthy soil are mostly disease free. Sometimes problems that look like disease are a result of growing conditions, such as blossom end rot on tomatoes, caused by shortage of water.

Here are some examples of problems you may encounter.

Chocolate spot (*Botrytis fabae*)

Brown spots appear on the leaves of broad beans in late spring, mainly when plants are stressed. This is often from soil being too dry, or too wet! The simplest remedy, for the following year's sowing, is to increase organic matter which holds moisture and improves drainage.

Late blight (*Phytopthora infestans*)

A terrible menace for potato and tomato leaves, but only when night temperatures are above 10°C (50°F) for 48 hours, with water continually present on leaves. This allows blight spores to propagate at will. At time of writing some new tomato varieties such as Resi are offering blight resistance and are worth a try for outdoor tomatoes in areas of wet summers.

- Undercover tomatoes should always be blight free, because you can avoid wetting their leaves by watering the soil only.
- For potatoes, instead of maincrop varieties which mature when blight spores are multiplying fast, grow second early varieties such as Charlotte. They do most of their growing before blight arrives, giving a harvest even in wet summers.
- In temperate areas it is safe to add blighted leaves and fruits to compost heaps, because blight survives only on living tissue and not in soil or compost.

Mildews

Some mildews are less a problem, more a growth control mechanism. For example, older cucurbit leaves in late summer are covered with white, powdery mildew (*Podosphaera xanthii*), yet plants continue producing cucumbers and courgettes, whose growth is fuelled by the healthy new leaves.

- Mildew is rare on healthy lettuce leaves, especially from autumn or spring sowings, but old leaves are colonised by spores which help them decay, especially after mid summer. Mildew is most common on lettuce that is out of season, from summer instead of spring sowings. In lettuces' natural cycle of growth, hearts form in summer before flowering, then seeds ripen in late summer and fall down to start growth either in autumn or spring, for hearting and flowering the next summer.

Downy mildew (*Pseudoperonospora cubensis*) is a growing problem for cucumbers and melons, and can destroy plants

Above:
Blossom end rot is not a disease; it is mainly caused by insufficient water

Below:
Blight on outdoor tomato plant in early autumn

October courgettes with healthy
new fruits despite mildew

First signs of onion mildew in early summer

White rot on onions in June

completely before they finish fruiting, or even start cropping in the case of melons. Undercover its spread is reduced by keeping leaves dry, but this is partial control only, and is not possible outside. First symptoms are mottled, mosaic-like yellow patches on leaves' top sides, and black mould underneath, easily confused with cucumber mosaic virus.

Damping off is a destructive mildew usually caused by *Phytopthora* and *Pythium* families, a result of seedlings being overwatered and/or growing too closely, with insufficient light or warmth. Infected seedlings can't be saved, but sow more thinly next time and water less often.

Viral diseases

Symptoms are bright yellow streaks or blotches appearing on leaves; sometimes leaves grow twisted and deformed, often quite suddenly. Many viruses are seed borne, occasionally even on 'virus-free' seed potatoes, but fortunately this is rare. Aphids spread virus, for example when they suck the sap of parsley and carrot leaves in spring and introduce motley dwarf virus, which makes leaves stunted and the plants are then worthless. Viruses are relatively rare, and are also difficult to identify with certainty.

Disease organisms that live in soil

These are not widespread but where present, their persistence is a problem. No dig is helpful be-cause it does not spread these organisms around, unlike digging and rotovating. Increased soil health also means that clubroot in particular causes less damage.

Bacterial soft rot (*Erwinia carotovora*)

An occasional disease of many plants, especially brassicas after the bacteria enters stems and leaves damaged by insects. You may smell its rottenness, before seeing leaves turning black on their stems and then going yellow. Once established on brassicas, the plants are unlikely to give much harvest.

Clubroot (*Plasmodiophora brassica*)

Fortunately rare in gardens, more common on old allotments where brassicas have been grown for decades, often with synthetic fertilisers. Clubroot spores persist for a decade and thrive in acid soil, so liming to achieve a pH above 7 is the main remedy. Affected plants develop swollen stems and may survive, but do not thrive, especially cabbages.

A course participant at Homeacres has cured his clubroot-infected soil and succeeded with brassicas by sprinkling a small handful of 50% diatomaceous earth (DE) and 50% garden lime in every planting hole. His soil is acid: on neutral or alkaline soils, add only the DE. See page 211 (suppliers).

Onion white rot (*Stromatinia cepivora*)

You see symptoms in mid spring, when infected garlic and onions suddenly turn yellow and fall over, from their roots being devoured by a bright, white fungus. It persists for 4-7 years, waiting for more allium roots to feed on, but we find that in healthy, undug soil it diminishes to the extent that after three years you can grow alliums again in that place, with little damage.

Chapter 6
DIY Potions for Your Garden, Home & Body

Homemade
herbal potions

Using homegrown plants to make products for your garden, home and body is empowering, and enables you to close the loop at home, increasing self reliance. One feels more positive, it's economical and gives us more control over what goes into and onto our bodies and home, because what we use to clean our houses is also absorbed into our bodies. Fresh ingredients and no wasteful packaging are far less polluting than using even eco-friendly store bought goods. Making these potions is also fun and creative.

Useful equipment

You will most likely have the equipment you need to make these recipes already in your kitchen.

Clean glass jars and bottles with lids
Heatproof containers
Tea towels
Large pan
Smaller pan
Colander
Sieve
Muslin/cheese cloth
Kitchen grater
Spice grinder or pestle and mortar
Large spray bottles (upcycled ones are fine)*
Smaller spray bottles
Pump action jars
Spoons
Jug
Funnel
Food processor or blender

* I prefer to store my homemade goods in glass as much as possible. You can buy spray containers that are entirely glass and metal. Or make your own glass spray bottle using a washed spray from an old product (this part is plastic) screwed onto a recycled screw top bottle. Alternatively, reuse well washed out old plastic spray bottles.

Store cupboard ingredients

Vinegar – cider, wine, malt
Sea salt
Oils – olive, sunflower, almond, etc.
Liquid castille soap
Natural soap bars
Bicarbonate of soda
Washing soda
Citric acid
Bentonite clay
Arrowroot
Other ingredients:
Beeswax
Candelilla wax – a vegan alternative for beeswax

A natural product made from the candelilla plant (from Mexico), candelilla wax can be used to replace beeswax in these recipes. Note that it can take a bit longer for the wax to harden. I buy the wax in pellet form, which is easy to melt.

Most of these recipes involve making a herbal decoction, infusion or sun tea. The quantities vary with some recipes.

How to make a decoction

To make a herbal decoction, add a cup of chopped fresh herb (½ cup of dried) to 4 cups of water in a pan. Bring to the boil, simmer with the lid on, then remove from heat and allow to cool. Leave overnight before straining. Store in a jar until needed.

How to make an infusion

Herbal infusions are made almost as one would a cup of herbal tea. Fill a strong heatproof glass lidded jar (preserving jars are ideal) to one third full with chopped fresh herbs. Top up with boiling water to almost full, then place the lid so that all of the valuable volatile oils remain. Leave overnight before straining into another jar.

Sun tea

If it is a bright day, make 'sun tea' by keeping the jar (prepared as for an infusion above) on a sunny windowsill for 4-8 hours, depending how strong you want the solution to be.

Infusing oil using a bain marie

Place a heatproof jar of oil and herb/root/flower in a solid pan that has a dishcloth folded at the bottom (to prevent the jar from breaking). I use one of the jars I use for canning, so that it will withstand this method. An earthenware cooking pot is another alternative.

Add water into the pan up to ¾ of the way up the jar.

Bring the water to a simmer, then turn to a low setting. Leave for 2 hours, checking regularly that the water hasn't evaporated.

Remove carefully using jar tongs or oven gloves, place on a wooden board and cool.

Infusing oil using the cold method

A jar with a lid
Dried or fresh herb/flowers/root
Olive or other suitable oil (coconut, grapeseed, almond)

Fill a clean jar loosely with herb or half fill if using dried.

Pour in olive oil or sunflower until the herb is completely submerged, use a pickling or fermenting weight if necessary.

Place the jar in a dark cupboard for 2 weeks, shaking daily.

Strain through muslin into another clean jar.

Recipes for the garden
(including some for the home and body)

Soapwort (*Saponaria officinalis*)

Soapwort is a hardy perennial herb that is native to Europe. It came to the United States with the first settlers, mostly likely because of its useful soapy qualities, where it has naturalised and is now widespread. The leaves and roots contain saponins, producing a soapiness when combined with water which has been used for centuries to clean the home, body and clothes. Soapwort dies back in the winter, regrowing again in the spring, the lush foliage reaching heights of 90cm (3ft) with pale pink lightly scented flowers that bloom from June into the autumn. The flowers are edible and can be added to summer salads.

Soapwort grows well in full sun to light shade, in most soil conditions, and is highly invasive. For most gardens, it is better to grow soapwort in a pot to prevent it from taking over. Due to its invasive nature, it can create excellent ground cover if you don't mind it spreading everywhere.

Soapwort can be propagated from seed in the early spring, taking around three weeks to germinate or from splitting existing plants, watering well until the new plants are established.

Soapwort flowering in the garden

Soapwort roots and leaves

With the exception of the flowers, the rest of the plant is poisonous and should not be taken internally. Do not use the soapwort liquid to wash pets.

Soapwort liquid makes an excellent gentle handwashing liquid for delicate laundry including silk, lace and wool. It is widely used in conservation on tapestries and other old fabrics which could be damaged by modern chemical detergents. It can also be used in bathing and to wash hair. A quick way to use the plant is to rub leaves on your hands whilst washing.

> To make a cleaning solution, chop 2 cups of fresh leaves and stems (or 1 cup of dried) and add to 3 cups of water. Simmer for 30 minutes, strain and store in a sealed glass jar or bottle for a week or so. Soapwort solution doesn't smell especially nice, so you can add a perfumed herb (lavender, lemon verbena, rosemary) before simmering if you would like a more fragrant solution.

> Alternatively, chop 2 handfuls of root into 1cm (0.5in) pieces using secateurs and add to 3 cups of water. Soak overnight, boil for 30 minutes, strain and store. Again, this keeps for a week.

The leaves are dried as you would other leafy herbs, in bunches or on trays in a well ventilated space. To dry the roots, wash and chop first into 1cm pieces using secateurs (it is very difficult to chop the roots once they are dried) and spread on the herb drier (see herbs/drying, page 92) for 2-3 weeks, until thoroughly dry. Store in glass jars.

TO WASH CLOTHES

Pour the solution into a large bowl and top with warm water (at the right temperature for your garment). Wash carefully as usual. Rinse with fresh water until the water runs clear.

TO MAKE A SHAMPOO

Make soapwort solution as above, adding ¼ cup of fresh (⅛ cup dried) scented and beneficial ingredients before simmering, for example:

Lemon verbena, lavender, basil, mint, fennel – for healthy hair, smells wonderful

Horsetail – strengthens hair

Nettle – strengthens hair, helps with hair loss, stimulates growth, treats dandruff

Sage, lemon balm, lemon grass, rosemary, lemon peel – for oily hair

Burdock root, comfrey, marsh mallow, elderflowers – for dry hair

Chamomile, calendula – for light hair

Rosemary, sage – for dark hair

Red rose petals, rose hips – for red hair

Label and store in a cool, dark place. It should last 7-10 days.

Soapwort is good for dandruff and itchy scalp. I have been told it is particularly good for cleaning dreadlocks.

Horsetail (*Equisetum arvense*)

Horsetail (also known as marestail) is a beautiful plant, sending up shoots resembling tiny trees in the spring. It is a great survivor, having been around for many millions of years (when its descendants reached heights of 30 metres!) and is known as a 'living fossil'.

It is highly invasive with fast growing rhizomes and roots which can go down 3m (10ft) and it can regrow from small pieces of root. Horsetail is extremely difficult to eradicate so do not introduce it to your garden – it will rapidly take over. I am always very careful when I bring any into the garden – it is one of the few weeds whose roots I do not risk putting in the compost heap.

It is however a pleasure to forage for and so useful – I usually find mine in the banks of streams and hedgerows here. Harvest the plant above the surface (not the root) for these recipes.

Horsetail is a powerful herb, rich in minerals, alkaloids and silica thanks in part to its deep roots. It has a wide number of uses in herbal medicine including treating bleeding, bone diseases, thinning hair, brittle nails, athlete's foot – consult a professional medical herbalist for horsetail's medical uses.

Making horsetail solution

To make the tea, pour 2 cups of fresh horsetail (1 cup of dried) into a large pan with 10 cups water and bring to the boil. Simmer for 30 minutes with the lid on, then remove from the heat and leave overnight. Strain and pour into labelled bottles. This keeps well for a month or so in a cool dark place.

Pour into a clean spray bottle before using.

Horsetail is easy to dry; simply hang the bunches in paper bags in an airy place for a few weeks: it becomes brittle when dry and easily crumbles, so paper bags prevent it disintegrating onto the floor. Always handle dried marestail wearing gloves as the silica in it can make shards stick in your skin. It isn't too much of a problem for leathery gardening hands, but it is wise to take precautions, especially when potion making with children. When the herb is dried, crumble into glass jars and store in a dark, dry place. It keeps for at least a year.

Dried horsetail can be added to compost heaps, sprinkled on the soil or mixed in with other plants for a nutrient feed as well as to make the tea.

In the garden and at home, horsetail's natural fungicide properties are highly beneficial. The tea is used to treat problems including powdery mildew, black spot, mildew on roses, peach tree leaf curl and it can also be used to make a root dip for propagating. It makes a magnesium rich spray that can be sprayed directly onto plants and the soil, aiding health and fertility. The tea is ideal for cleaning greenhouses and cold frames (I make a solution of 50/50 horsetail tea and a herb or citrus vinegar, see page 56 and 115).

In the home, spray horsetail tea on mildew and mould, or add to other herbal preparations when cleaning floors, worktops, etc. It has been used for centuries as a pan scourer – handfuls of horsetail and lots of elbow grease!

HORSETAIL HAIR TONIC

This mineral-rich rinse is full of silica that can help encourage strong hair

- 1 cup fresh horsetail (or ½ cup dried), chopped
- 2 cups water

Put the ingredients in a pan and simmer for 10 minutes. Leave to cool, strain and store in a labelled jar.

After shampooing, pour a cupful over the hair and massage. Leave for 10 minutes then rinse.

Comfrey (*Symphytum*)

Comfrey is an absolutely wonderful plant, excellent for adding fertility to the garden. It is best to grow Bocking 14 in your garden. The more invasive wild comfreys are not a good idea to grow at home or your allotment, unless you have a lot of wild space that can cope with its invasive nature. Bocking 14 will provide a huge number of juicy leaves and flowers for wildlife without taking over. It is sterile and propagated from root cuttings, so ask a friend for some or buy from the many suppliers online. Both kinds have wonderful flowers much loved by bees.

Due to its invasive nature, wild comfrey is best foraged for. We harvest wheelbarrow loads from wild areas down the lanes here without upsetting the ecosystems there as it regrows very quickly from mid spring right through to autumn and beyond, if it is a mild winter. Never add the roots or flowers to your compost heap; it is too invasive and could spread in your compost. If you have a large supply growing wild locally, there is no real need to grow it at home too, unless you want to harvest the roots to make comfrey oil.

Harvest comfrey by holding the leaves in bunches and cutting just above the crown. During the summer, comfrey can regrow within 2 weeks. Hang bunches of comfrey tied with string regularly during the summer for use during the winter and early spring. Alternatively, use a dehydrator. To maximise space, crumble dried comfrey into large jars or tubs with close fitting lids. You can use this to make comfrey liquid – stir two handfuls into a bucket until thoroughly mixed and use as a liquid feed, removing the 'rose' from the watering can so that it doesn't get blocked with particles. Dried comfrey leaves can also be used as a soil conditioner, sprinkled onto the soil or mixed with potting compost and added to the compost bin to boost the process. To make a fine powder, whizz in a coffee grinder or food processor.

Comfrey is an excellent compost ingredient and bioactivator, adding essential nutrients and minerals, which draws from the subsoil using roots of up to 3m (10ft), one of the reasons why it is difficult to eradicate! It can help heat up the compost heap, reducing composting times significantly: a mixture of comfrey and nettles is particularly effective.

To use as a mulch, chop the leaves and spread on the ground at a depth of around 5cm (2in). This is especially beneficial for fruit bushes and trees or on ground that is not cropping – in the vegetable garden I find that an unrotted mulch provides a habitat for slugs and other pests so it is better used as a liquid feed there.

We use two methods for making comfrey liquid with fresh leaves. I like to make these at new moon: they are ready just after full moon.

1. Loosely fill a container with leaves, top up with water, cover and leave for around 2 weeks. Strain into another container (I use a large colander) with a close fitting lid

1 Containers packed with nettles and comfrey

2 Packing the leaves in

3 A brick in the bucket helps to stabilise the tower

4 Stacking the pots on top of the bucket

– it stores well for months. To use, dilute 1 part comfrey with 12 parts water in a watering can. Be warned, it is very smelly – wear your worst clothes when straining and using!

2. To make a stronger feed without adding water you need a bucket and one or more containers with a hole at the bottom – such as another bucket or large plant pot. They need to fit snugly (see photo). Pack comfrey (nettles are good here too) into one of the containers with a hole in and put on top of the bucket. Repeat with another container and put on top, if you wish. Cover and leave for at least 2 weeks. Gradually a dark liquid will ooze into the bucket. Use immediately or store in bottles. To make a liquid feed, dilute 1 part comfrey with 20 parts water.

To use as a foliar feed or in a watering can with a rose attached, strain the liquid through a fine sieve, muslin or coffee filter so that it does not clog up the nozzle/holes.

Flowering comfrey provides food for bees and other beneficial insects

INFUSING THE OIL USING HEAT METHOD

Place the jar of oil and root in a solid pan that has a dishcloth folded at the bottom (to prevent the jar from breaking). You can also use a canning jar.

Add water into the pan up to ¾ of the way up the jar.

Bring the water up to a simmer, then turn to a low setting. Leave for 2 hours, checking that the water hasn't evaporated.

Remove carefully using jar tongs or oven gloves, place on a wooden board and cool.

Strain and bottle as above.

COMFREY OIL USING COMFREY LEAF

2 cups fresh chopped leaves or 1 cup dried chopped leaves
2 cups olive oil

Put in a jar and use either method described above.

N.B. Do not use comfrey oil on broken skin; it is so good at healing that the skin could heal over dirt in a wound, causing infection.

COMFREY SALVE

Use on the skin for bruising, sore muscles and bones, mild sunburn, mild skin irritation.

2 cups comfrey infused oil
30g/1oz grated beeswax (around 2 tablespoons) or
    30g/1oz grated candelilla wax

Using a bain marie, gentle warm the oil. Stir in the beeswax until melted. Remove from heat.

Pour into wide mouthed jars. As it cools, it will become semi-solid.

Alternatives: Other oils that work well with comfrey to make a healing salve include calendula, plantain, lemon balm, eucalyptus and lavender. Replace up to 50% of the comfrey oil with the other herb infused oil.

USING COMFREY ROOT

I harvest comfrey root around the spring and autumn equinoxes. Dig out a good-sized chunk of root with a sharp spade and scrub the earth off in a bucket of water. Peel using a sharp knife and chop into 5mm (0.19in) sized cubes. Use the root fresh or dry (see herb drying methods, page 92).

Comfrey root makes an excellent comfrey oil for use on the skin, by infusing the root in oil. You will need:

Fresh or dried comfrey root
Olive oil (coconut, almond, grapeseed)
A lidded jar

If you are using fresh roots, spread them out and let them air dry for 24 hours before making this.

Half fill the jar with root. Pour the oil over it until it is well covered, with 2.5cm (1in) oil above the root.

Replace the lid and shake. Gently shake it every day for 2 weeks, then strain through muslin (etc.) – this can take a long time – and bottle.

Label the bottle – contents and date – and use to make comfrey salve and cream.

A large harvest of comfrey root

Making comfrey oil: olive oil and peeled, diced comfrey root

Infusing the root in the olive oil

Nettles (*Urtica dioica*)

Nettles are rich in iron, copper and calcium. Ladybirds lay their eggs on nettles (ladybird larvae eat hundreds of aphids each) and they also provide a home for many butterflies including tortoiseshell, comma and peacock. Nettles are highly invasive and grow abundantly in the wild, so there is little need to grow them at home unless you have lots of space.

I am happy to harvest nettles with my bare hands. I pinch out the shoots with my fingertips unless I am pulling up whole plants, in which case I wear thick gloves. Nettles seem to send warning messages to nearby nettle plants as the stings get stronger with each plant.

Nettles are an excellent compost ingredient and activator. Remove any seedy flowerheads and cut into 10-15cm (4-6in) pieces with a spade or secateurs. I dry nettles in bunches (like comfrey) for winter use in feeds and as a soil enhancer.

Nettle liquid feed is an excellent fertiliser, helping plants to build up resistance to pests and diseases. Make in the same way as comfrey feed – either entirely using nettles or a mixture of nettles and comfrey.

You can add other weeds and herbs to the comfrey and nettle brews, or make one entirely from the weeds, those with long tap roots like borage, dandelion, dock, plantain, yarrow, parsley and burdock are particularly beneficial.

We add raw nettles to smoothies (the powerful blades mean that they do not sting), to soups and to pestos. Spring, when the first fresh nettles and cleavers are emerging, is a good time to make this tincture with cleavers (goosegrass – *Galium aparine*). It is a good general tonic and is said to help with allergies and muscle cramps.

NETTLE AND CLEAVERS TINCTURE

You will need:

- A large jar with a close fitting lid
- Nettle tops
- Cleaver tops
- Vodka (or other neutral tasting spirit)

Chop the nettles and cleavers – you need enough to half fill your jar, so how much you use depends on the size of your jar!

Fill the jar with vodka to just below the top and put on the lid. If you are making other potions, it is a good idea to label your jar so you know what it is.

Put in a cool place, somewhere you'll remember it (perhaps near to the kettle) and shake every day for two weeks.

Strain, discard the pulp into the compost bin and pour into small bottles with dropper lids.

To use: put 3 drops in a small glass of water daily. You can pop it directly on the tongue but it does taste quite strong!

If you use dried leaves, fill the jar ½ full.

NETTLE HAIR TONIC

This is a mineral rich rinse for hair that can help stimulate hair growth, increase circulation in the scalp and help with dandruff.

- 1 cup fresh nettles (or ½ cup dried), chopped
- 2 cups water

Put the ingredients in a pan and simmer for 10 minutes. Leave to cool, strain and store in a labelled jar.

After shampooing, pour a cupful over the hair and massage. Leave for 10 minutes then rinse.

Pot marigold (*Calendula*)

Calendula is a lovely flower to grow, comes in many beautiful sunny shades of orange, yellow and red, is very beneficial for the garden and is also a powerful ingredient in potions. It is very easy to grow. Sow in the spring and plant out in the garden and polytunnel in May and June; it rarely suffers from problems with pests and is reasonably hardy. During mild winters, I have had fresh calendula flowers in the polytunnel right through the winter.

Bees and other beneficial insects are attracted to its bright flowers; wild birds enjoy eating the seeds. Calendula self seeds easily, so is ideal for wild areas too. To harvest the seeds, simply gather dried seed heads, separate the seeds from their curved, crinkled shells as much as you can by shaking, spread on a cloth lined rack (see herb drying page 92) until fully dry and store in labelled jars or paper envelopes.

The petals are eaten raw in salads and have been added to food for centuries, adding colour and flavour to rice, desserts and cocktail ingredients. Calendula infused vodka, oil and vinegar is edible and can be used in cooking too.

In the garden, calendula repels chewing and leaf cutting insects. To make an insect repellent spray gather whole plants, or break off some stems. There are two ways to make the spray:

INSECT REPELLENT SPRAY: QUICK METHOD, USING A BLENDER

- 1 cup full of flower heads, stems, leaves (½ cup dried – dry whole calendula stems as 'drying herbs')
- 2 cups water

Put in the blender and whizz until thoroughly chopped and blended.

Pour into a container with a lid and leave for 24 hours.

Strain into another container.

Calendula

INSECT REPELLENT SPRAY: HAND METHOD

- 1 cup full of flower heads, stems, leaves (½ cup dried)
- 2 cups hot water

Mash the calendula in a pestle and mortar (or large bowl using a cocktail muddler or potato masher) until well mashed together. Cover and leave for 24 hours.

Strain into another container.

Both keep for a couple of weeks in a cool, dark place.

To use:

Dilute 1 cup of mixture with 2 cups of water and 1 cup of soapwort solution.

Or, dilute 1 cup of mixture with 3 cups of water and a squirt of eco washing up liquid.

Pour into a squirt bottle and use on affected plants.

CALENDULA FLOWER TEA

Steep 2tsp fresh petals (1tsp dried petals) in 1 cup boiling water for 10 minutes. Strain and drink. It is said to be good for colds, tummy ache and menstrual cramps.

Alternatively, allow the tea to cool and soak a folded flannel in it. Place over the eyes to soothe sore, puffy eyes.

The tea makes a nice hair rinse too.

CALENDULA OIL

- A jar with a lid
- Dried or fresh calendula petals
- Olive or other suitable oil (coconut, grapeseed, almond)
- Fill a clean jar loosely with calendula petals or half fill if using dried.

Pour in olive or sunflower oil until the petals are covered.

Place the jar in a dark cupboard for 2 weeks, shaking daily.

Strain through muslin into another clean jar – compost the petals.

Use to soothe and calm sensitive skin, cracked skin, sunburn, sore skin, nappy rash, insect bites, as a massage oil and facial oil.

This keeps for 6 months or so in a cool dark place.

CALENDULA TINCTURE

Make in the same way as the oil but use vodka instead of oil.

Store in a dark bottle or jar.

Calendula tincture, diluted 50/50 with water, is excellent for cleaning wounds, treating acne, rashes, infections and minor burns.

This keeps for at least a year.

Dried calendula petals

CALENDULA VINEGAR

- A jar with a lid
- Calendula petals
- Cider vinegar

Half fill your jar with fresh calendula petals (or quarter fill with dried) and fill the jar to just below the surface with vinegar (leave about a centimetre). Shake well.

Make as tincture above.

This keeps for at least a year.

Calendula infused vinegar can be added to salad dressings. It is soothing for minor sunburn, diluted 50/50 with water and applied directly to the skin or add a cup to a warm bath. It is a good hair rinse and diluted 25/75 with water (rose water is lovely) makes a nice skin toner. Alternatively, dilute 25% calendula/25% witch hazel/50% rose water for oily or spotty skin.

Use it diluted 50/50 with water in a spray bottle as an all purpose cleaner or undiluted to clean glass, mirrors or in the fabric softener/rinse aid parts of domestic appliances.

Yarrow (Achillea millefolium)

Yarrow, of which the native white flowered variety is widespread in the British Isles, can also be bought in a variety of gorgeous bright colours – yellow, red, electric pink. It attracts and feeds many beneficial insects including butterflies and hoverflies. Grown near other herbs, yarrow can increase their potency, fragrance and yield, although caution should be taken as it is invasive. It has been used as a healing herb for centuries, most notably as a healer of wounds and is a natural dye plant. We mainly use it as a potent ingredient in composting.

Dried yarrow can be used in sachets or pot pourri to repel moths and flies.

It is a powerful compost catalyst; its deep roots bring up minerals including copper, phosphorus and potassium: the biodynamic dose for a 1 cubic metre compost heap is one single leaf, chopped up. It is often used in permaculture fruit tree guilds as a natural pest control.

Chamomile (*Anthemis nobilis* and *Matricaria chamomilla*)

Chamomile is widely used in many herbal remedies including a soothing bedtime tea and a healing oil and salve (make an oil as calendula, then make a salve as on page 62).

The oil and salve helps to soothe minor sunburn and skin problems, eczema and rashes. As with calendula, the cooled tea is a lovely compress for sore eyes. Pour a cup of chamomile tea into the bath to relax and soothe itchy skin.

In the garden, it has the reputation of benefiting nearby plants, attracts beneficial insects and the flowers and leaves are excellent additions to the compost heap. Chamomile has antifungal properties which makes it a useful cleansing herb.

CHAMOMILE VINEGAR FOR CLEANING

- A jar with a lid
- Calendula petals
- Cider vinegar (or other light vinegar – white preserving vinegar, white wine vinegar)

Half fill your jar with fresh chamomile flowers (or quarter fill with dried) and fill the jar to just below the surface with vinegar (leave about 1cm). Shake well and leave for 2 weeks to infuse, shaking every day.

Strain into another lidded container and label. To use, dilute 50/50 with water in a spray bottle or use neat to clean glass and surfaces in the greenhouse or home.

See also soapwort for its use in shampoo (page 49).

Garlic based insect sprays

These are very powerful insecticides to remove aphids, chewing insects and to get cabbage white caterpillars off brassicas and should really be used as a last resort. Indeed, the only time I have used them has been on stressed, aphid infested overwintered houseplants (it does feel strange to be dealing with aphids in January).

Usually good soil and plant care (including effective use of barrier methods) means that aphid or caterpillar attacks are minimal. However, if it seems as though you may lose a whole crop to pests, this could be a useful solution.

For cabbage white infestation, try encouraging wasps to help you first. They love to feed on caterpillars. Squashing a few on the plant releases a scent which entices the wasps to your brassicas. Wasps have an unfortunate reputation yet are very beneficial insects ecologically, not only feeding caterpillars, house and blow flies and to their young but also are useful pollinators. (In my experience, the wasps are so busy collecting their food we can co-exist happily in the garden without any problems, however don't do this if you or someone near you has an allergy to the stings, obviously!)

JUST GARLIC

- One whole bulb of garlic
- 6 cups water

Whizz them in a blender until puréed. Pour into a jar with a fitted lid and leave for 2 days.

Strain into another jar and keep in a cool place until needed.

The garlic spray has a reputation as a preventative to discourage cabbage white butterflies as the smell is said to mask that of the brassicas. I have not tried this, mainly because of wildlife concerns and it seems a bit of a palaver when good netting is so effective.

GARLIC, MINT AND CHILLI

This is for most garden insect pests, including chewing insects.

- 3-4 hot chilli peppers (quantity depends on the size and potency of your chillies)
- 3-4 whole cloves garlic
- 1 cup mint leaves – any kind of mint; it is a natural insect repellent
- 6 cups water

Whizz in the blender as above.

To use both sprays:

Pour into a spray bottle and add a squirt of eco washing up liquid (or replace one cup of liquid with soapwort solution). Spray on the affected plants once a week or after heavy rain.

Important considerations! Always use care and protection when using these sprays. Wear eye protection and do not breathe them in. Do not spray when children or pets are present or when beneficial insects are flying. Always check your plants for ladybirds and other insects first. A healthy population of ladybirds or hoverfly larvae can sort out an aphid problem without any intervention.

Infusing garlic in water for the garlic spray

Pounding dried chamomile in a pestle and mortar

Chilli (*Capsicum*)

All types of chillies make a potent deterrent for mice, rats and other rodents including squirrels. Sprinkle fresh or dried chopped chillies to discourage them from eating pea, squash and other seeds either in the greenhouse or garden. Always be very careful when chopping and sprinkling chillies. Wash your hands thoroughly and especially avoid touching the eyes or other sensitive areas.

Southernwood (*Artemisia abrotanum*) and **wormwood** (*Artemisia absinthium*)

Both southernwood and wormwood have strongly aromatic leaves that repel insects. Wormwood is perhaps best known for being an ingredient in absinthe!

Dried and crushed, the leaves deter flies, mosquitoes, mice and – so I am told – snakes. You can make a deterrent insect spray in the same way as the tansy one below.

Tansy (*Tanacetum vulgare*)

Tansy was used as one of the 'strewing herbs' in medieval times, along with other pungent herbs including thyme, rosemary, lemon balm and lavender, to help deter insects. Walking on the herbs released their aromas and natural oils.

It is easy to grow, with beautiful flower heads in late summer made up of many 'buttons'. Tansy will grow in most soils and can become invasive.

Dried crushed tansy leaves repels ants, flies, fleas, caterpillars and other insects. Sprinkle on the ground in the greenhouse and sheds to deter these pests; it smells rather like camphor. Rich in potassium, the herb is an excellent compost ingredient and the flowers attract many beneficial insects.

Tansy planted by the kitchen can help to deter flies, or hang bunches to dry in the window.

This spray is a preventative – it doesn't kill anything – but still be careful when spraying as flying insects won't enjoy being squirted.

TANSY INSECT SPRAY

1 cup fresh tansy leaves (½ cup dried)

4 cups hot water

Put the leaves in a heatproof container (a pan or large preserving jar with a lid) and pour on the hot water. Cover and leave for 24 hours to infuse.

Strain and pour into a spray bottle. Apply to all of the surfaces of the plant you are wishing to protect.

It can be stored in the fridge for up to a week, properly labelled. Tansy spray is toxic and should be labelled accordingly.

cleaning

Cleaning solutions for the home

I first became interested in exploring natural alternatives for home care when I realised that chemical cleaners were making me feel ill: symptoms included headaches, sore throat, sneezing, sore eyes and rashes on my skin. These alternatives smell wonderful, they feel good to use and your home smells fantastic afterwards. Caring for our home is a natural, nurturing instinct and a form of self expression. When our home feels good, we feel good!

There are more recipes in Chapter 12, page 115, including powerful cleaning solutions made from citrus.

Making cleaning potions

Herb vinegar for cleaning

Useful cleaning herbs: these have excellent potent properties to help keep your home smelling great and hygienically clean.

Chamomile	Parsley
Eucalyptus	Pine
Lavender	Rosemary
Lemon balm	Sage
Lemon verbena	Thyme
Mint	

Vinegar is also a powerful cleaner, deodorising, and killing bacteria, mould and germs.

This vinegar is useful for all kinds of cleaning tasks. Use it neat to remove limescale or inside the toilet.

You will need:

- A glass jar with a lid
- Herbs of your choice
- Cider or white vinegar (you can use brown; it just won't look or smell quite so pretty)

Loosely fill the jar with fresh herbs (or half fill with dried), then pour on the vinegar, leaving about 1cm space at the top. Put on the lid and gently shake.

Shake the jar every day for two weeks then strain the vinegar into another labelled jar. This keeps for at least a year but is so useful it rarely lasts that long!

Parsley, sage, rosemary and thyme, ready to infuse in vinegar to make a powerful cleaner

Parsley, sage, rosemary and thyme infusing in vinegar

TO MAKE A MULTIPURPOSE CLEANING SPRAY

For a simple, powerful cleaning spray pour the solution into a spray bottle and use.

For areas prone to mould or mildew, pour 1 cup horsetail solution into the bottle and top with the vinegar.

For a more soapy cleaner, pour 1 cup of soapwort solution into the bottle and top with the vinegar, or add a generous squirt of eco washing up liquid (or liquid castile soap).

FRAGRANT KITCHEN AND BATHROOM SCRUB

This is useful for areas that need a slightly abrasive scrubber for limescale, such as bath rims, and sinks.

- 1 cup sea salt, finely ground
- 1tbsp finely ground dried herbs (if you have none of your own dried, I have found the contents of a peppermint teabag work rather well here)

Mix together and store in a jar. To use, dip a damp cloth or sponge in and scrub. Use a toothbrush for taps. Rinse and spray with the multipurpose spray to make your kitchen and bathroom shine.

Finely ground dried herbs, salt and bicarbonate of soda to make scouring powder

Homemade scouring powder

NATURAL HOMEMADE SCOURING POWDER

- 1 cup bicarbonate of soda
- 1 cup finely ground sea salt
- 1tbsp of finely ground herbs of your choice (optional)

Mix together and apply as above.

For a soft, creamy scrub, drizzle washing up liquid into either scrub, stirring until the desired consistency is reached.

WOOD CLEANER/FURNITURE POLISH

Mix 1 part vinegar with 3 parts olive (or other suitable) oil in a jar.

Put on the lid and shake thoroughly to mix.

Use on the wooden handles of tools to protect them, on wooden furniture, etc. Do a test spot first to make sure this is suitable for your wooden furniture.

This is a good recipe for using up culinary homemade oils and vinegars that are past their best.

LAUNDRY LIQUID, SOMETIMES KNOWN AS 'GLOOP'

Variations of this recipe are found widely on the internet which is where I first came across this thrifty way to make a detergent for the washing machine. I use one of my scented vinegars (or sometimes just plain malt vinegar) in the softener drawer.

- 4 litres of water
- 1 cup of flowers or scented herbs of your choice
- 1 bar of unscented soap
- ½ cup (120g) washing soda

You will need a large pan and storage containers – ice cream tubs or wide mouthed glass jars are ideal.

Pour 4 litres of water into a large pan and add 1 cup of fresh flowers (half cup of dried) for example chamomile, rose petals, lavender, feverfew. Bring to the boil and simmer for 5 minutes then remove from heat, put the lid on and allow to brew for 30 minutes. Strain and compost the flowers.

Meanwhile grate the soap using a cheese grater.

Pour the liquid back into the pan and bring back to the boil. Add the grated soap, stirring until it has melted. Remove from heat, add the washing soda and stir until dissolved.

Leave to cool.

Decant into your containers – you will see now why it is called gloop!

Use ½ cup per load, placing directly into the drum using a small sturdy plastic container. Add some herbal vinegar to the softener drawer before washing in the machine as usual.

Gloop may also be used for handwashing and directly on stubborn stains prior to washing.

Infusing flowers in water to fragrance laundry gloop

LAUNDRY POWDER

This is placed in the laundry soap drawer, like commercial products. Pour some regular or home scented vinegar into the softener drawer.

- 1 bar of good quality natural soap,* diced or 140g/5oz pure soap flakes
- 1 cup household washing soda
- ½ cup citric acid
- ½ cup bicarbonate of soda
- ¼ cup sea salt
- 20 drops essential oil of your choice, if you have used unscented soap (optional)

* I use a naturally scented soap for this because it smells lovely, e.g. lavender, peppermint, citrus

Put everything in a food processor or blender and whizz until finely ground. Store in clean dry jars with well fitting lids. Use 2tbsp per load.

Useful plants to help clean the air at home

These houseplants help to remove toxins from the air within the home, including formaldehyde, trichloroethylene and benzene. Simple, effective and they look lovely, too.

- Spider plant (*Chlorophytum comosum*)
- English ivy (*Hedera helix*)
- Peace lily (*Spathiphyllum*)
- Gerbera daisy (*Gerbera Jamesonii*)
- Chrysanthemum
- Aloe vera
- African violets (*Saintpaulia*)

Natural, homemade cosmetics

HOMEMADE LIQUID CASTILLE SOAP

- 1 bar of castille soap (140g/5oz)
- 8 cups spring or filtered water, brought to the boil

Grate the soap using a kitchen grater or food processor.

Place in a large heatproof with the water and mix together until the soap has dissolved.

Leave until cool and pour into labelled jars.

HOMEMADE SHAMPOO USING CASTILLE SOAP

- ½ cup herb or flower infused water (of your choice; for ideas see the soapwort recipes)
- ½ cup liquid castille soap
- 1tsp of a gentle mild oil – avocado, sunflower, jojoba, olive, coconut, sweet almond, hemp

Pour your ingredients into a jug, mix together and pour into your container. Replace the lid and label.

You can add essential oils to this shampoo if you wish.

To use, pour some into your hands and rub together to make a lather, then massage through hair and scalp. Rinse with warm water, then use a conditioner (if desired) followed by a herbal hair vinegar rinse.

This shampoo lasts around 2 weeks as there is no preservative in the solution. The quantities here are for a family of three, so adjust them to suit your needs.

LEMON AND CUCUMBER SHAMPOO

- 1 whole lemon, seeds removed, chopped
- 1 whole cucumber, chopped

Put them both in a food processor and blend until pulped very finely.

Pour into a jar or bottle, label and replace the lid. This will keep for 2-3 days in a cool place (compost any leftovers).

You can if you wish peel the lemon and cucumber before processing. Use the lemon peel in one of the lemon peel recipes (page 114) and the cucumber peel as a skin tonic (simply wipe over your clean skin) or place on the eyes to cool and relax tired, puffy eyes. (Make sure the cucumber doesn't have traces of lemon on of course!)

Massage through your hair and scalp (being careful not to get any in your eyes!), then rinse thoroughly with warm water.

Finish with a herbal vinegar rinse, if desired.

Making cosmetics: candelilla wax, homemade shampoo, a bar of castille soap, deodorant, toothpowder, dried rose and calendula petals.

HERBAL VINEGAR HAIR RINSE

This hair rinse will help to remove residues from your hair, reduce tangles and help to leave your hair shiny.

> 1 cup herbal vinegar (see page 57)
> 1 cup cooled, boiled water
>
> Pour the liquids into a spray bottle. Shake before use then spritz over your hair after shampooing and conditioner. Rinse with warm water.

You can pour the vinegar rinse over your hair, but I find spritzing is less likely to get vinegar in the eyes!

Suggestions for herbal infused vinegar that is good for hair:

Citrus	Nettle	Rosemary
Lavender	Rose	Sage

HERBAL HAIR CLEANSER – THIS CAN BE USED IN PLACE OF SHAMPOO IF YOU ARE GOING 'NO POO'

Going 'no poo' means stopping using detergent based shampoos and conditioners to allow your hair to restore its natural balance. Some people just use water. Others use bicarbonate of soda or vinegar solutions on their hair. The method takes 4-6 weeks, after which time many find that their hair is fuller, softer and healthier than when they used regular shampoos.

> ½ cup fresh herbs (e.g. rosemary, lemon balm, mint, lemon verbena, chamomile)
> 2 cups boiling water
> 2tbsp bicarbonate of soda (baking soda)
>
> Put the herbs in a heatproof container, pour the boiling water over and push the herbs down so that they are submerged. Leave to brew for 30 minutes, strain and cool. Once the herbal infusion has cooled, stir in the bicarbonate of soda until it has fully dissolved. Pour into a container, replace the lid and label.

To use, massage ½ a cup of cleanser (more or less, depending on hair length etc.) through the hair and scalp for 2-3 minutes and rinse with warm water.

Finish by using a herbal vinegar rinse.

ROSEMARY HAIR CONDITIONER

> Oil – coconut, olive, sweet almond
> Fresh rosemary sprigs
> A heatproof jar (one used for canning is ideal) or earthenware cooking pot.
>
> Half fill the jar with rosemary sprigs and pour over the oil until it is fully submerged.
>
> Place in a solid pan which has a dishcloth folded at the bottom.
>
> Add water to the pan, ¾ of the way up the jar.
>
> Bring the water up to a simmer, then turn to a low setting. Leave for 2 hours, checking that the water hasn't evaporated.
>
> Remove carefully using jar tongs or oven gloves, place on a wooden board and cool.
>
> Strain, bottle and label.

To use as a conditioner, massage 1-2tsp (depending on length and thickness of hair) of oil through your hair and scalp. Wrap your hair in a warm towel and leave for 30 minutes to an hour. Wash with warm water then apply a vinegar rinse (as above).

Experiment with other herbs or flowers.

HOMEMADE TOOTHPOWDER

I first came across the idea of using a powdered clay based toothpowder when I met a woman selling it at the Offgrid Festival three or four years ago. Until then, I had been using a fluoride free toothpaste from the local whole food shop (no artificial sweeteners, SLS etc.) which was fine – however trying this was a revelation! It made my teeth feel really clean and felt so much healthier and pleasanter in my mouth than toothpaste. It lasts a long time, is cheap to make and easy to store. This toothpowder keeps my teeth clean, helps to remove toxins and also can help (according to what I have read) remineralise my teeth.

Bentonite clay naturally detoxes and can help eliminate toxins, and it is also full of minerals which are beneficial for gums and teeth.

Bicarbonate of soda, which gently whitens and polishes teeth, is an ingredient found in many commercial brands of toothpaste too.

Sea salt is also rich in minerals, removes tartar, whitens teeth and is beneficial for oral hygiene. I make a sea salt mouth wash sometimes, a teaspoon dissolved in warm water, a technique recommended by a dentist.

You need:

1tbsp of sea salt, finely ground –
    I grind salt crystals in a herb grinder
4tbsp bentonite clay
4tbsp bicarbonate of soda
A glass jar

Put everything in the glass jar and replace the lid.

Shake it to mix well!

Right:
Sea salt, bentonite clay and bicarbonate of soda to make toothpowder

Below:
Adding the ingredients for toothpowder

And there you are – a jar of toothpowder. If you like, you can add some finely ground dried mint, sage, fennel or lemon balm for flavour but I like it just like this. I keep a small jar of this in my bathroom cabinet, refilling it from the larger jar when needed. This helps to keep the powder dry and fresh.

To use, just dip your toothbrush in the powder and brush and rinse as normal.

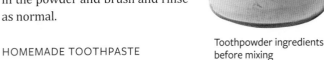

Toothpowder ingredients before mixing

HOMEMADE TOOTHPASTE

If you prefer something creamier.

½ cup homemade toothpowder
½ cup coconut oil
Finely ground herbs or spices (as above) optional

Mix together thoroughly and store in a labelled jar. To use, place a pea sized amount on your toothbrush.

HOMEMADE DEODORANT RECIPE

1 cup arrowroot powder
⅔ cup baking soda
⅔ cup coconut oil which has been infused with fragrant herbs (or use 30 drops of essential oils)

Mix together thoroughly in a jar. I apply it with my fingers.

HOMEMADE HERBAL DEODORANT SPRAY

½ cup herb infused witch hazel
½ cup complementary herb or flower water
A small spray bottle

Firstly, make the infused witch hazel by putting your chosen herbs or flowers in a jar and pouring over witch hazel until the herbs are completely submerged with an extra 5cm/2in of witch hazel on the top. Replace the lid and put somewhere cool and dark to infuse, shaking every day. Infuse for 2-4 weeks, depending how strongly scented you wish the infusion to be. Strain through a muslin lined sieve and pour into a labelled jar or use straight away to make the spray.

Mix the infused witch hazel with the flower/herb water and pour into your spray bottle. Spray to apply.

As with all deodorants, it is not recommended to use them on broken skin.

Suggested herbs and flowers to use in deodorants:

Basil	Lemon balm	Rose
Calendula	Lemon Grass	Rosemary
Kaffir lime	Mint	Sage
Lavender		

FIRE CIDER

This powerful brew is an excellent tonic to deter winter chills. Dilute 1 part fire cider with 5 parts boiling water, sweetened with honey or other sweetener if desired. It keeps for about a year. This makes 4-5 cups (using 236ml US cups).

Peel (where necessary) and dice the ingredients quite small, into ³⁄₁₆ in/0.5cm pieces

- 1 cup horseradish
- ½ cup ginger root
- ½ cup garlic
- ½ cup fresh turmeric (omit if you can't get it)
- 1 cup onion
- 2 or 3 hot chilli peppers
- 2tbsp fresh rosemary
- 2tbsp fresh thyme
- 1tbsp black peppercorns
- Zest and juice of 2 organic lemons (or 1 lemon and 1 orange)
- 6 cups raw apple cider vinegar

Place all of the ingredients in a large jar and replace the lid. Shake well and put in a cool dark place for 2 weeks, shaking daily.

Filter the ingredients through a muslin lined sieve and store in a clean labelled jar. Store in the fridge or a very cool place.

Freshly dug horseradish

BASIC HOMEMADE SALVE RECIPE

- 250ml/8.5floz infused oil of your choice
- 50g/1.75oz grated beeswax or grated candelilla wax

Using a bain marie, gently warm the oil. Stir in the beeswax until melted. Remove from heat.

Pour into widemouthed jars. As it cools, it will become semi-solid.

To make a softer salve, reduce the wax to 40g/1.5oz or for a stiffer salve (to use in a lip salve or deodorant tube) increase the wax to 60g/2.25oz.

Choose one oil or mix your own soothing or healing combination. St John's wort oil will make a salve beneficial for aches, insect bites and minor burns; chickweed to soothe skin irritations; calendula for wounds and bites; it is gentle enough for nappy rash, lavender to soothe and calm; mint for sore feet; rosemary for sore joints; rose petal oil for scars; stretch marks and sun damaged skin.

HOT MUSCULAR OIL AND SALVE

This is a powerful spiced oil which helps warm and soothe aching joints. We find it useful for back pain and arthritis. Do not use on broken skin and avoid contact with eyes and sensitive areas after use until you have washed your hands carefully.

- 25g/1oz each of ginger root, rosemary, St John's wort flowers, cayenne powder (or 4 chillies), mint
- 500ml/17floz Olive oil

Chop the ginger, chillies (if using), mint and rosemary and place in a large jar with the St John's wort flowers and cayenne powder. Replace the lid and leave in a cool, dark place for two weeks, shaking daily.

Strain through muslin and store in a clean jar.

For salve pour into a bain marie. Add 50g/1.75oz beeswax or candelilla wax for each 250ml/8.5fl.oz of oil. Melt over a low heat stirring until combined and all of the wax has melted, then pour into sterilised jars or tins.

Allow to cool, label and replace the lids.

Chapter 7

Transforming Waste into Compost

Your compost heap is both dustbin and transformer, in the sense of alchemy, 'transforming base metals into gold and finding an elixir of life'. When things go well, the transformation is exciting: on courses at Homeacres there are always bright eyes when we look at the compost heaps, and lots of questions too, so let's dive in there.

Winter compost heap before turning in April, one of its plywood sides removed to show the profil. First ingredients were in December

Kit

Unless you have a large space for composting, sides are worthwhile to contain heaps and keep animals out.

Compost bins of plastic are tidy, lightweight and work well for a small garden.

Aerators are long metal poles with either a push-pull spike at the bottom, or a corkscrew. The latter is more robust and in say five minutes of screwing down, then pulling up, you improve compost by mixing ingredients and introducing air.

A long-handled, four prong manure fork is good for handling compost: the thin prongs slide in and out more easily than a garden fork.

Compost with life, less hot

You can make great compost in cool conditions. Heaps made in winter rarely rise above 35°C (95°F), because of lower ambient temperatures and the relative absence of green ingredients. Nonetheless, after one turn in spring and maturing through summer, the compost is superb by autumn.

Pathogens such as viruses and parasite eggs are killed when the temperature stays over about 50°C (122°F) for a few days, but there are also micro-organisms of cooler composting processes that kill pathogens. Composting is a biological as much as a thermal process. Heat is not vital, unless you want compost really fast, or to kill masses of weed seeds – they die at about 60°C (140°F).

Compost in October, four months after completing the heap; it was made in winter so it was never hot

Inset, left:

Early spring, Rob, a volunteer, turning the same heap finished two months earlier, for use six months later

Inset, below right:

The same compost in early summer, eight months since starting the heap and after one turning

BIODYNAMIC COMPOST

A study at Washington State University in the 1990s (*Biological Agriculture and Horticulture* 2000, Vol 17 pp.313-28) found that adding biodynamic preparations to a compost heap raised its temperature by 3-4°C (5-7°F) for eight weeks and gave compost with 65% more nitrates and a different microbial balance, compared to a similar heap that received no preparations. How they work is not explained by science. You can make your own (see 'Activators' on page 66) or you can buy them.*

* www.biodynamic.org.uk

Homeacres' compost heap in November, with a nice mix of garden and kitchen waste

Time from start to finish

There is no need to rush the process, even though it's possible to make compost within a month. Commercial operations, using machines to shred ingredients and turn heaps, create something black and friable in as little as three weeks. However this is not finished compost and its blackness is more related to charcoal.

In gardens, unless you invest a lot of time and money, such speed is neither achievable nor desirable; see 'Temperature' below.

- Homeacres compost is ready within 4-12 months, depending on the season
- Heaps started in spring and turned in summer, are ready by autumn
- Heaps started in summer and turned in autumn are ready by winter, usually
- Heaps started in winter take longer and are the first to mature by the following autumn.

Bins are 1.7×1.7m (5.5ft), makes one tonne of compost, and the waste of a three quarter acre (0.3ha) garden takes six weeks to fill one bin in summer, and four months in winter.

Is a cover necessary?

Problems arise from water displacing air, so that is the main reason for covering with polythene or any kind of roof. In dry climates, covers retain moisture. We cover finished heaps but not those in the making, except when using plastic bins, as their covers are so easy to remove and replace. A downside of covers is how they protect rats from predators such as cats.

The two ingredient types

'Green' means high nitrogen, mostly alive recently, and not always green in colour. Green ingredients are weeds, crop residues, kitchen wastes, grass cuttings, coffee grounds, fresh animal droppings and leafy prunings.

'Brown' means higher carbon content, therefore often derived from wood, and usually drier than green. Brown ingredients are twigs, bark, straw, hay, soil, paper, cardboard and wood ash, but not coal ash.

Some soil is good and there is usually enough on weed and plant roots. Add rockdust to increase trace elements, while lime is generally not necessary, unless your soil is acidic below pH 6.

Should you water ingredients?

Extra water is needed only when there is a predominance of brown and dry materials. When half the additions are green and fresh, moisture is more likely to be over-abundant.

Check maturing compost for moisture by squeezing a handful and counting the water droplets coming out: if more than two, your compost is too wet rather than too dry.

From top:

An axe for chopping broccoli for compost – the stems look green but count as brown. They are woody.

After axe-work, compost heap chopped brassicas

A layer of fibrous twiggy material added to balance the green of grass cuttings

Sometimes the brown/green mix is quoted in 'carbon/nitrogen' terms, say with a recommendation of 30 carbon to 1 nitrogen. This is a different measure to 'brown/green' and does not mean 30 brown to 1 green, because green wastes contain carbon. Aim for 40-50% brown and 50-60% green ingredients. This is a guideline not a rule.

The foot long thermometer probe reads 63°C / 147°F which is quite hot enough!

Mature green waste compost is only slightly warm as the woody part continues to break down

Recently added grass and straw in summer quickly reach a high temperature

Ingredient proportions

Garden wastes rarely come in perfect proportions, and the mix varies seasonally. Add whatever waste is available, from a brown predominance of prunings and leaves in winter to a green majority of weeds, clippings and crop residues in summer.

Green leaves contain moisture so take care in summer to add enough brown to hold air in the heap. Or make a separate pile of fresh greens to wilt for a week or so, before adding to the main pile. Heaps with more green than brown need extra aeration.

Ingredient size

Smaller pieces are best so that ingredients break down faster, through rapid access by bacteria and fungi. Use a knife to cut stems into 10-15cm (4-6in) lengths, or a rotary lawnmower for larger amounts of stem wastes, and for tree leaves too. Use an axe to cut and crush brassica stems. Shredders are a good option for large gardens with many wood prunings, but they are often noisy and have a tendency to jam.

Temperature

Biological processes are harmed by temperatures over about 75°C (167°F), but this happens only when heaps are turned every few days, which feeds oxygen to thermophilic bacteria and makes them more active. Should the temperature reach 80°C (176°F), most life dies.

At Homeacres the heaps heat up within about three days of adding the first green matter, then stay at 60-70°C (140-158°F) in the top part, while more additions arrive in ensuing weeks. The thermometer you see in the photos is at the end of a foot long metal probe and is a good investment.

Activators

These can speed up composting and improve the end result, although if your process is giving good results, you are adding 'activators' already. Many common ingredients are powerful initiators of composting and help to ensure good results. Examples are regular additions of green leaves, nettles, horsetail/equisetum, comfrey leaves, small amounts of fresh animal or human manure, and urine. A key activator is oxygen.

Biodynamic gardeners understand activation in a more esoteric sense and use yarrow, stinging nettles in flower, chamomile flowers, dandelion flowers, oak bark and valerian flowers, prepared in special ways and placed in finished heaps in tiny amounts. You can use local activators rather than expensive purchased ones; Maye Bruce's book has advice on this.*

Perennial Weeds

There is wasteful advice that one should not add roots of invasive perennial weeds, such as bindweed, docks and couch grass. At Homeacres they all go in and decompose, adding their minerals and strong life-force to the compost. Should

* www.pssurvival.com/ps/composting/common_sense_compost_making_1946.pdf.

any survive somehow, simply remove their roots, which are clearly visible, while spreading the compost.

The only time to be careful of adding perennial weed roots is if there are long periods between subsequent additions, and in bins without lids, so they can regrow on top. In a regularly filled heap, every addition is soon smothered. If adding frequent masses of perennial weed roots, use a bin with solid edges of plastic or plywood, to prevent regrowth out of the sides.

Containers, structures

Pallets are often available for free and you can simply tie them together at each corner, or hammer four fence posts into the ground and tie them to these. We do not find that pallet sides' supposed admission of air makes better compost than solid

The sides can be solid wood or pallets; here some weeds are growing out of the side where there was a pallet

sides of plywood. Once heaps are filling, there is not much airflow in and through the composting ingredients around each side.

Enclosures which hold warmth are good, such as old bales of hay and straw, which can then be added to future heaps.

Turning and/or aerating

Oxygen speeds up composting and also prevents or rectifies an airless (anaerobic) state, which smells of sulphur and methane and results in black sludge, instead of dark brown compost. If your compost has pockets like that, using an aerating tool is one way to sweeten it.

To turn (move) a heap you need time, energy and an empty space next to any recently finished heap, whose main heat has dissipated, say a month after the last addition. Fork everything onto the empty area, and in the process shake out any lumps to mix and aerate them. Then cover and leave for two to six months before using.*

Composting in smaller gardens

Movable, cone shaped plastic compost bins are an alternative to permanent compost heaps. They are long lasting, light, easy to move about and come with fitted lids. You could have two, so that one is composting while you fill the other.

* www.youtube.com/watch?v=TPcYXGqt9CQ

HOTBINS

To produce more compost faster in a domestic garden, and to compost cooked food waste, Steph bought a Hotbin. It's moveable and vermin proof. All vegetable based waste can be put in the regular heaps, but the omnivorous teenagers in her house produce mixed food waste and bones.

The Hotbin runs at a temperature of 40-60°C (104-140°F) even in winter, thanks to its thick expanded polypropylene (EPP). There are no smells and it's the size of a wheelie bin, compact enough for use in a domestic garden. When empty, it is light enough to move to wherever you need it.

As well as food waste, Steph adds animal bedding and poo, nettles, comfrey, shredded paper and card, garden waste and perennial weeds. There is lovely compost in around three months.

The main disadvantage – apart from the price – is getting the compost out of the bottom hatch, without all of the uncomposted material falling from above.

Other domestic composters that can safely compost meat and fish waste at home include the Green Cone, Green Johanna and Bokashi bins.

Brandling worms indicate the compost is nearly ready to use

This trowel was found after being lost in the compost heap for six months

Turning after four months ... the compost needs more time

They are light enough to put next to where you want to use the compost, then just lift it off when the compost at bottom is ready to spread.*

Worms and timing

Brandling worms (*Eisenia fetida*) are small, shiny and bright red, about 5cm (2in) long and they are prolific breeders in damp, decaying organic matter. They help to convert almost finished compost into something special, and appear after the temperature cools, when ingredients are about half-decomposed.

Worm eggs are in most soil, so adding weeds and plants with soil on the roots is enough to ensure they arrive. By the stage that worms appear en masse, compost is almost ripe. The longer compost is left in a heap, the finer it becomes after being digested by worms, and the less there is in volume.

Solving problems

Slimy and smelly (anaerobic) compost happens after adding lots of green material, or from too much rain entering a heap. Turn the heap or use an aerator, and cover to keep rain out: within two to three months you will have sweeter if not perfect compost, and still more black than dark brown.

Dry and uneven compost may happen in regions of low rainfall; again, turn heaps while also sprinkling some water from a fine rose, and firm ingredients even with your feet, to bring them more into contact with each other. You can walk on heaps when ingredients are half brown and fibrous, but not if there is plenty of moisture and green matter.

Lack of breakdown can happen if ingredients are too long or fat, so that they have not packed down, and micro-organisms cannot access them. More cutting and chopping is needed at the filling stage.

---

* www.youtube.com/watch?v=Kf6CGj7xpFE

Chapter 8
Longer Seasons

Extending the growing season increases the productivity of your productive space by creating microclimates. This can be as extensive as a large system of heated glasshouses or as simple as a small potted garden on your windowsill. Growing year round makes optimum use of your garden, helps your budget, adds another dimension to your growing skills, along with the pleasure of harvesting fresh, vibrant vegetables full of vitamins and flavour throughout the winter.

Gardening encourages you to go outside during the darker months, which has many recognised health benefits. It is amazing how a day that seems dark and gloomy from indoors is actually not bad at all once you are outside. It is emotionally uplifting, increases energy levels and you can make the most of the shorter daylight hours, appreciating more fully the fresh air and any winter sunshine. Noticing the changes around you helps to make the winter months seem shorter, especially with the first signs of spring. Afterwards, the warmth of indoors with some homemade nourishing food is lovely.

Of course in some areas, it isn't possible to garden outside during winter time: then it is a time to be cosy, enjoy your stored foods from the summer and plan your growing year.

Overwintered crops in Steph's polytunnel in March. The carrots in the foreground were sown on 14th October

A wide range of crops and flowers in the polytunnel in August

An effective way of extending the seasons is to make sure that you have everything that you need for the months ahead: seeds, compost, pots and trays, fleece, netting, etc. Steph has spent many an evening beside the fire making paper pots for the spring using a cardboard tube and newspaper, stored in stacking crates until needed. It is also a good time to check over your equipment, clean and oil your tools (see page 116 for homemade wood oil), repair any damage and read the big pile of books you just didn't have time to explore, during the busy summer months!

Homeacres is a commercial market garden and so as well as growing for an almost self sufficient home, Charles needs to grow crops that provide for course lunches and give some income year round. This forms the basis for his teaching and writing.

When Steph ran a large private estate kitchen garden, in addition to wanting homegrown vegetables year round, the clients also wanted some produce out of season. Even with the help of a heated greenhouse, this was a challenge. Restaurants want reliability and continuity. With the gardens on show to customers year round, there is a need for them to be both productive and attractive.

In Steph's smaller garden, extending the season reduces the need to go shopping, saving money and resources, as well as feeding the family healthy food. It is wonderful to be able to go into the polytunnel in the depths of winter and harvest fresh greens to eat with tomatoes, aubergines and peppers that were grown there in the summer and preserved in the kitchen. At the allotment, leeks, parsnips, Brussels sprouts and kales are harvested throughout the winter, with purple sprouting broccoli in late winter/early spring along with autumn planted spring greens and cabbages as the spring progresses.

Here in the UK, some protection from British weather enables us to grow a wider range of food successfully and increase yields, including plants which otherwise wouldn't crop very successfully here. We can grow tomatoes outside, for example, but they are more abundant and less prone to blight and other problems grown undercover than outdoor ones. Consider your climate and location to decide what works best for you.

A polytunnel, greenhouse, cold frame or cloche allows you to grow earlier crops including peas, new potatoes, strawberries, Florence fennel, herbs, spring cabbage and very early broadbeans.

As a commercial grower, during the winter Charles concentrates on cash crops in his polytunnel and greenhouse, mainly salad leaves. Steph's undercover spaces are to feed a family, so in addition to salad she grows:

Beetroot for roots & leaves	Kale: Cavolo nero and red
Broccoli raab	Russian
Broadbeans	Leaf celery
Bulbing onions	New potatoes
Carrots	Oriental greens for cooking
Chard	Peas
Early potatoes	Pea shoots for cooking and
Edible flowers	salad
Florence fennel	Radish
Garlic (inc. elephant garlic)	Spring cabbage
Japanese bunching onions	Spring onions

Herbs including parsley, dill, coriander, French tarragon, chives, mint and lemon verbena.

There are also perennials that overwinter in there, for example more tender perennials in pots from the garden. Very cold sensitive perennials, including chillies, lemon and lime, are brought indoors to overwinter.

These are mostly sown in mid September for planting in late October after the summer crops have begun to be harvested. Having the plants ready means that they can go in as soon as space becomes available. Carrots, radish, broad beans and garlic are sown direct. The soil always needs a really thorough watering first to help the plants to establish.

Polytunnels

There is a lot of choice when it comes to planning a polytunnel. They are extremely versatile, with a wide choice of width, height and length. Online there are many tutorials for how you can make one yourself from upcycled materials and timber, so it is possible to make one for even a very small space.

Some considerations:

Your location

Consider how close you are to the road and other properties. Before buying a polytunnel, it is a good idea to check the planning regulations for where you live. In urban areas, there are often rules about how high your polytunnel can be, what percentage of your garden it can take up, how close it can be situated to boundaries and the road. A phone call or email to your local planning office should reveal any rules you need to take into consideration. This usually is not a problem in very rural areas or if you have lots of land. There may also be rules about fixing the structure to the ground.

Weather conditions

Exposure to high winds and extreme weather will influence

HOW TO MAKE PAPER POTS USING NEWSPAPER AND A LOO ROLL TUBE

Cut newspaper into strips 30cm (12in) long and the width you need: the height of pot you want plus 3cm (1.25in) longer – so if you want 5cm (2in) tall paper pots, the strips need to be 8cm (3.25in) wide.

Wrap around the loo roll then tuck the excess inside the tube to form a base.

Carefully remove the tube, repeat until you have as many pots as you need.

Place neatly in old mushroom trays or similar, fill with compost (a jam funnel helps to prevent spills) and sow your seeds. The pot biodegrades in the soil.

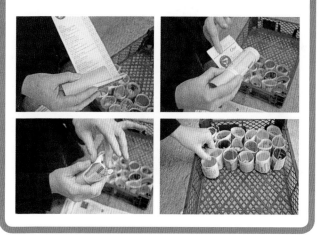

---

your choice of structure, crop bars, how it is anchored (you may need to use anchor plates and/or concrete), strength of the polythene, etc.

Straight or curved sides

If you are buying a second hand polytunnel you may not have much choice here, but if buying new, straight sided polytunnels offer far more flexibility than curved ones. You can plant taller crops closer to the polythene which increases productivity. Also, gardening in a more upright position is more comfortable.

How to secure the polythene

Should you bury the polythene in a trench or fix it with wooden batterns or aluminium base rails? Burying the polythene is ideal because it helps increase stability by anchoring the whole structure to the ground and the plastic creates a useful barrier to weeds and pests outside of the tunnel. However in some situations choosing a wood or metal base rail provides the ideal solution. You do not have to dig a long trench, reducing the amount of physical digging work.

In smaller more urban gardens where space is limited, there may not be enough room for a trench. In Steph's garden, the polytunnel had to fit in an area with a hedge on one side and a concrete path on the other. Choosing a straight sided tunnel with base rails gave an extra 24m (80ft) of growing space, which would have been lost. Usually you need to stabilise the structure with base plates fixed to the legs and buried, so there is some digging involved.

Clockwise from top left:

June growth of summer crops, including tomatoes and cucumbers

Charles' polytunnel in October: last tomatoes, some veg for autumn harvests and salad plants for the winter and spring picking

Overwintering salads in Charles' polytunnel in January

Size of the doors, one on either end

Ensure doors are wide enough to be accessible for a wheelbarrow and to provide sufficient ventilation. We have doors that can be lifted out; sliding and swinging doors are other options. Charles' double doors are specially constructed by him in four pieces, covered with polythene, so that he can increase and decrease ventilation as he wishes. Steph's single doors are approximately 60% polythene and 40% mesh, which provides year round ventilation. During the day in the summer, Steph lays the door on its side, with the mesh covering the entrance, to provide a lot of airflow but discourage neighbourhood cats from visiting. If it gets very cold in the winter, a 'curtain' of polythene hung over the door increases warmth. During the summer, a curtain of bird netting hung over the doors allows fresh air, bees and other

beneficial insects into the tunnel but keeps out unwanted butterflies and birds.

Crop bars and other fixings

Crop bars are so useful all year round. You can also get special fixings for the hoops that allow you to have crop bars along the sides and braces for shelving. If you are feeling creative, make 'floating' shelves from wire, timber, large plastic trays, 'S' hooks, chains, tension wire, etc. There are a lot of ideas on the internet with tutorials.

Ventilation

We leave a gap at the top of the doors, year round, to allow for a continuous flow of air. Ventilation is very important in polytunnels even during winter months, to reduce fungal diseases and other problems. Local wrens have discovered that this gives them year round access to the tunnel. As they feed on tiny insects, we are sure they are helping with pest control.

Polythene

There are several different kinds of polythene to choose from which allow different levels of light through. Some also have heat-retentive or anti-condensation properties; research thoroughly to decide which best suits your needs. It is worthwhile buying a quality polythene which will last. Buy a roll or two of repair tape at the same time so that you always have some in case of tears. We discovered that brooms with old towels wrapped around the bristles and another length of wood strapped to the handle to increase the length are extremely useful for guiding the huge sheet of plastic across tall hoops.

Irrigation

There are different kinds of irrigation available, however we prefer to water using a hose or watering cans filled from the water butts. Automatic sprinkling and ground irrigation systems are less time consuming perhaps, but hand watering provides the opportunity to garden at the same time – weeding, observing any insect damage or other problems,

Charles' greenhouse, November

Autumn planted vegetables in Steph's polytunnel, in March: spring cabbage, chard and garlic

Cucumbers, beans and tomatoes in August; the beans were sown originally for an early crop

side shooting, enjoying growth, discovering wildlife – and enables you to water according to the needs of individual plants. Stakes hammered into the ground at the top of the beds (we use lengths of copper plumbing pipe) act as useful guides for the hose, preventing accidental damage to plants as you pull it along. A sprinkler attachment which can be fastened to a hose is a useful option if you are doing a lot of watering of small plants, and can be used elsewhere in the garden if needed and shared with the neighbours.

Maintenance

We clean the polythene every year. On a damp and drizzly winter day, tie old sheets together, soak in a trug of water, fling one end across the polytunnel and, with a friend on the other end, gently move the wet fabric across the structure, cleaning the mould off. A soft bristled brush and a bucket of water (infused with a suitable herbal cleaner from Chapter 6 if you like, such as horsetail solution for mould or mint and lemon balm for freshness) is useful for cleaning the inside of the polytunnel, especially the first 1.2m/4ft which can get very grubby during the summer.

Setting up a no dig polytunnel or greenhouse

The beds inside a polytunnel and greenhouse are created using the same methods as setting up outdoor no dig beds, with composted mulches.

Steph didn't have enough compost for a 15cm/6in mulch for her polytunnel which was going on the lawn in late March,

so she removed the turf and stacked it (this rotted down and was used as a mulch two years later). A 7.5cm/3in mulch of well rotted manure and homemade compost was spread on the beds with an inch of municipal waste compost on the paths. Removing the turf was a lot of extra work and in doing so removed a lot of beneficial nutrients and soil organisms, but provided a solution for this set of circumstances, meaning she could sow and plant straight away.

Alternative solutions, if you don't have enough compost, include covering the whole area with cardboard and making the beds on top of that, planting into holes cut in the cardboard (taking care to remove any weeds which seek the opportunity to poke through these holes) or sowing directly into the compost mulch. Or make the beds on top of the grass and then cover with a temporary light-excluding polythene/paper/card mulch, making holes as necessary. This method is not suitable for direct sowing.

A main difference might be varying the width of the beds to suit the space. In Steph's 3.6m (12ft) wide polytunnel, there is a 1.75m (5ft 6in) wide main bed running down the middle, to take full advantage of the height for growing tomatoes etc. There are two paths of 40cm (15in) and narrower side beds measuring 60cm (2ft). Here, bailer twine fastened along the full length of the tunnel, wrapped around the crop bars for extra support, is used to support plants and as a washing line in the winter.

Each spring as the winter crops are cleared, the beds are mulched with 1-2in (3-5cm) of well rotted compost. This provides enough fertility for all of the summer crops and the winter plantings too.

Staging provides storage space underneath for pots, trays and other propagation equipment. Steph's greenhouse is connected to an electrical outlet and uses electric heat mats with adjustable thermostats for propagation. These are great for starting off seeds that require warmth and keeping tender plants frost free during unexpectedly cool springs, but of course come with the cost (financial and environmental) of the electricity. One solution could be connecting the greenhouse to solar panels. We would love to explore this possibility one day. A more low tech sustainable solution is a hotbed.

A polytunnel also creates an indoor sanctuary for wildlife. During the summer months Steph has the doors half open at all times, allowing access for bees, butterflies, moths etc. She grows flowers as companions, to use in recipes and also as food for wildlife, including night scented flowers for the moths. During the winter months, toads move into the greenhouse and polytunnel. If you have the space, a small pond adds another dimension to a polytunnel.

Undercover space offers so much potential for stacking uses. At home, Steph uses hers to dry out firewood and laundry. A chair creates an outdoor place to sit and read during very wet weather. It is useful for seed saving because it protects the plants, ensuring the seeds ripen. Container plants of herbs brought in from the garden can, if not too cold, keep cropping almost through the whole winter.

In Steph's polytunnel a small wooden bench across the rear door becomes an all-weather potting station for early spring sowings, with compost and trays kept dry underneath. Toads love hibernating under module trays!

Greenhouse or polytunnel?

We have grown in both; here are Charles' comparisons:

- Greenhouses hold a little more warmth and their plants suffer slightly less pest damage

- For this small difference, new greenhouses are not a good investment, but second hand ones or homemade structures are worthwhile

- The wooden frame of Homeacres greenhouse is pretty, but keeps out some light; aluminium frames are better from that point of view

- His investment in automatic-opening windows has paid off, but the polytunnel also self-ventilates because he left a slight gap above doors and below the doorframe, to allow some air all the time; therefore he can leave the doors in place during windy and cool weather, without humidity building up

- Greenhouses often need hard foundations with some concrete, so they leave a legacy in soil. In contrast the footprint of polytunnels is light, and most polytunnels can simply be dismantled and moved if necessary.

Making a hotbed

Charles builds a hotbed in his off grid greenhouse to raise all the early plants for his garden, using fresh horse manure including straw, free from a neighbour. The structure is made from four sheets of plywood, 4×4ft (1.2×1.2m), supported on two sides by the greenhouse walls, with the other two pieces kept in place with stakes and wire; it's very quick and easy. Extra sheets of plywood are added as the heap is built, to increase the depth of manure.

In mid February, we pile the manure in using a fork, Charles dances (!) on top to firm it down and then more manure is added, followed by more dancing, until it is about 1.5m (5ft) high and level. A pallet placed on top creates the propagating 'bench'. A hotbed sinks quite quickly, so is topped up with more fresh manure in late March or April to ensure warm enough temperatures for the germination of tender plants (melons, cucumbers, etc.).

Filling the wheelbarrow from the trailer, which we had filled with fresh horse manure and bedding, from the stables in the village; this is then tipped into the hotbed structure inside the greenhouse

Charles 'dancing' on top of the hotbed, to firm down the straw

A pallet on top provides a stable area to place trays

A hotbed with trays on 14th February

Seedlings growing
well in mid April

Compost thermometers are useful to check the
temperature of compost heaps and hotbeds

In late May, when the hotbed is no longer needed, it's either left in place to decompose into compost, or removed to an outdoor heap.

The hotbed increases the temperature in the greenhouse only slightly. Ventilation is important, particularly in the first few days, so that ammonia gases do not damage your plants.

Hotbeds can also be used to provide a warmer micro-climate in polytunnels for growing in directly, topped with 20cm (8in) of well rotted compost for the plants to grow in. Steph used one in a polytunnel at work to bring on earlier crops, constructed from layers of fresh chicken manure and bedding, comfrey, nettles, grass clippings, weeds, human urine and alpaca bedding (straw, poo, urine, fur), using what she had to hand in that location.

Compost thermometers with 30-90cm (1-3ft) long probes are useful to keep track of the temperature within the hotbed.

Outside, a similar structure with a homemade polythene cloche on the top successfully grew tender aubergine plants to maturity, even though they are more suited to a tropical climate; the cloche was removed in high summer, when the aubergines were flowering.

At Homeacres, we made some longer hotbeds and grew early radishes, carrots, spinach, pea shoots, spring onions, coriander, dill and lettuce. To conserve the warmth, outdoor hotbeds need a cloche cover or a cold frame 'light', a wooden frame with polythene stretched over or an old window. However, covers can blow off in high wind and may need screwing down, which slows access to the bed for watering and picking.

After two years of doing this, bringing in three tonnes of fresh manure each February, and a half tonne of compost for the beds on top, the early outdoor hotbed crops started to feel expensive in terms of time and effort. Whereas the smaller amount of manure for an undercover bed feels worthwhile. The one pallet on top of this germinates 4,000 seeds every year and gives vital warmth to plants such as basil and tomatoes.

Cloches and cold frames are more enduring and less time hungry than hotbeds.

Growing indoors – salad in upcycled crates or pots

Using Charles' method of picking the outer leaves, you can grow a small salad garden on your windowsill throughout the winter. Grow any varieties of lettuce, mixed orientals and herbs such as parsley, chervil, sorrel and coriander. These plants can supply you with a small bowl of fresh salad most weeks throughout the winter. In milder areas, grow them in a cold frame or simple plastic greenhouse too.

You'll need:

Pots/containers that are the right size for your growing
  space
Trays which are the right size for your pots
Store bought potting compost
Well rotted homemade compost or pelleted comfrey or
  chicken manure or homemade liquid feed
Young plants

Fill the containers with a mix of 50/50 potting and homemade compost or 100% homemade, if you have enough, or just potting compost.

If you are upcycling a plastic mushroom crate, line it with newspaper before filling.

Plant your salad 10-15cm (4-6in) apart and water. (See Chapter 16 for growing and picking tips.)

A selection of salads growing in recycled crates

Young vegetable plants growing in module trays in the greenhouse; they will be ready to plant when previous crops are cleared, to ensure continuity and increased harvests

To have leaves ready for the winter months, you'll need to sow these by mid September and plant from late September to mid October, taking into consideration where you live.

Homemade reflectors can help the salad grow if there is low light. (See Appendix, page 212.)

Growing indoors – sprouted seeds and pulses

They are delicious, fresh, crunchy, full of vitamins and minerals and can be grown in the smallest of spaces. You can buy manufactured tiered sprouters but they are very easy to make.

You'll need:

Making sprouts: the jar is inverted on the dish drainer after each rinse

- Wide mouthed jars – cleaned thoroughly
- Muslin and something to secure it – a rubber band or if you are using the kind of canning jar which has lids which are in two parts, use the ring part.
- Seeds and pulses – e.g. radish, lentils, mung beans, alfalfa, broccoli, fenugreek, chickpeas, sunflower, peas, beetroot. Always use chemical free untreated seeds good for sprouting as some seeds that are sold for growing plants have been treated and are not suitable for eating in this way.

Measure your seeds and pulses by pouring into the clean, dry jar – they should take up ¼ of the jar or less.

Wash the seeds and pulses in fresh water – pour them into a sieve and rinse – then pour into the jar, fill it with fresh water, fasten the muslin over the top and leave to soak at room temperature for 12 hours.

Drain, refill with water, swish the seeds about in the water, then drain again. Place the jar upside down at an angle which allows the air to circulate and the water to drain – a dish draining rack works well for this. Do not let them dry out completely.

N.B. Make sure the jar is out of direct sunlight.

Repeat the rinsing and drain 3 or 4 times a day. When they are ready (2-7 days, depending on what you are using), rinse again in fresh water and pour into a sieve to drain thoroughly.

Store in a covered bowl and eat within 3-4 days. Eat raw in salads and sandwiches, sprinkle on top of dishes, stir into soups and stews just before serving or cook in stir fries. Sprouted chickpeas make an amazing raw hummus.

Chapter 9

Storing Produce after Harvest

Keep the flavour and freshness, where possible

Two lovely results of growing plants in lively, undisturbed soil are

- Extra healthy vegetables
- They store well after harvest.

Salad leaves, for example, stay alive for several days after picking, when kept moist.

Harvests in June, mostly fresh and leafy, can be stored for a short time in bags in the bottom of the fridge

When to harvest

Leaves keep best when picked in early morning, damp and fresh. It is also possible to harvest limp leaves, on a sunny afternoon, then to revive them in a bucket of water until they re-moisten and become firm again.

Roots and fruits can be harvested at any time of day; some say the flavour of roots is better when picked in the evening but it's a small difference. For young and tender roots, the best time to harvest is just before eating.

Maturity of fruiting vegetables

Growing your own gives you the chance to harvest peas, beans, tomatoes, sweet corn and courgettes at the stage of ripeness you like the most. Experiment to see how flavours and textures evolve as pods and fruits grow and mature. A nice way of storing beans over winter and for longer; is to leave pods to dry or almost dry on the plants, then shell out the seed. (See Chapter 15 Top Vegetables for Pods and Fruits.)

Mulching to protect winter roots

Laying straw and hay over the ground before hard frost keeps the soil warmer and allows midwinter harvests, especially of Jerusalem artichokes and parsnip. The mulch may also offer a home for rodents and slugs, and if your plot is frequented by them, it is best to harvest roots in the autumn.

Pre-frost harvests of leafy vegetable plants

Before a hard freeze, you can pick and store leafy and frost-tender plants with some roots attached of about tennis ball size. Use a trowel to lever plants out, then place in a shallow, polythene lined box in a frost free place. Celery, chicory and endive stay in fair condition for up to a month.

Leeks can also be lifted and stored like this for many months, in areas of deep frost where the soil is too hard for winter harvests.

Late autumn harvest of endive with their roots, to store for up to three weeks in a shed

Storage guide, short term

The main criterion for storing produce after harvest is temperature, and there are two main temperature bands used here. Refrigerator temperature is 3.5-5.5°C or 38-42°F; room or ambient temperature is 15-21°C or 60-70°F, at which temperature many vegetables and fruits store better than in a fridge.*

Other considerations when storing

- Fruits give off ethylene gases while ripening, so keep them separate from vegetables that you wish to store for more than a day or two, because ethylene hastens maturity and then decomposition. Ethylene producers include avocados and tomatoes, but not apples and watermelons.

- Storing produce in polythene bags is good only for leafy vegetables, to keep them damp and alive. For some other produce, sealed bags can accumulate carbon dioxide and spoil the taste.

---

* Based mainly on Charles' experience. More details are in this document by the University of California http://ucce.ucdavis.edu/files/datastore/234-1920.pdf

Artichoke, globe

Best eaten straight after harvest as they dry and toughen with age, otherwise store at ambient temperature.

Artichoke, Jerusalem

These resist moderate frost and keep well in the ground, until required. Soil is best washed off straight after harvest, because it's more difficult later; or store with soil if keeping them for several months; eat before early spring, when new shoots become prolific.

Asparagus

Spears are the immature stage of stems and want to keep growing: store in a polythene bag in the fridge, or no more than three days at room temperature, after which the buds start to open and stems become fibrous.

Aubergine

Best flavour is freshly picked, though fruits keep well at room temperature for up to a week, gradually going soft, sometimes a little seedy and bitter too.

Harvests of early autumn, many can be stored for longer than earlier in the year

Beans broad/fava

Young pods with small and bright green beans want eating fresh, within a day. Older pods with mature beans, which have meaty flesh inside a skin, keep for 3-5 days at ambient temperature.

Beans, dry seed

Once fully dry, storing is easy, in a jar for up to two years and at any temperature. Shelled beans which are still moist want cooking within two or three days, or can be frozen.

Beans French, runner, green

Tender pods of summer beans keep 3-5 days in a bag in the fridge, but they toughen with time.

Beetroot

The first harvests in early spring taste sweeter when eaten fresh, and store cool. Beetroot keep well and in winter the roots resist some frost, but are best harvested before -3°C (27°F); store unwashed, in boxes or sacks, as cool as possible without freezing.

Brussels and flower sprouts

Leave on plants until needed, especially because sugars increase in cold weather; below -10°C (12°F) there is a chance of rotting.

Cabbage greens/collards

Cabbage leaves are hardy to frost and the main risk is from birds. After harvest store moist and cool; fridge temperature is best in a polythene bag.

Cabbage hearts
including Chinese cabbage

Hearts except savoys are burst open by ice, so cut before it freezes, then keep cool as for cabbage greens. Chinese cabbage have a high water content and want using first; they can store for up to a month in a fridge.

Calabrese, broccoli, cauliflower

Small broccoli heads resist some frost; large calabrese and cauliflower heads hold more water and are damaged by freezing. Keep all these in a fridge after harvest, because after 2-3 days at ambient temperature they discolour and are less tender.

These store for different times: winter cabbages, four types: white, red, Savoy, Chinese

Aubergine Black Pearl at Homeacres in October, final harvest before planting salad for winter

Brussels sprouts Doric F1 in December, can be harvested until March

Preparing to store in November, using back of knife to trim off all celeriac leaf

Carrot

Frozen carrots turn to mush, so harvest before frost gets into the soil, when air temperatures are below -4°C (25°F). To keep through winter, store unwashed and in sacks, cool but frost free. For summer use, wash at harvest and then they keep well in a fridge, not in a bag.

Celery

Full of water, stems wilt quickly and are best cut for immediate use, or kept in a bag in the fridge, with some moisture on stems and with all leaves trimmed. Celery is damaged by frosts of -1°C (30°F) or lower so before that happens in autumn, twist out plants with their roots on, to store in a frost free shed. It's possible to earth up with soil and compost, but this encourages slug damage.

Celeriac

The easiest root vegetable to store because of its high dry matter content, and a reluctance to sprout. Leave in the ground as long as you can because it can double in weight during autumn. Harvest late autumn and store with a little soil on the roots, cool or up to 10°C (50°F).

Chard and leaf beet

Eat fresh, or keep leaves in a polythene bag at fridge temperature, for up to five days. For having fresh leaves in winter, leaf beet plants are more frost hardy than chard.

Chicory and endive hearts

Firm hearts want picking before frosts of -2 to -3°C (27-29°F), while loose hearts can be left in the ground, to cut or pick from when you need leaves.

Chilli/hot peppers

Chilli fruits gradually shrivel on the plant after colouring; pick fruits as they attain full colour and then dry on a tray in a windowsill, or use a needle to run cotton thread through their stems and hang at room temperature.

Courgette/zucchini/summer squash

Cool is best, to keep these immature fruits fresh, in the fridge and not in a bag; they are good to eat for several days, and keep better with stalks on, so cut through their stem when picking, rather than snapping them off.

Cucumber

They keep well at room temperature, and for at least a week when home grown; a bag is not necessary as their skin seals in the moisture.

Endive hearts, see chicory

Florence fennel

This watery root vegetable turns to brown mush after freezing, but keeps well in a fridge or below 10°C (50°F) for at least a week. After that, bulbs start to make new shoots and need trimming of outer leaves; they are still good to eat but less tender.

Garlic, bulbs

Keep warm and well ventilated after harvest, so that bulbs are thoroughly dry. Then store in a dry and mild place at 10-20°C (50-68°F), either hanging in bunches or plaits or (with stems cut off) in a box, and they should store until sprouting at some point in the spring. Softneck garlic stores a little longer than hardneck.

Garlic, green

To eat as green garlic, pull at any stage in spring; eat the stem and leaves as well as any developing bulb. Green garlic stores well at room temperature, and if reasonably mature it develops into a dry bulb if kept for long enough.

Herb leaves

Mostly these store well in a bag in the fridge and for a fortnight on average, except for basil which wants to be less cold at 7-10°C (44-50°F), and it discolours after about a week.

Kale, as for cabbage greens

Kohlrabi

In summer, eat straight after harvest as the bulbs turn slowly more fibrous in warm temperatures. In autumn, harvest before moderate frost and store in cool dampness, where they are good to eat until late winter.

Leek

Delicious eaten fresh in summer, autumn, and even in winter if the soil is soft enough that you can remove them. Summer and autumn varieties want picking before hard frost, while winter varieties stand in the ground and grow again in early spring. Harvested leeks store best in a bag in the fridge, for up to a month, or in a cool shed with some roots and soil left on.

Dry, bunched indoor-stored garlic for winter

Autumn, these kohlrabi can be harvested at any time before a moderate frost

Before the final chilli harvest in autumn; chilli plant on left is four years old

Onions were dried undercover after pulling, then tied in bunches and stems cut off, to hang until needed

Lettuce, hearts

Similar to chicory except for having less frost tolerance, and firm hearts want picking before any chance of freezing. On the other hand a brief spring frost causes little or no damage.

Melon/muskmelon

Keep checking ripening melons on the plants, for softness and colouring around their stalk, and a lovely aroma. If fully ripe when picked, eat within a day or two and before the flesh softens with a loss of acidity and flavour. Store at room temperature for up to two weeks, not in a fridge, and separate from vegetables.

Oca

Wash at harvest time and lay in a tray or crate, on a sunny windowsill to sweeten the flavour, then store in a dry, cool place 5-10°C (41-50°F) until needed. Tubers maintain good condition for months, until they sprout in early spring.

Onion bulbs

Dry and store as for garlic, with or without dry stems and in dry air (70% humidity or less) if possible, so indoors is better than outdoors in winter. Bulbs should keep until sprouting in early spring and some varieties do this sooner than others; Stuttgarter often keeps the longest.

Onion and shallot when young – salad/spring/green onions

Harvest with roots on, peel off yellowing leaves and rinse, store moist in a bag in the fridge for up to a week.

Oriental leaves, as for salad leaves below

Parsnip

The roots are high in dry matter so tolerate a hard freeze, during which starches turn to sugars. Weather permitting, they can be harvested any time from autumn until early spring, before they sprout many leaves in spring warmth, when the new leaves are taking nutrients from the roots.

Peas, all kinds

Harvest pods as short a time as possible before eating or preserving, for maximum sweetness. If needing to store them, keep pods in the fridge.

Pepper, sweet/bell pepper

Keep at room temperature. When harvested green but reasonably mature – full sized and thick walled – they should colour up and sweeten over a fortnight or so.

Potato, early

Top flavours are at harvest time, even in the first hour after pulling the smooth, shiny tubers; otherwise store at room temperature with soil on, and eat as soon as possible to enjoy that taste of early potato.

Potato, main

Tubers store for up to nine months at a cool 5°C (41°F), but less cool is possible for eating within a few months of harvest. Some varieties start to regrow sooner than others, and we find that Charlotte sprouts obligingly late, yet also grows fast once planted.

Parsnips harvested early spring after a winter in the ground, before and after washing

Pumpkin and winter squash

Fruits need to be hard-skinned and well coloured before cutting through the plants' trailing stem on either side of the drying neck, so that it does not snap off the fruit. Store in dry warmth, as for garlic. Pumpkins have a high water content and mostly need eating before winter solstice, while winter squash (Kuri, Buttercup, Acorn etc.) are good to eat until spring, when kept at room temperature.

Radish

Spring radish are best eaten fresh, otherwise store without leaves for a few days in a bag in the fridge. Winter radish are larger and have more dry matter; store like turnips, cool and damp until early spring.

Salad leaves including lettuce, mustards, rocket, purslane, corn salad, sorrel, pea shoots, endive

Cool is best though not too cold: 7°C (45°F) is gold standard temperature for storing most salad leaves. Winter salads with more brassica leaves keep well in a fridge.

Selling leaves to shops, where a few bags may sit for days on a shelf, has shown that moisture in the bag keeps leaves alive and in good condition. So after washing your leaves, drain off the excess but leave some moisture on, before putting them in a polythene bag.

Spinach, as for salad leaves

Kuri squash harvest from six plants; they keep for months once dry and hard-skinned, on a sunny windowsill here

Swede/rutabaga

These are hardy roots and resist frost to -12°C (10°F) or lower, so outdoor storage is possible, often better, because mild winters cause stored roots to sprout leaves, even to go soft if temperatures are above 10°C (50°F).

Sweet corn

Most traditional, open pollinated varieties start to lose sweetness after harvest, whereas modern supersweet hybrids retain sweetness for longer. On the plant, cobs have just a week or two of top ripeness – pick too early and kernels are pale and small – harvest too late and kernels become starchy and less sweet. Bingenheim Seeds have done pioneering breeding to increase sweetness of open pollinated varieties and their Damaun (early), Mezdi (mid) and Tramunt (late) varieties have grown and stored well for us.

Charles with Tramunt sweet corn on 11th September

Tomato

Tomatoes keep well and taste better at room temperature, ripening all the time. At summer's end you can pick mature but still green tomatoes and keep them at 15-21°C (60-70°F), to eat as they ripen over the next month or two, although they are less sweet and more mild in flavour than freshly picked tomatoes.

Turnip

Turnips rot after a frost of -3°C (27°F) so lift before this is likely, with a little soil on, to store in boxes in a cool and damp place.

Watermelon

As for melon, except you have more time to eat them when ripe and they store for 2-4 weeks at room temperature.

Yacon, as for oca

Christmas abundance, about a half of this has been stored, 19th December 2015

Chapter 10
Storing & Preserving your Harvest

Preserving the abundance of nature and your homegrown harvests for the winter months triggers an ancestral feeling of security, preparation and contentment. There is the pleasure of knowing that you have some of your own preserves or stored vegetables; it is practical, looks beautiful and feels homely. Eating home-grown foods in the depth of winter brings good memories of sunshine, growing, harvests and foraging. You don't have to be self sufficient; just a few jars of preserves and bunches of homegrown garlic feels good.

Storing food gives a sense of security and self reliance, a feeling of preparedness for the winter months; the harvest is in, and there is the promise of many delicious wholesome meals made from your own produce. Increasing your own food security reduces the dependence on shops and saves money. You do not have to buy onions, tomato sauce or jam, pay for fuel to get to the store or get tempted into buying items you don't need whilst shopping.

Home preserved food tastes better and is more nutritious too. There is a shorter time between plot and freezer, jar or cupboard. You know exactly what is in prepared sauces, preserves and canned goods.

Preserving food in season bought from farmers' markets and local growers offers the opportunity to store other delicious flavours; after all most people do not have the space (or climate!) to grow everything they want to eat. It is also an excellent way of using up abundance found in the supermarket reduction areas.

Using a dresser to store homemade preserves, garlic and squash

Where to store veg for the winter and spring – finding storage places in your home/garden

A large purpose built area for storing homegrown abundance is just a dream for most people, so embrace the challenge of seeking the storage potential of every space, thinking of your whole home as a larder. Steph uses almost every room in her house. Ideal places are cool or room temperature (depending on what you are storing), avoiding areas which are damp or freezing, and of course where there are no rodents.

Hang bunches of onions, shallots and garlic tied with string in the kitchen. Brass cup hooks fixed onto shelves and beams are ideal. Sometimes Steph makes plaits with the dried garlic or onion leaves which look lovely, but bunches tied and twisted together work just fine too. They are easily accessible for cooking and keep right through the winter. Any which have lost their leaves are stored in fabric bags and used first.

Winter squash store well indoors and look beautiful arranged on shelves lined with newspaper or tea towels. Make sure they are ripe and dry before storing. Dry them off with old t-shirts or towels. Store them anywhere you can: the kitchen, living room, hallway, conservatory; be creative. Any damaged ones are stored separately so we remember to use those first as they will be prone to rot. Extend the life of winter squash with rain softened stalks by drying in an airing cupboard or other warm airy place, for two weeks.

Jams, chutneys, canned (bottled) produce, dried beans and dehydrated fruit, vegetables and herbs are stored in glass jars.

We keep some ready to be used on the kitchen shelves and store the rest in a cool dark place until needed, not just the kitchen cupboards but also under the stairs, under beds, in the wardrobe, on bookcases… be creative! Turn a wardrobe or understairs cupboard into a larder using old shelving, cup hooks, recycled boxes and hanging storage bags. A built-in bench in the kitchen has hinged seats which can be lifted to reveal a large storage area. There is often useful space below cupboards or on top of cupboards and appliances (the top of the fridge for example).

During the summer months, when the abundance can get a little overwhelming some days, a fridge or cold larder is an excellent place to store fresh produce before preserving.

A frost free shed is ideal for most root vegetables and apples in paper potato sacks or crates. We have stored potatoes harvested in July right through until the following late spring this way. If rodents are a problem, use rodent proof containers. A large metal trunk and metal dustbin which were being thrown away (a few small holes in them allowed air to circulate) have proved useful for this. We don't use clamps or sand boxes as we have found this is a far simpler and quicker way to store root vegetables. Storing beetroot and carrots in sand is a real palaver. As well as the expense and fuss of buying suitable sand (builder's sand usually has chemicals in), you need to wash the sand off outside to avoid blocking the kitchen sink, which isn't especially pleasant during the winter.

Tip...

Preserving and storing: Keep a record of what you have and where it is so that you don't lose anything! This also helps with menu planning, which saves on trips to the shops.

Storing root vegetables in a frost free shed at Homeacres

An understairs cupboard is used to store homegrown and other produce

At Homeacres, storing squashes, onions and garlic with overwintering pots of chillies

Freezing

Freezing is a quick, simple and safe way to store the harvest. Most vegetables are blanched before freezing. This stops the activity of decay causing enzymes. Prepare the vegetables to the desired size and bring a large pan of water to the boil. Meanwhile fill the sink or a large bowl with iced water – you want to cool the vegetables as quickly as possible. When the pan of water is boiling, add the vegetables, bring back to the boil and cook for 1 minute. Drain the boiling water off and plunge the vegetables into the iced water until they are cool, then drain in a colander. If you don't have ice, run the vegetables in a colander under the cold tap or pour jugs of cold water over them, turning until all of the vegetables have cooled down.

Prepare soft fruit by removing any leaves, twigs, etc., washing and checking for insects.

Store the fruit or vegetables in containers with the contents and weight written on a label. There are several mysterious frozen items lurking in the freezer from those busy moments when one thinks: "Of course I'll remember…!"

During busy times, you can store fruit and vegetables for making wine, chutney, jam, sauces and other preserves in the freezer, enabling you to make them later in the year. It is lovely to defrost some summer fruit and have a jam making session on a cold January day. Weigh before freezing and write the weight as well as the contents on the label. You will thank yourself later!

Most of our tomatoes are stored using a water bath canner but when there isn't time, we wash and freeze cherry tomatoes whole. They are delicious popped into a soup, stew or casserole during the winter where they keep their shape and burst with flavour. Larger tomatoes are quartered, drizzled with olive oil and roasted at around 180°C/356°F/gas mark 4, usually and frugally when roasting something else to make full use of the oven. These make gorgeous soups, sauces and the basis for so many dishes (curries, pasta, stews) during the winter. Frozen fruit is a wonderful addition to smoothies.

Freeze homemade stocks, pesto, herbs and leftover wine in ice cube trays and then store in freezer containers to add extra flavour to winter cooking.

To freeze herbs in an ice cube tray, place the chopped herbs in the tray until mostly full and then top with olive or another light oil. Leave overnight, pop out of the tray, label the container and store. Alternatively use water instead of oil.

To make a quick, simple, vegan pesto suitable for this, add several handfuls of basil with a good glug of olive oil (enough to blend it so you may need to add more when processing), whizzed in a blender until puréed and frozen. Add a couple of garlic cloves before blending if desired.

How to freeze food without plastic

Most freezer containers are rectangular or square plastic lidded boxes or plastic freezer bags. These are easy to label, freezer safe, washable and reusable, the bags too if you buy the stronger ones. (Hand wash, make sure they are thoroughly clean, turn inside out and hang on the washing line. Do not reuse plastic bags that had contained meat or fish.) Of course you can always use recycled ice cream tubs, etc.

However there are concerns about the environmental consequences of using plastic, especially so-called disposable plastic and problems that may be associated with chemicals leaching from the plastic into the food. So we are working towards reducing plastic in our kitchens. Here are some alternatives:

Glass jars – Many preserving jars are also freezer proof (always check with the manufacturer). It is easier to use square and rectangular jars from a space saving point of view, but cylindrical jars work fine too. It is important to leave proper headspace so that the jars don't crack as the frozen ingredients expand. This varies according to the jar, so check with the manufacturer (this information is available online). Some jars have a line on the side which is a 'freezing level'. Lids range from metal, silicon and plastic (not ideal but most of the large canning manufacturers have BPA free plastic lids; they are reusable many, many times and do not touch the contents). Always defrost the glass jars thoroughly before using to prevent cracking.

dehydrate

Clockwise from left:

Tomato abundance

Tomatoes, cut in 6mm (¼in) slices, ready for drying in a dehydrator

Dehydrating tomatoes

Dehydrated tomatoes

Glass containers – These are square, rectangular or circular and mostly come with BPA free lids. Some manufacturers offer stainless steel lids but these are more expensive. Usually these glass containers are oven proof too once defrosted, ideal for freezing complete meals. (Always check with the manufacturer.)

Stainless steel – These have stainless steel or plastic lids. we use containers sold to store lunches in. They are not oven proof. Stainless steel ice cube trays are available for freezing small portions of herbs etc. as well as making ice.

Dehydrating

Dehydrating preserves food without the need for additives or salt, until it is needed. It is useful for modern lives as the dehydrated food takes up less space, has a long shelf life and retains much of the nutritional value. We store our dehydrated fruit, vegetables and herbs in glass jars in a cool, dark place.

In the UK, dehydrating food in the sunshine is mostly a dream, so we use an electric food dehydrator in which a fan extracts the moisture. It fits on the counter and is easy to use, with clear instructions for the recommended temperatures and times. Smaller dehydrators are widely available. It is worth making sure it has a timer as dehydrating times can be long. Charles has a large rectangular 9 tier dehydrator; Steph's is a circular one with 10 trays (which can be removed when dehydrating smaller quantities, to save electricity) and takes up less counter space.

DEHYDRATING TOMATOES

Always use firm, fresh tomatoes – damaged or soft ones are better used in sauces and chutneys.

Charles' dehydrator is powered by electricity from solar panels at Homeacres, so it is 'almost' sun dried! Slice the tomatoes into 4mm (0.25in) thickness and spread out on the dehydrating trays. Charles likes to place these in the sunshine for a few hours before putting in the dehydrator. Follow the instructions for your machine. At 60°C (140°F) they can take between 4-8 hours, depending on the moisture in the tomatoes and the thickness of the slices.

They store beautifully for at least a year – we use recycled large glass jars in a dark cupboard.

HOW TO DEHYDRATE FOOD WITHOUT A DEHYDRATOR

Use your oven on the lowest setting (around 49°C/120°F to 60°C/140°F is good). Spread the sliced produce on baking trays and put in the oven. You can leave the door ajar to keep the airflow up, but do be careful if you do this, particularly of children or pets. Check the drying produce regularly and also the temperature using an oven thermometer.

The 'simmering oven' of a solid fuel cooker is ideal for dehydrating.

DEHYDRATED VEGETABLE STOCK POWDER

This is a flexible recipe; adapt it to suit what you have. Key ingredients are onions, celery, carrots and garlic.

- 2 medium onions
- 4 garlic cloves (we like garlic, but you may prefer 2 or 3 cloves)
- 3 large carrots
- 2 stalks celery
- 1 large leek
- 1 medium parsnip
- 1 large potato
- 3 medium kale leaves, stalk removed (or use cabbage leaves)
- 2 medium tomatoes
- Handful of parsley including stalks
- 4 sprigs aromatic herbs – sage, rosemary, thyme

Thinly slice the root veg, tomato and garlic and chop the leaves into small pieces

Arrange the vegetables and herbs on the dehydrator, keeping the same kind together. Dehydrate according to the directions on your machine.

Check every hour as they take different times to dehydrate due to different water content – the parsley will be ready before the onion, for example and remove anything that has dried.

When everything has dried, leave to cool.

Put in a food processor or blender, add any extras you want – sea salt, black pepper, dried chilli, other dried herbs or spices such as dried turmeric or ginger – and blitz. You may need to do this in several batches. If so, for each batch, place into a large bowl and mix with a spoon when it is all done.

Store in glass jars in a cool, dry, dark cupboard.

Dehydrated vegetables and stock powder

As there are so many different types of oven it is difficult to say how long this will take, so check with your manufacturer.

Apples, pears and some other fruits may discolour during this process. To prevent this, sprinkle with lemon juice 30 minutes before drying.

OVEN DRYING TOMATOES

Cut the tomatoes in half (or quarters for large ones), mix with a little olive oil to help prevent them from sticking and spread on baking trays. Preheat the oven to 140°C/120°C fan/gas mark 1/the 'simmering oven' of an Aga. Put in the oven, leaving the door ajar if it is safe. Check regularly because dehydrating times will vary: usually tomatoes take from 2-6 hours.

Air drying herbs

When dry, check your herbs for any sign of pest, mould or decay before storing in glass jars in a dark place until needed. Usually, you use half the quantity of dried herbs to fresh so if a recipe calls for 1tsp fresh herb, use 1tsp dried.

IN BUNDLES

Harvest herbs in the morning after any dew has dried but before the sun gets too hot. Remove any dead, diseased, old or wilted leaves.

Many herbs can be dried in bunches, tied with string and hung in an airy, warm, dry place. Put the bunches inside paper or cloth bags and tie at the top, if you want to catch any falling, dried herbs, otherwise just hang as they are. Check every few days. This method takes 1-2 weeks, depending on the type of herb.

Herb butter

5g/0.2oz/¼ cup finely chopped fresh herbs of your choice
125g/4oz/½ cup butter at room temperature
1tsp freshly ground pepper
(1tsp freshly ground sea salt, only if using unsalted butter)

Mix all of the ingredients together in a bowl then use to fill ramekins or place on a homemade waxed cloth or greaseproof paper and roll into a cylinder shape. Place in the fridge until cool, then slice into circles.

This will keep for 2 weeks in the fridge or for 6 months in the freezer.

Herb vinegar

1 cup of herb leaves
4 cups vinegar (use white wine or cider vinegar)

Put the herbs in a large glass jar and pour on the vinegar. Leave in a cool place, shaking daily, for two weeks, making sure that the leaves are always below the surface of the vinegar. Strain and bottle. Store at room temperature – it will last for about 6 months.

ON HERB DRYING RACKS – ALSO IDEAL FOR DRYING FLOWERS, COMFREY LEAVES AND NETTLES

Plastic mushroom crates, lined with muslin or paper towels, make excellent stacking herb dryers. They are usually available for the asking from greengrocers and can last for years. Spread the herbs in sprigs or leaves across the racks and leave to dry in a cool, warm, airy place, checking regularly. Again, this takes a few days to two weeks, depending on the herbs.

Alternatively, bamboo steamers make useful herb dryers. This is a good way of using steamers which are too damaged to be used for cooking.

Large woven bamboo circular drying trays are effective; ours are from Thailand.

Make a three tier hanging drying screen from old frames. You will need:

3 old wooden frames from a thrift store
Window screening or fine metal or plastic mesh or muslin
Paint (if wanted)
Hammer and small tacks or a staple gun
Eye hooks
Metal chain or strong string
S hook
Drill

Remove the glass, backing panels etc. from the frames and clean thoroughly checking for any sharp edges. The largest frame will be at the bottom, the smallest at the top.

Paint the frames if you wish and allow to dry.

Cut the screen/fabric to the right size for your frames and staple to the edges on the underside of the frame. Keep the fabric taut whilst doing this.

Drill small holes in each corner of the front of the frames and insert eye hooks. Repeat on the underside of the frames for all except the one which will be at the bottom.

Cut the chain to 20cm (8in) lengths and attach to the bottom frame and the corresponding underside of the next frame. Repeat with the middle and top frames.

Attach the chain to the top frame and then fasten all 4 pieces together to make a pyramid shape. Attach another piece of chain to the centre; attach this to an S hook.

Hang somewhere cool and airy (but not windy).

Freeze-drying herbs

After checking as above, remove the stalks and chop long herbs such as chives or lemongrass. Make sure they are thoroughly dry: if necessary, leave on a clean tea towel for several hours and pat dry before freezing. Spread across a baking sheet and place in the freezer overnight. When frozen, remove and store in the freezer in a labelled container.

wax cloth covers

Wax cloth food covers, a reusable alternative to plastic wrap

HOW TO MAKE

Candelilla wax pellets

Spread the candelilla wax over the cloth

Spread the melted wax across the cloth using a soft brush

Dry the waxed cloths

Preserving herbs in oil

Infused herbal oils add a delicious dimension to salad dressings, meals, drizzled over bread and much more. They are easy to create and make lovely gifts.

You'll need:

- A glass jar with a lid
- Fresh herbs (if you are using dried, use half the quantity of herb)
- A light neutrally flavoured oil – I usually use olive; you can also try grapeseed, avocado, rapeseed (canola) or sunflower
- Sieve and muslin for straining
- A glass bottle with cap for storing and a label

Half fill the glass jar loosely with the fresh herbs (¼ fill the jar if using dried). Pour on olive oil until it is a centimetre below the top of the jar.

You need to make sure that all of the leaves are submerged in the oil so that they don't go mould; a preserving weight can be useful here. Leave in a cool place, checking daily for 2-4 weeks, depending how strongly flavoured you would like the oil to be.

When ready, drain through a fine sieve or muslin (compost the herbs) and store in a clean jar or bottle.

You can make your own unique blends mixing homegrown herbal infused oils with oils infused with citrus, bought spices (peppercorns, ginger, star anise) and nut or seed oils such as walnut, almond or sesame.

There is a risk of botulism in homemade infused cooking oils, so always store in a refrigerator and discard after a month – remember to label with the date of bottling. Bring to room temperature for 20-30 minutes before using, returning any remaining oil to the fridge.

Rather than throwing away flavoured oils which are no longer fit for consumption, make homemade wood treatments (see page 116). We are happy to use them in body scrubs, for example the homemade foot scrub (see page 116), but do take the usual precautions and do not use on the very young, pregnant women etc.

DIY waxed cotton food wraps

These are excellent for storing food in the larder or fridge, for sandwiches, to use as covers for bowls; indeed, anywhere that you might use plastic bags or plastic wrap. Washed in cool water with a mild detergent and rinsed, the wraps will last for several months and can be re-waxed when needed (or use as firelighting strips if they have got past reusing).

You will need:

- Beeswax or candelilla wax – pellets or grated – about 15g/0.5oz per wrap, depending on the size
- 100% cotton fabric cut to the size you want
- Baking trays, use old ones
- Pastry or paint brush (used only for this, not for baking too!)

Preheat the oven to 180°C/356°F/gas mark 4.

Place the fabric on the baking trays and sprinkle lightly all over with the grated wax. Put in the oven. Check regularly.

When the wax melts (around 5 minutes) remove from the oven and spread the melted wax evenly all over the fabric so that it is completely covered.

Hang to dry.

Preserving, an overview

Always follow instructions carefully to avoid botulism, mould or other problems and discard if you have any concerns or doubts.

Preserving is a huge, fascinating topic encompassing such a wide variety of methods, techniques and recipes that it merits several books in itself. Different countries and cultures have multitudinous techniques and methods for preserving food, some of them extremely ancient, with associated folklore, histories and traditions. They not only preserve the harvest but also preserve a culture's identity and way of life.

Having a stock of preserves give a good feeling of abundance, economy and food security. There is also the advantage and convenience of using homemade goods for quick meals during busy times – open a few jars and supper is almost ready.

Make sure all equipment is in excellent condition. Check all jars, bottles, lids, etc. before using and recycle any that are damaged. Washed glass containers can be sterilised before use in the oven at 140°C (284°F) for 20 minutes or boiled in a water bath or large pan of water with a tea towel folded at the bottom for 10 minutes. Keep hot in the oven or water bath until ready to use. Boil lids for 10 minutes and drain on a clean cloth or draining rack.

Whole tomatoes in the electric canner

Cooling the preserved tomatoes on a towel

Home preserves: canned tomato sauce, dill cucumbers and whole tomatoes (left); chutney, canned tomatoes, medlar jelly, tomatillo salsa (right)

Bottling/canning

Bottling, which is known as 'canning' in many countries although the produce is stored in glass, is a brilliant way to preserve much of your homegrown harvest. The results look stunning, it is reassuring to have stored food for winter months and they also make thoughtful gifts.

Always follow proven tested recipes and directions carefully, noting whether your ingredients are low or high acid foods. You can make low acid ingredients more acidic with lemon juice, vinegar or citric acid, which can then be canned in a water bath – always follow directions for this carefully.

We use a Weck water bath electric canner and jars (both the jar and lid are glass), with rubber seals. They come in an extraordinary choice of sizes and beautiful shapes and are reusable many times. The rubber seals have a 'pull tongue' which faces downwards when the processing has worked

HOW TO MAKE A WATER BATH CANNER
USING KITCHEN EQUIPMENT YOU ALREADY HAVE

Safety – It is advisable to use the back of the stove where possible to reduce the risk of accidental tipping. Follow the usual safety considerations for boiling liquids, being particularly aware of the safety of yourself, children and pets. Have everything to hand before you start.

You will need:

Homemade water bath 'canner', a large pan with a folded tea towel at the bottom

Removing the hot jar carefully with preserving tongs

A large pot with a fitted lid, such as a stock pot, which is deep enough to submerge the jars a couple of inches below the water level

A circular rack that fits in the bottom of your pan, a canning rack or cake cooling rack, or use a folded tea towel

Oven gloves

A ladle

A spoon

A funnel

Tongs to handle the jars – preserving tongs are best if you have them. If not, cover the 'grabbing' ends of your kitchen tongs with thick rubber bands to increase the grip

Jars with lids

Fold the towel and place it level at the bottom of the pan and fill halfway (or more, depending on the height of your jars) with water. Bring to the boil.

Carefully place your filled jars (sterilised and filled according to instructions) into the boiling water using tongs and oven gloves. Take care that they do not touch the sides or each other. There should be 5cm/2in of water above the lids of the jars.

If there is not enough water, top up with boiling water from the kettle, pouring into the gaps between the jars to prevent them cracking.

Bring to a rolling boil for the length of time specified in your recipe.

When they are ready, turn off the heat and ladle some of the water into another container to make it easier to grab the jars by the lids.

Grab the jars one at a time just under the lids using the tongs and carefully lift the jars onto the prepared surface – a wooden board with a towel spread across it. Be aware that there may be boiling water trapped in the tongs so wear thick gloves and exercise caution.

Leave until cool. Check that the jars are properly sealed according to the manufacturer's instructions before labelling and storing.

correctly, an easy way to check that all is well. The advantage of an electric canner is that you can set the correct temperature and time, switch on and then go and do something else whilst it is processing. However, it is easy to make your own water bath canner to use on a stove (see above) or even outdoors. In warmer climates, many people create an outdoor kitchen for canning in the summer.

Pressure canners are ideal for preserving low acid foods (with a pH higher than 4.6) which must be heated to 116°C /240°F to destroy botulism spores. You can buy stove top and electric pressure canners. They are very expensive in the UK so we have never tried one, but are much more widely available and affordable in America. In addition to knowing the correct time to process, pressure etc. you also need to know your altitude which can affect canning times as at higher altitudes, internal canner temperatures are lower.

Equipment needed for jams, chutneys, marmalade, pickles, etc.

You will need:

- **A large preserving pan** with a good, solid bottom. It is worthwhile using a proper maslin pan, with a wider top than base and lip, especially for preserves that need 'reducing' when cooking, such as chutneys. They are widely available for all kinds of cookers, but do check before buying that you have the right sort for your hob. It is worthwhile buying the sturdiest you can afford; it should last for decades.
- **Jars and lids**. Use new or recycled jars, checking that there is no damage and recycling any that are imperfect. We are happy to use recycled lids which have been carefully checked for damage or rust and sterilised. Replacement lids for jam jars in different sizes are widely available. There are some beautiful jars on the market now if you want something special for gifts.
- **A jam thermometer**, if you want one. We don't use ours much – making jam is such a visual process you can tell when it is ready but for other recipes knowing you have reached the right temperature is very useful.
- **Preserving funnels**: not necessary but very useful. We have several stainless steel ones in different sizes for the different jars. They avoid spillages and waste.
- **Wooden stirring spoons**, spatulas, slotted spoon for skimming – we use our regular kitchen ones.
- **Something to remove bubbles** from the jars before putting the lid on – you can buy special purpose made tools, or carefully use a flat bladed knife. We use some glass stirring rods (the heat resistant sort used in chemistry labs).

Cooking tomatoes to make sauce for canning

- **Jar lifting tongs**, useful for removing jars if you are sterilising them in boiling water (see page 95 for how to make your own)
- **A jelly bag** and means of supporting it, a purpose made jelly bag stand or an upside down stool
- **Muslin and sieves** for straining
- **Waxed discs**
- **Oven gloves** for handling hot jars
- **Jar labels** – bought, homemade, upcycled – pens, decorative homemade covers, recycled string and ribbon to make gifts look pretty

Pickles and chutneys

Chutneys are a mixture of vegetables and fruit, chopped and cooked to a pulp in vinegar with sugar and spices added whereas pickles are chopped vegetables, fruit and spices stored in vinegar. Both are a flavoursome addition to sandwiches, on the side of curries and other main dishes, stirred into soups and stews, mixed into vegan or meat loaves and sausages, used as a glaze (fruit chutneys are wonderful on winter squash; add a little water before spreading if they are too thick), puréed and used as a dipping sauce or ketchup.

Chutneys store very well, often for 2-3 years, usually need at least 2-3 months to develop their flavour and they mature well.

Pickles require pickling vinegar, which is a spiced malt vinegar. With a bit of planning you can make your own by infusing spices in vinegar. This widens your choice of vinegar – malt, cider, wine, etc. – and you can experiment and make your own blend of spices to steep in the vinegar too, really personalising your pickles.

You'll need:

A large glass jar with a lid

Vinegar

Spices – choose from mustard seeds, peppercorns (black, Sichuan, white, green), cinnamon sticks, allspice, fennel, cloves, star anise, bay leaves, coriander seed, chilli pepper, dill seeds, ginger, mace, juniper berries, cardamon, celery, cumin

For each litre of vinegar you will need 30g/1.5oz of spices. Mix your chosen whole spice blend in a small bowl and measure the quantity you need. Store any leftover spices in a small labelled jar for another time. Write down your own special spice blend in a notebook so that you can remember what you used.

Measure and pour the vinegar into the large glass jar, add the right quantity of spices and mix. Store in a cool, dark place for at least a month. Strain the spiced vinegar (compost the spices) and use or pour into clean labelled jars until you need it.

Jam, jelly, marmalade

These taste so much better homemade and are an effective way of storing gluts of fruit including those more usually treated as vegetables (such as marrow or green tomatoes jam). There are so many combinations to explore, from traditional hedgerow jams to more exotic fruits and vegetables.

Jams usually need quite large quantities of sugar. It is possible to make a reduced sugar jam (using less sugar, not a chemical replacement, which we do not recommend) but this will be runnier and need storing in the fridge. The high sugar content and boiling process kills micro-organisms and bacteria that could spoil the jam. We mostly use an unbleached cane sugar.

There are some recipes using alternatives to sugar which are worth exploring, with honey, stevia and concentrated fruit juices, or try raw vegan fruit jams, which have a much shorter life (3-4 days) but are very delicious.

Fruit pectin and acid helps the jam to set. Some fruits are high in pectin – apples, plums, currants, crab apples, citrus, gooseberries, damsons, quinces – whereas others are low, such as strawberries, peaches and rhubarb. You can balance this out by mixing a high pectin fruit with a low one, or buy pectin. There is also jam maker's sugar available that has pectin and acid added.

A jelly is made with the juice of the fruit, which is boiled and then strained before being boiled again with the sugar. These are beautiful, jewel like creations. I especially like redcurrant or medlar jelly as an addition to wine based sauces for special meals – rich and sensual in the darker months.

Fruit cheeses and fruit butter (neither contains dairy!)

Fruit butters have a lower sugar content than jam and therefore have a short storage life of a few weeks. Once opened they should be consumed within a few days and stored in the fridge or a cool place. They are made from pulped fruit, boiled with sugar and spices. Use as a marinade, on yogurt, on granola, as a glaze, spread on toast and other baked goods.

Fruit cheese is a more solid preserve which, turned out onto a plate, can be sliced and served as you would a dairy cheese. A cheese has a higher ratio of sugar to fruit pulp and has a longer storage life of four months. They taste better if allowed to mature for a couple of months before opening. Store in the fridge once opened and eat within 3-4 days.

For a longer shelf life, pour your cheese or butter into freezer proof jars and freeze. Defrost before use.

Fruit curd

These are traditionally made with fruit juice, zest, eggs, butter and sugar. In the UK we usually think of citrus curds (lemon, lime, orange); for a change, try passionfruit, apricot and apple.

Homemade curds last around six weeks in a cool place, three months in the fridge and need to be consumed within a week once opened. You can extend the storage life by processing in a water bath canner.

Vegan fruit curds are made using coconut (or other non-dairy) cream, arrowroot, fruit juice and zest and sugar or a sweet syrup (maple, agave). They keep in the refrigerator for 10-28 days, depending on the ingredients you use (the recipe will give you this information).

Ketchups, sauces and relishes

There are far more possibilities for ketchups, sauces and relish than tomato! Damson, chilli, tomatillo, blueberry, elderberry, beetroot, peach, apple – so many possibilities. You can regulate the salt content and replace the sugar in recipes with an alternative if you wish.

APPLE KETCHUP RECIPE

- 2kg/70oz apples, any sort, peeled, cored and chopped
- 1kg/36oz onions, finely chopped
- 3 cloves of garlic, chopped
- 2.5cm(1in) piece root ginger, finely chopped
- ½tsp cayenne pepper
- 1.25l/42floz cider vinegar (or malt)
- 2½tbsp sea salt
- 1kg brown sugar

Cook the onions and garlic until soft in a preserving pan, add the other ingredients and slowly bring to the boil, then reduce heat to a simmer. Stir until the sugar has dissolved then simmer covered for about an hour. Remove from the heat and puree using a stick blender.

This makes about 2.5l/85floz of ketchup.

Pour into prepared sterilised jars and can according to the instructions on your canner.

Fruit vinegars

Use to make salad dressing, gravy, drizzle over sweet or savoury dishes or drink as a cordial. To make fruit vinegar, crush the fruit, covering with vinegar and steeping for up to 5 days. Next, strain the liquid, measure the quantity and simmer with spices (if using) plus 30-50g of sugar for every 100ml of fruit vinegar, according to your taste. A spiced blackberry or elderberry vinegar with hot water makes an excellent warming drink for colds during the winter. Edible flowers (e.g. elderflower, rose, lavender) can be used to make a vinegar in this way too.

To make a sugar-free fruit vinegar, take a large clean jar and put 300g of fruit in (e.g. raspberries, blackcurrants, elderberries). Pour on 700ml vinegar (cider, red or white wine), seal and store in a cool dark place for two weeks.

Strain the fruit through a sieve lined with muslin into a large jug, then decant into clean, sterilised jars or bottles. Label, date and store in the fridge. This lasts for six months.

The vinegar soaked fruits are edible and will keep for a few days in the fridge. If you find the taste too strong, they can be composted.

Fermented foods

Fermented foods, including kimchi, kefir, kombucha, vegetable pickles, miso, tempeh and sauerkraut have increased in popularity recently, but have been part of people's diets for more than 9000 years. Important as part of the culture and culinary identity for many, in some countries a meal which did not include some fermented dishes would be incomplete. They expand the palate, including more tart, sour flavours and have a wide range of health benefits, including promoting healthy digestion and gut bacteria.

The range of possibilities for fermenting is enormous – wine, beer, milk, nuts, fish, meat, eggs, tonic drinks – as well as pickles, chutneys and sourdough breads. We are very much at the start of our journey exploring the possibilities of wild fermenting our homegrown vegetables and fruit, although we have made wine and beer for decades. Charles' sourdough bread using his homemade Homeacres sourdough yeast and home ground flour (we buy the organic grain in) is a popular part of our course lunches. The recipe is on page 118.

Preserving food in oil

Preserving the harvest in oil is an ancient technique in which the hot oil poured over the cooked vegetables acts a sealing agent, protecting food from spoiling and imparting a delicious flavour. We mostly use olive oil, sometimes mixed with other mildly flavoured oils. This method is used to preserve cheese, fish and meat too. We preserve our tomatoes, peppers, aubergines and artichokes this way; it is also a wonderful way of preserving gluts of mushrooms from foraging or bought from markets. Once opened, the preserves can be used in cooking or eaten straight from the jar. Use up the oil in cooking and salad dressings.

These will last a couple of weeks refrigerated. To ensure a long shelf life, can in a water bath canner (according to the instructions for your machine and the recipe) or freeze small jars, bringing to room temperature before using.

Cordials

A lovely way of preserving fruit to be enjoyed all year round, some cordials can also be beneficial for health, especially those high in vitamin C (elderberry, rosehip) or including healing herbs and spices. Cordials are usually made by simmering fruit in a small quantity of water in a large pan, cooling, straining then bringing the fruit liquid to the boil with the right quantity of sugar, honey or other sweet preservative (according to your recipe; alternatives include agave, coconut sugar, maple syrup – each will lend a different taste to the finished cordial) and simmering for 5-10 minutes before pouring into hot, sterilised bottles and sealing. The cordial can be further preserved in a water bath canner.

Sugar free cordials are canned to prolong their shelf life, or frozen. If you do not like the tart flavours of elderberry, blackberry or similar, experiment with using some homemade stevia liquid in the cordial (see page 122).

An alternative is to use a Steam Juicer which uses steam to extract the juice. The resulting juice is good for making cordials, jelly, puddings, cocktails, syrups and soups.

The remaining fruit from either method can be used in puddings or as a base for homemade fruit wines.

Storing fruit in alcohol

There are many variations of alcohol soaked fruits, including the German Rumtopf, in which the whole season is preserved in alcohol. It traditionally started with the first fruits and end with the last fruit harvests of autumn, layered as they became available in a large ceramic lidded container with sugar and rum. Once the Rumtopt is full, it is left for a further 4-6 weeks. The boozy fruit and syrup is served in all manner of deserts; the strained liquid can also be served as a liqueur.

Alternatively, place your washed and dried fruits in a large glass lidded jar, sprinkle with sugar and add the alcohol of your choice: vodka, gin, rum, brandy, whisky, bourbon, whatever you fancy and have to hand! Use in desserts (the fruit is amazing in trifle), served with cream (dairy or whipped coconut cream or nut creams), ice cream; the liquid can be drunk as a liqueur or mixed into cocktails. The fruit adds a festive dimension to savoury dishes, stirred into sauces or served warmed as an accompaniment. These preserved fruits look very beautiful and make excellent gifts.

Autumn preserving – plum jam, blackcurrant jam, blackcurrant cordial, blackcurrant vinegar, bramble liqueur. apple sauce, bottled blackberries

Homemade alcohol:
wine, beer, cider and infused liqueurs

Making your own alcoholic drinks opens up a whole new realm of flavours and combinations which are usually unavailable in shops. There are some wonderful recipe books available full of interesting combinations for alcoholic brews. Many of mine were found in thrift stores and are from the 1940s and 50s.

Wine

Almost everything you grow can be made into a delicious country wine. Do be careful though; some can be extremely potent! The equipment needed is fairly simple – a large fermentation bucket with a lid, some demi johns with fermentation locks, wine bottles (we reuse these) and new corks. Use fruit, herbs, wild weeds and vegetables. One of my favourite homemade wines uses mangold, a large root vegetable which I grow just for this purpose.

Beer

You can use your own wild yeast to make the more familiar beers from hops and malt, and also ginger or root beer. Nettle beer, made from foraged plants, has been used as a tonic for centuries. Try other wildcrafted beers using foraged ingredients – recipes include dandelions, mushrooms, walnuts, horehound and heather.

NETTLE BEER

- 900g/2lb nettle tops, carefully picked from young fresh nettles
- 450g/1lb demerara or unbleached sugar, preferably organic
- 30g/1oz cream of tartar
- 2 lemons, thinly peeled rinds and juice
- Brewer's yeast
- 4.5 litres/1 gallon of water
- Optional – 5cm (2in) root ginger, sliced

In a large pan, bring the water to the boil with the nettles, lemon rind and root ginger, if using. Boil for 30 minutes.

Meanwhile, activate the yeast (if necessary) and pour the sugar and cream of tartar into the fermentation vessel. Strain the hot liquid carefully onto the sugar. Stir and leave until lukewarm, then add the yeast. Stir, cover and leave in a warm place for 5 days.

Strain through muslin and bottle in very strong sterilised bottles. It is important to only use bottles which are designed for fizzy drinks; do check that yours are suitable, otherwise they can explode which is very dangerous. (Do not use wine bottles or similar.)

It is ready to drink after a week.

Mangelwurzel is an old English name for the mangold *Beta vulgaris* (also known as field beet, usually grown as animal fodder). The leaves can be eaten like spinach or chard; the roots used as you would potato or swede. In south Somerset where we live, mangelwurzels were hollowed out on the last Thursday of October and made into lanterns known as 'Punkies', a tradition which still continues in some parts. Children would walk the streets after dark, singing the Punkie Song:

> It's Punkie Night tonight!
> It's Punkie Night tonight!
> Adam and Eve would not
>   believe
> It's Punkie Night tonight!
> Give me a candle
> Give me a light
> If you haven't got a candle
> A penny's all right

A mangelwurzel growing at Steph's allotment

Mangelwurzels make a particularly potent and delicious wine. Indeed we refer to the effect as feeling 'mangelwur-zelled'!

My recipe is based on one in a 1950s book: *Home Made Country Wines* by Dorothy Wise. It makes approximately 1 gallon of wine.

MANGELWURZEL WINE

- 1800g/4lb mangelwurzels, washed and sliced into 2.5cm (1in) pieces, no need to peel
- 1800g/4lb sugar, preferably unbleached and organic
- 10cm (4in) piece of root ginger, sliced
- Thinly peeled rinds of 2 lemons and 1 orange, preferably organic
- Juice of the lemons and orange
- 4.5 litres/1 gallon water
- Wine yeast

Place the mangelwurzel slices and citrus peels into a large pan with the water. Boil until the root is tender.

Meanwhile, pour the sugar into the fermentation bucket and activate the yeast (if necessary). When the root is soft, strain the contents of the pan onto the sugar and add the citrus juices. Stir until the sugar has dissolved and leave until lukewarm; now add the yeast. Stir, cover and leave for a further 24 hours in a warm place.

Transfer into a sterilised fermentation jar, insert the airlock and leave somewhere warm to ferment. This takes around 2-3 months. Then siphon off into bottles, cork, label and store for at least a year.

Cider

Every year in the autumn, Charles harvests apples from his orchard and the surplus from neighbours to make gallons and gallons of apple juice using his apple press. Some of this juice is bottled and preserved in large cauldrons set on open fires in the yard, some made into cider in large plastic barrels. On a smaller scale, Steph uses windfalls and gifted surpluses to make 'Cottage Cider', again based on a recipe in *Home Made Country Wines, Beer, Mead and Metheglin*, written in 1957.

COTTAGE CIDER

I use any apples that I have for this recipe. It is particularly good for using up windfalls and damaged apples that won't store. Using homegrown, organic apples means that you do not need to use a yeast to make this drink. If you are using shop bought, then add a cider yeast to the brew.

- 5.5kg/12lb apples, chopped by hand or use a mincer or food processor
- 500g/1lb raisins or sultanas, chopped
- 700g/1.5lb unbleached granulated sugar
- 4.5 litres/1 gallon warm water
- Cider yeast, if using

Put the apples, dried fruit, sugar and yeast (if using) in a large fermenting bucket. Pour on the water and stir. Leave in a warm place for two weeks, stirring every day, pushing down the pulp as you stir.

Strain through muslin and decant into a sterilised fermentation jar. Insert the airlock and leave in a warm place until fermentation has ceased. This can take several months, depending on the fruit and time of year. Then move to a cooler place for a further month before siphoning into strong bottles (see nettle beer for information about bottles).

The cider can be drunk now, or left for the flavour to improve.

Infused liqueurs

Always use a good quality alcohol to make fruit, flower, leaf, root, spice and herb infused spirits; a poor quality alcohol can make you ill. They can be drunk neat, in cocktails, added to winter puddings, or mixed with hot water for a warming drink. It makes a lovely gift with a very long shelf life. Use vodka, gin, rum, brandy, whisky, bourbon, tequila, whatever seems most appropriate for your ingredients. Experiment with the quantity of sugar and your ingredients – many infusions taste far more interesting if less sweet. You can also use alternative sweeteners, including homegrown stevia.

One of Steph's favourite infusions is simply blue butterfly pea flowers infused in vodka or gin for a couple of days, which makes the most amazing electric blue liquid which turns a stunning violet with the addition of a little lime or lemon juice.

Bramble liqueur – blackberries infusing with vodka and sugar to make a delicious cocktail ingredient

Blue butterfly pea (*Clitoria ternatea*) is a tender perennial from tropical Asia. In the UK, it is a half hardy annual, dying quickly with the first frosts even in a polytunnel.

N.B. The flowers of edible peas are safe to eat, but the flowers and seeds of sweet peas (*Lathyrus odoratus*) are toxic and should not be consumed.

AUTUMN FRUIT LIQUEUR IS SWEET, FRUITY AND POTENT

You need:

- A large glass jar or bottle, one with a wide lid so it is easy to get the fruit in and out
- 700g fruit, fresh or frozen – blackberries, raspberries, elderberries
- 350g sugar, I use unbleached soft brown
- 1 litre vodka, gin or brandy

Put the fruit and sugar in the jar, top with alcohol and stir to dissolve the sugar. Put on the lid and store for 3 months, shaking twice a week. Strain through muslin or a sieve and pour into labelled bottles.

This recipe works well with most other soft fruit.

Salting and smoking

We have not tried preserving in salt or by smoking, but these ancient methods offer more possibilities for the home preserver. There are some fascinating preserving books available which cover these methods.

Chapter 11

Saving Seeds

Great seeds come with understanding more about vegetables' growth

Saving seeds is a fine way to close the loop, especially when so few of the seeds we buy are even produced in our own country, and most are grown using synthetic chemicals.

Some discolouration of pea pods after a damp summer, now dry and ready to shell for seed

However, consider these points before starting:

- The number of seeding plants you need for genetic maintenance, by cross-pollination
- The area of garden that these plants will take up
- Misbehaving weather, such as rain when seeds are ripening
- The time needed for harvesting and winnowing.

Seed saving requires commitment, space in the garden, time and knowledge. When you are successful, the results make it worthwhile.

Steph rubbing chervil seed over a sheet

Why save seed

Multinational corporations own and control around three quarters of the seed trade. They own heirloom seed companies, not that you would know, and many sellers of vegetable seeds now buy much of their stock from outside.

The dwindling number of independent seed producers include Franchi from Italy ('Seeds of Italy' in the UK), Real Seeds and Seed Cooperative in the UK, and Bingenheim Saatgut in Germany. The last two grow biodynamic seed.

- Seed freshness is the major ingredient of rapid germination and vigorous growth – when under a year old they just want to grow. A problem with bought seed is the absence of this information, because it says only 'packeted year ending', which reveals nothing about when the seed was grown and harvested.

For seed sellers, the tests to certify germination percentages, which legally must be only 70% in the UK (and for flower seeds there are no legal minima), are mostly performed in laboratories. The warmth and light encourages extra germination which does not translate to healthy growth – even if they germinate, the seedlings are weak and stunted.

Every year we do sowing comparisons with two batches of the same vegetable, from different companies' seed, recently purchased. Some batches germinate poorly, alongside successful growth of other suppliers' or home-saved seeds, all sown and grown in the same conditions.

Usually an email of complaint to the worst performer is explained in terms of how seeds are managed, together with a free packet of seeds. This is no help when one has wasted a part of the growing season, compost, and precious space in the greenhouse too.

SUITABLE WEATHER

Seeds ripen in warm, dry weather, so in damp climates you need extra skill and probably a polytunnel to achieve viable seed harvests. Lettuce for example takes one whole season to grow and set seed, including some dry weather in autumn, otherwise ripening seeds may go mouldy before harvest. This is one reason why seed farming is concentrating in fewer areas of best climate, with dry air and a long growing season.

Lettuce seed freshness: mixed bought seed on left, home-saved seed on right

For root vegetables, seed saving also means saving (not eating!) your best roots, so that you can plant them to flower, say 10-12 together. As a result, you have larger seed harvests than you are likely to need. Therefore it's worth cooperating with other gardeners and growers so that harvests can be shared, in return for seed of vegetables grown by others.

Climbing French bean in tunnel, Cobra for seed

Onion plants late summer, ripening their seed in the polytunnel

Inbreeders and outbreeders: the vital knowledge

Inbreeders

Some vegetables breed true and well from the seed of just one plant. Kate McEvoy of Real Seeds* says you could build a population of pea seeds from one heirloom pea, because each pea variety grows the same from each seed, without any cross-pollination from nearby pea plants of different varieties. Also in this category are lettuce, French bean and non-hybrid tomatoes.

Outbreeders

Most vegetables are outbreeders and to keep their seed, you need space for several plants of the same variety flowering together, to be sure of cross-pollination. When outbreeders flower alone, their seeds grow weak plants with 'inbreeding depression', characterised by poor germination and uneven growth.

To save seed of leeks, onions, brassicas, runner (pole) beans, sweet corn, beetroot and spinach, it is recommended to grow at least six and up to 12 plants. Possibly three or four would suffice but it's a risk.

Sometimes you can reduce the numbers of flowering outbreeders, as we found with just three plants of Medania spinach in the polytunnel. We had planted 40 the previous August and picked leaves from October until June following, then let three plants flower and set seed on stems 1m (3ft) high, tied to bamboos. They were overshadowed by tomato plants, but in early August we rubbed out some worthwhile seed from the dry stems, then winnowed and sowed it straightaway. They grew into vigorous and long-lived plants, and the following August we sowed this same seed again, by now a year old, and it gave 90% germination with strong growth for 10 months.

* Seed saving info www.realseeds.co.uk/seedsavinginfo.html

One plant of coriander Calypso, sown the previous autumn, wintered in tunnel, needs more plants to cross pollinate = lots of space needed

F1 hybrids

Vegetable breeding in the last decades has concentrated on hybrid varieties, many of which grow excellent vegetables, with high yields and good flavour. Unfortunately from a seed saver's perspective, they don't breed true. For example, do not save seed of hybrid tomato varieties such as Sungold and Rosada F1, because they grow uninteresting and flavourless tomatoes (having tried this!).

F1 seeds are the result of firstly inbreeding two generations of plants to achieve desirable traits, then the two lines are cross pollinated, sometimes in a forced way. This gives precisely one generation of a desired outcome, but if you sow seeds from those plants, you get a random mix of undesirable traits.

Seed packets write 'F1' if they are hybrids. The process does not involve genetic modification, nor is it a natural method. The results are predictable, consistent and profitable, the reason for seed producers favouring work on F1 hybrids, rather than on open pollinated strains.

The result is poor maintenance (plant selection and seed saving) of many open pollinated varieties such as Gardener's Delight tomato. In the 1980s this was small and sweet, the gold standard of cherry tomatoes, but most 'gardener's delight' seed now grows considerably larger and less sweet tomatoes. Same name, different produce.

Space, more space and isolation

At the flowering and seed developing stage, some vegetables are economical of space, especially tomatoes, peas and beans, which are seeding anyway as part of the food harvest. Lettuce and alliums (onion family) make reasonably compact heads. On the other hand brassicas, chenopods and beetroot need room to branch out.

Another factor is outbreeders' need for a certain isolation distance, from relations that flower at the same time, to avoid unwanted cross-pollination. Leeks may cross with ornamental alliums, brassicas with brassica weeds, and carrots with hedgerow umbellifers such as Queen Anne's Lace (wild carrot).

Quoted isolation distances are for open ground, while insect growth is slowed by hedges, fences and buildings, therefore it's difficult to give precise figures.

The risk of cross-pollination is reduced by growing seed plants of the same variety in a polytunnel, or by making an isolation cage.*

Seeds that pollinate by wind need the longest isolation distances to maintain varietal purity, up to two miles (3km) for beetroot and chard, and further than that for maize, whose pollen is so light.

Harvesting seeds

The easiest harvests are from certain fruiting vegetables, which already contain seeds when we normally pick them. For example, leave pea and bean pods to turn brown and dry on the plants, then gather and shell out their seeds.†

---

† A clear and useful book is *Back Garden Seed Saving* by Sue Stickland, eco-logic Books, 2008

Harvested Czar pods, November (late!), riper on left and barely ripe on right

Same Czar after shelling, drier on left and damper on right, both need more drying, or eat the ones on right

---

* Isolation cage of bamboo and netting
www.realseeds.co.uk/isolation%20cages.html

Treading on borlotti pods to shell out the seeds is a faster way to open them

The next process is winnowing borlotti beans on an afternoon of light breezes

seed harvesting

Right, from top:

Leek seed rubbed, next it needs winnowing

Dry seedpods of brassicas after walking on them

Brassicas in a bucket after winnowing mustard seed, June

Stay observant

When flowering is mostly finished and seed pods are developing, watch for drying of these pods, usually to a pale brown colour, within about a month of the first flowers drying. Check often, to see if any dry seeds can be shelled out or if any may be falling.

Waiting too long can waste a lot of good seed, for example onions are prone to drop seeds without being obviously ready, and during a thunderstorm one August, almost a whole crop of parsnip seed was washed to the ground.

Gently pull out plants such as spinach, lettuce and brassicas when about half their seed pods or clusters are dry. Hang in a dry, airy place for a month or so, with a sheet underneath to catch any falling seeds, then break seed pods by hand rubbing, or by walking over plants on a cotton sheet placed on concrete.

Winnowing

Do this outside in a breeze. Winnowing is to blow away fragments of pea, bean or other pods, lettuce fluff and fragments of dry spinach leaf.

Careful use of two buckets in a gentle breeze gives sufficiently clean seed for home use. Let seed drop from one bucket to the other in a steady flow, and watch the seed going in rather than fluff flying out, to be sure that the precious seed itself is falling correctly. Repeat two to four times, in gentle winds only, and beware of gusts.

Often there are still some unwanted bits after winnowing, and you can pick out the larger ones. Mostly the non-seed residue is dry, small, and does not affect keeping quality or germination percentages. Clean the seed as much as you can, without worrying that it looks less perfect than bought seed.

Black Russian is open pollinated, so good to save seed from fruits

One plant of Grenoble Red lettuce seeding, 11 months after sowing

Self sown Lollo Rossa at flowering stage in late summer

If you produce a lot of seed, it's worth building an apparatus which fits to the end of a vacuum cleaner.* As seed is funnelled in, the lighter debris is sucked out, but make sure you calibrate it for seed to fall rather than go into the cleaner!

Some veg to save seed from

Tomato inbreeder

Be sure that you are saving seed of an open pollinated variety rather than F1 hybrid variety.

Most tomatoes do not cross with different varieties nearby, except for potato leaved and currant varieties, and the first fruits of some beefsteak tomatoes, when they grow from an initial large 'king' flower.

At harvest time, squeeze and scrape out seeds of one or more fine and fully ripe tomatoes, into a cup or jar, add water and leave to ferment for a few days in warmth. Off smells suggest removal of germination inhibitors, and this technique also helps identify the best seeds, which sink to the bottom when you stir lightly.

Drain off the scum and wash seeds with more water, sieve them and spread on a plate, rather than cardboard which they stick to. Once dry they need rubbing to separate individual seeds.

Lettuce inbreeder

Because lettuces rarely cross pollinate, it's fine to let two or three different varieties flower near to each other. In zone 8/9, our best seed harvests are in a polytunnel, or sometimes outdoors from plants sown as early as possible.

Choose the plant that pleases you most and insert a bamboo cane beside it, to remind you not to harvest. When about to flower, tie the flower stem to this bamboo; six weeks later and about a fortnight after the pale yellow flowers are fading, check for readiness by rubbing out seeds of the first fluffy, plump clusters. If it's wet weather and the leaves are decaying with mildew, twist out the whole plant and hang it upside down in a dry, airy place.

A month later or when fully dry, rub each flower cluster over a sheet to catch the falling seeds; sometimes we rub the heads between two blocks of wood. There will be a lot of debris; pick larger pieces off the top and a gentle winnowing helps clean most of the rest.

* Seed cleaning machine www.realseeds.co.uk/seedcleaner.html

Broad (fava) beans outbreeders

Fortunately these outbreeders tend to look inwards, and a distance of just 50m is usually enough to maintain purity. As with peas and other beans, it's worth marking say four plants for seed, then leave all their pods unpicked. You can harvest the black, dry pods about a month after the last food harvest, from the same sowing.

Peas and French beans inbreeders

These are easy because they breed true, and pods for seed are usually dry within a month of your last harvest to eat. At this time of summer for peas and early autumn for French beans, the weather is likely warm and dry enough to ripen seeds on the plant, then harvest pods when pale brown and crisp. Pod out seeds straightaway and leave in a bright, airy place for two or three days before bagging up in paper.

French beans include borlottis.

Runner (pole) beans outbreeders

These are famously promiscuous with any other runner bean plants up to half a mile away. Apart from that, they are simple to save seed from, when you've sown the plants by early summer, and are in zone 8/9 or warmer. This ensures enough summer weather for seed development and ripening. In Somerset we pick these seeds from early to mid autumn, until the first frost.

Squashes, marrow outbreeders

To prevent cross-pollination you need either to grow only one variety, while hoping that near neighbours have the same one or none at all, or to hand pollinate. This is a precision job.

- Enclose one each of a soon-to-open male and female flower, in breathable polythene or paper, secured with a rubber band around the stem.
- Next day, just possibly two days later, remove the bag from the now-open male flower, peel off its petals, remove the bag off the female and quickly rub the male's pollen onto female stamens, then quickly recover the female flower until it has withered.
- Mark the developing fruit so you recognise it at harvest time. For courgette/zucchini, this means allowing the pollinated courgette to grow to a marrow with hard skin.
- Seeds can be scraped out and then washed, just before you cook the fruit's flesh.

Sometimes a cross of neighbouring squashes of different variety is not a problem, as long as they are all squash. One year we kept seed of Kabocha squash which had grown near to some Kuri squash plants, and their fruits were mostly similar to the original Kabocha. Best not keep seeds of squash grown near to courgette or pumpkin, as their fruits would probably be an undesirable mixture.

Aquadulce broad bean
seed drying on plant

Czar runner beans in early autumn
– yellow pods hold the drying seed

save seed

All these squash grew
from seeds of the same
fruit, Kabocha, which had
grown near to Uchiki Kuri

Rosada variety is an F1 hybrid so best not save its seed, but you can save side shoots

Side shoots of one-month-old Rosada tomato plants, late autumn

side shoots

Tubers, bulbs, shoots to save

Potatoes

Virus contamination is the problem to avoid, revealed by bright yellowing of leaves; see page 45 (Chapter 5). From potato seed bought in spring, we find that saving seed for planting the next spring gives good results. A third year is more risky as perhaps other diseases build up and for the cost of some seed, each of which can give over 2kg (4lb) potatoes, it's safer to buy new seed every other year.

You can use slightly green potatoes for seed, of any size larger than eggs. Create extra seed by cutting big tubers in half, lengthwise and through the stub-end which was joined to last year's plant.

Garlic

Save the money you would spend on expensive seed by keeping the best bulb(s) from your harvest, then plant the largest cloves. We have done this for 16 years consecutively, even after years when there was much rust. From what we observe, rust is caused not by infection of seed, rather by weather conditions, as witness the rust free garlic every year in Homeacres polytunnel, out of the rain.

Tomato side shoots

These root easily, starting from shoots 2-3in (5-7cm) long, pushed into a pencil size hole in a small pot of moist compost. Any variety is possible, and you need somewhere to keep the plants alive through winter – frost free, not too warm and reasonably light.

You may have quite tall but thin plants by early spring, almost falling over. In that case, simply pinch off the top and replant it to root again, to have sturdy plants by mid spring as soon as frosts have passed. If plants are still too forward before you are ready, take some of their side shoots to make new and smaller plants.

Difficult vegetables for seed saving

Here are some problems we have encountered:

- In a damp summer, outdoor onions developed mildew on their leaves before seeds had developed and the harvest was tiny, for the space and time involved, with poor germination the next spring. In contrast, onions planted for seeding in the polytunnel gave more seed and fair germination next spring.

Medium size and home-saved potato seed placed on surface, then mulched over with compost and hay

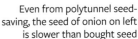

Even from polytunnel seed-saving, the seed of onion on left is slower than bought seed

- Outdoor spinach grew tall, sprawled and was difficult to support, then other plants needed the space in mid summer, before its seeds were dry, so we removed it before harvest.

- To save space we left only one plant of Red Frills mustard to flower, then had a plentiful harvest with good growth from the sowings, but the second year of doing this gave depressed seeds with weak germination – for brassicas you need space to grow enough seeding plants.

How long to keep seed?

Keep seeds cool, and most importantly keep them dry: for example with a small pack of silica gel in your seed packet container. A sealed container can go in the fridge, but for seed packets a fridge environment is too damp.

Home-saved seed stays viable for two or more years, especially legumes, tomatoes, brassicas and lettuce. Alliums and especially umbellifers keep less well: parsnips are famous for storing badly, though we find that speculative sowings of two-year-old (bought!) seed come up well, helped by the moisture retention of compost on undisturbed soil.

Best keepers are brassica seeds for up to five years, and tomato seeds for up to eight. However the vigour of growth from old seeds may be reduced.

Something different

Potato seed germination, from their 'apple' pods (if absence of blight allows them to ripen in early autumn), takes up to three months. Harvest results of the tiny potatoes are uncertain; it's akin to sowing apple pips, but unlike with apples you at least have a result in the first year. From any good harvests, which are small, keep the best tubers to plant again, and name your new variety!

- Poppies of edible-seed varieties are fun to grow and not difficult. Sow in spring, space at 10in (25cm), gather the seed heads as soon as they show brown, before they drop thousands, spread on a tray to finish drying. Then store in a glass jar and use in salads and bread.

Red Frills mustard seeding needs a lot of space

Edible poppy seeds, 205g from 20 plants

Chapter 12
Food for Thought

What we eat is an important part of cultural identity. Recipes handed down through generations invoke a connection to the past and our shared experience. People displaced from their homelands through war, migration or environmental disasters would travel, if they could, with seeds that reflect the harvests of their ancestral homes, to introduce into a new land. Traditions around food help to bind families and communities together. Seasoning or the traditional ingredients of something as simple as a soup or winter stew reflects the different cultural histories. Food can be an expression of identity and a celebration of freedom.

Rich smells from the kitchen invoke memories of childhood, other lands and different times. Cuisine historically has reflected a person's social status, from peasant dishes to the feasts of the ruling classes. The criteria of what represents wealth or good breeding has changed over the centuries and differs from region to region. In Elizabethan England, being able to afford to consume quantities of sugar was a conspicuous display of wealth, which led to rotten teeth being considered fashionable as it demonstrated affluence, an idea that is strange to us today.

What we eat is very much bound up with our identities, not just culturally or nationally, but also how we want to be perceived by others: it is a statement. Food is identified with increased consumption and consumerism. We are encouraged to identify with everything from junk food

**Homegrown
plant based lunch**
(Homeacres courses)

Lunch

brands, highly sugared confectionery and drinks, to obscure ingredients (which usually have to be imported), so-called superfoods and a myriad of diet choices in the West. This has led to ill health, consumerism and food waste on a scale that is seriously damaging our environment.

We are becoming increasingly aware of the power of multinational corporations and the effect this is having on our diets, food sovereignty and the ability to grow our own food, save seeds and the consequences for people, communities and the environment. The manipulation is becoming clearer, as is the evidence of the health problems, addictive nature and environmental consequences of certain ingredients like sugar, palm oil, margarine and high fructose syrup.

Food, a fundamental necessity for life, is being repackaged as a lifestyle. Many superfoods are indeed tasty and full of beneficial vitamins and minerals, but so are many less mysterious and exotic fruits and vegetables which grow well and naturally where we live. It is far better to look around oneself at nature's larder locally, than import a particular berry or grain from thousands of miles away, often at the expense of the people of that country (as in the case of quinoa).

The waste generated by 'food fashions' is extraordinary. We are encouraged to buy unusual oils, grains, commercially mixed sauces, dried fruits, etc. which often form a small part of a particular recipe, then languish in the back of the cupboard or fridge until discarded, often barely or even not used at all.

Even when the superfood of the moment is something less exotic – kale, spinach, broccoli – the reverence and claims for the vegetable detract from the real message of good nutrition. Eating greens should be part of one's daily life, not a fad.

In the West, food stores are packed with a huge range of different foods from across the globe: seasonality is rarely acknowledged and even when it is, often the seasonal part of a recipe is just one ingredient, cooked with out of season and imported goods.

On the surface we appear to live in a shopping environment that offers a wide range of choice yet the Western diet is actually lacking in nutrient diversity as we tend to eat the same foods over and over again. Supermarkets limit choice, especially with the kinds of foods they promote which regularly contain high levels of salt, sugar and processed ingredients. People usually eat too much processed foods, the same grains and meat products and not enough vegetables. We are fed a myth that convenience food is fast, easy and affordable whereas made from scratch food is expensive, difficult and too time consuming.

Of around 50,000 edible plants grown in the world, we primarily eat just 15. Corn, soybean, wheat and sunflower dominate because they are easy to grow (especially chemically) and harvest and they are profitable. Much of the food we eat is grown on soil that is mineral deficient and suffering from decades of aggressive chemical farming practices; it is sadly increasingly deficient in nutrients.

We think that the key to good health is a balanced diet including as many seasonal ingredients as possible. We need to eat a wide range of minerals, amino acids, essential fatty acids and vitamins that our bodies need and can't produce themselves: this can not be provided by a single food group.

Taking control of how your food is grown and what you eat is a political act, particularly crucial now that so much of the world's food production and availability – and therefore the health of whole populations – is becoming under the control of a few corporations. Growing your own enables you to increase the variety in your diet. The vegetables, fruit and herbs will be healthier grown in a vibrant soil full of life.

Food and recipes: a toolkit for amazing food

Food gives us energy and sustenance. It is wonderful that we are aware of so much choice and variety, with international recipes opening up new culinary horizons. I love exploring different ways with spices, herbs, vegetables and other ingredients learned from recipe books from other cultures and countries. Cooking from scratch, one is very much in the present, enjoying the pleasure of everyday moments. It can be an art form.

Sometimes of course after a busy day it just isn't possible to create a homegrown meal and this is where home preserved food can help, or indeed the occasional takeaway or something from the supermarket stashed in the freezer for emergency feeding of hungry families. Cooking your own food is a pleasure but in real life we also have to go out and work, do chores, take the children to the dentist or after school classes, have social activities; the unexpected occurs, life happens. We need to be kind to ourselves.

Homegrown, seasonal food is delicious; you need less emphasis on elaborate sauces and exotic ingredients, allowing the flavours to shine. There is a beauty to delicious fresh food, fresh vegetables, good bread, and homemade preserves.

When growing your own, even if it is in just a few pots, the anticipation of delicious, nourishing meals starts with the sowing of a few seeds, nurturing the growing plants and the exhilaration of the harvest. Then the pleasure of creating your own nourishing dishes, relishing the flavour all the more because you know the provenance of your food.

Homegrown food can be very exciting, in many ways more so than the novelty of imported delicacies. There are amazing colours, unexpected textures, gorgeous appetising fragrances and extraordinary flavours. You can experience the true flavour of freshly harvested vegetables grown with care in healthy, vibrant soil, a surprising sweetness. The food has the energy of the place where it has grown and the energy of those who have grown it.

Very few of us can grow everything we need and be entirely self sufficient: enjoy the achievement of what you can do. Although we grow almost all of our fresh fruit and vegetables we buy oranges, lemons, ginger root, coffee beans, culinary oils, spices, vinegars as well as pulses, grains, nuts and dried fruit such as sultanas, apricots and raisins. We buy organic and fair trade as much as possible. Locally, this supports small community shops and internationally, smaller growers, such as small scale olive oil producers in Europe. (There are many issues about the real sustainability of fair trade enterprises in some other countries, whether they are genuinely creating valuable business opportunities and benefiting the communities there or perhaps preventing the people from producing food crops they need. This is a huge topic, too big for this book, but is perhaps something you may wish to consider when choosing certain brands of imported goods.)

Eating seasonally, including using home preserved foods

The recipes here include a range of foods, bringing the vegetables to the foreground. Living with an awareness of the seasons gives one a sense of what is available to eat now and a preparedness for future harvests and meals. In the late summer, we'll eat fresh tomato soup for lunch then go outside to plant cabbages for spring.

Growing your own brings the opportunity to reconnect with the traditional pleasures of eating seasonally, increasing the awareness of what is available where you live at different times of the year, both in the kitchen garden and in nature when foraging.

There is a sense of achievement, a connection with the past, sharing the pleasure of your homegrown abundance with a good meal. Far from being limited, seasonal cooking is liberating and inspirational. Deciding what to make with that week's harvest is fun.

Every course day at Homeacres, I have an idea of some of the things I will make for the lunch but the actual menu for the day is created that morning, when we have gathered together the fruits of our labours, including home preserves such as dried tomatoes and cumin seeds and stored ingredients (onions, garlic, winter squash), plus the few store bought ingredients we use (oil, vinegar, mustard, etc.). It is exciting deciding what we will eat, a flexible decision which also reflects the weather and other considerations: is it cold, hot, raining, and do some of our guests have dietary requirements?

An awareness of seasonality helps your budget too when shopping in markets, etc. You can buy seasonal fruit and vegetables which you can't grow at home, often cheaply and certainly with more flavour than out of season foods which may have travelled long distances or spent many months in cold storage. Use these to make fresh meals and also preserves to store. This can include some imported goods, such as Seville oranges in late winter for making marmalades.

Taster menu tip

One way to really explore the textures and flavours of your homegrown produce, in particular fruit, herbs and vegetables which you are new to growing, is to have regular seasonal 'taster menu' meals. Harvest your delicious food and serve it simply as it is, cooked and raw (except for veg which needs to be cooked of course). So, I would serve beetroot raw, grated and sliced thinly, boiled and roasted, for example.

This gives an opportunity to fully appreciate your food with all of your senses and to experience different combinations, expanding your own recipes at home.

Upcycle your peelings!

The UK throws away more food than any other country in the EU – 15 million tonnes of food wasted – mostly by the food industry and supermarkets. Fortunately there are many schemes emerging which enable some of this food to be used, but there is still the need for a huge change to ensure that food is not wasted.

We do not consider composting to be 'waste', but before adding leftover bits of veg and peelings to the compost heap, here are some suggestions for things you can make to make use of odds and ends left over from making your dinner.

Using up citrus peelings

Citrus fruit is imported into the UK, so it is good to use as much of the fruit as possible. I grow small lemon and lime trees but average around three or four fruits a year, as we don't really have the climate.

Dried citrus peel make useful firelighters for your open fire or woodburner, the natural oils help the fire to start and they smell lovely too. Dry the peel on a tray or herb drying rack in a warm, dry airy place – in the airing cupboard, beside the fire (being aware of safety of course), on a sunny windowsill or even outdoors in the sunshine if it is summer. You can also dry them on a metal tray on top of a woodburner or stove, keeping an eye on things to make sure they don't burn – the smell is gorgeous, like roasting citrus fruits!

If you're using peels for culinary use or on your skin, I recommend using organic fruit which has been washed and dried with a clean tea towel.

A quick and simple use for lemon peelings is lemon peel tea: pop the peel of one lemon in a teapot, pour on freshly boiled water, allow to brew for 5 minutes, strain and serve. Add honey, agave or other sweetener if desired. This is a very healthy brew, a good way to start the day and to aid digestion after meals.

The first strawberries of summer

HOMEMADE CITRUS CLEANER

This is very simple and makes a beautifully fragranced and powerful cleaner. Citrus contains d-limonene, a natural solvent which breaks down oil, making it very effective.

You will need:

- A glass jar with a lid
- Citrus peelings – orange, lemon, satsuma, lime, grapefruit etc.
- Cider or white vinegar

Loosely fill the jar with peelings, then pour on the vinegar to cover all of the peels, leaving about 1cm (0.5in) space at the top. Put on the lid and put somewhere dark for two weeks. (You can leave it for longer, a month or so – this will make a more powerful cleaner.)

Strain the vinegar into another labelled jar. This keeps for at least a year but is so useful it rarely lasts that long!

For a simple, powerful, multipurpose cleaning spray pour the solution into a labelled spray bottle to half fill it, then top up with water and use.

CITRUS SCOURING POWDER

Put some homemade peels into a herb grinder and blend until powdery.

- 1 cup bicarbonate of soda
- 1 cup finely ground sea salt
- 1tbsp of finely ground citrus peels

Mix together and store in a jar. Dip a damp cloth or sponge in and scrub. Use a toothbrush for taps. Rinse and spray with a homemade citrus or herb spray to make your kitchen and bathroom shine.

For a soft, creamy scrub, drizzle in washing up liquid, stirring until the desired consistency is reached.

Use left over citrus skins to make a powerful home cleaner

citrus peelings

Citrus zest seasoning

Before squeezing, grate orange, lemon or lime zest. This can be frozen until needed and added to salad dressing, sauces and baking. Or dry the peels, blend in a herb grinder until powdered and store in a labelled jar.

To remove sticky residues

To help remove residue of sticky labels etc., squeeze the citrus skin to release the oils, rub the sticky area vigorously, then clean.

Cleaning taps

We live in a hard water area, so limescale build up is a problem. I was given this solution for limescale on chrome and stainless steel taps by a plumber. Put some citrus peels (you can also use all of the fruit halves after squeezing) in a blender with enough water to help it mix and whizz until it is a lumpy soupy consistency. Spread this over some rags and wrap around the taps. Leave for an hour or so, wipe off carefully with the plug in so it doesn't go down the drain (put in the compost) and scrub the taps with an old toothbrush dipped in salt. When all of the limescale has gone, bring the tap to a shine by rubbing with lemon skin and wiping with a rag, or spraying with citrus cleaner.

In the dishwasher

Put citrus fruit halves into the dishwasher after squeezing along with your crockery etc. They help keep the dishwasher clean and fresh and help reduce limescale.

Simple room fragrancer

Put the citrus peels into a pan of water and simmer on the back of the stove or on top of the woodburner. Check to make sure it doesn't boil dry.

LEMON OIL (WORKS FOR ORANGE AND LIME TOO)

Only use peels which have no flesh on and which are perfectly dry – leave for an hour or so on a clean cloth to dry thoroughly (to avoid mould growing in the oil).

Put the lemon peels in a large jar and add the oil. You need 1 cup of olive to the peel of 2 lemons. Top up with more oil if the peels are not completely covered by at least 1cm (0.5in) of oil.

Replace the lid and place in a dry, cool dark place, such as a cupboard, for two weeks.

Strain the oil through a sieve lined with muslin, discarding the peels into the compost bin. Pour into a labelled jar and use in recipes and to make DIY skin care products.

To make an 'instant' infused oil, add the finely chopped peel of 2 lemons to a cup of olive oil in a saucepan. Gently cook over a low heat for 10-15 minutes, then remove from heat and leave to cool. Strain and bottle as above.

You can use coconut or other light culinary oil in place of olive.

CITRUS OIL FURNITURE POLISH

¼ cup vinegar (any light vinegar; for extra power use homemade citrus peel vinegar)

¾ cup citrus oil

Pour the ingredients into a jar, replace the lid and shake thoroughly to mix. Apply with a clean cloth and buff with a soft rag.

Use on the wooden handles of tools to protect them, on wooden furniture, etc. Do a test spot first to make sure this is suitable for your wooden furniture.

CITRUS INFUSED SPIRITS

I always buy reputable alcohol for these infusions. Use for baking, cooking and in cocktails in place of shop bought extract. They can of course also be drunk neat in shot glasses and make nice presents.

You will need:

Vodka, gin, tequila, rum (I use vodka to make citrus extract for cooking)

Finely chopped or zested peel of citrus fruits, pith removed

A jar with a lid

Put the peel in the jar and carefully pour the vodka over the peels until it is covered by 1cm (0.5in) of alcohol. Shake vigorously, then store in a cool dark place for a month, shaking every few days.

Strain as above and pour into a clean, labelled jar.

Skin scrubs

These are very easy to create and make lovely gifts. You can get creative and add herbs (fresh when infusing the oil, 1tsp dried and ground as part of the scrub) or add a few drops of complimentary essential oils. Any skin nourishing oil is good for these recipes.

As with all skin oils, be careful when using in the bath or shower as they make the surfaces slippery.

CITRUS SKIN SCRUB

This is an invigorating skin scrub which is lovely to use in the bath or shower.

½ cup citrus oil

½ cup sea salt

½ cup Epsom salts

1tsp dried, ground citrus peel – optional

A labelled jar with a lid

Finely grind the sea and Epsom salts if they are coarse. You can use 1 cup sea salt if you don't have any Epsom salts.

Put all of the ingredients in the jar and mix thoroughly. Store in a cool, dry place.

N.B. Do not use on acne, sore or broken skin: it will sting!

CITRUS SUGAR SCRUB

⅓ cup citrus oil

⅔ cup sugar – I use unbleached cane sugar

1tsp dried ground citrus peel – optional

Mix thoroughly and store in a jar.

Using up veg odds and ends

Usually when grating and preparing food, I have various odds and ends of vegetables left over – peelings, the end of a carrot after grating, leaves, onion skins, kale and herb stalks, tops of leeks. These make a delicious base for soup, stews and stocks.

I keep a glass box in the fridge to put these if there are not enough scraps to use immediately. You can have a similar container in the freezer too. Make sure the scraps are clean and not mouldy before storing and using.

These can be dehydrated to make the vegetable stock powder (page 91, Chapter 9) or used to make a liquid stock.

ODDS AND ENDS STOCK

This is a guideline recipe – every time you make it, it will in particular brassicas, so only use a little.

You will need:

Vegetable scraps, chopped
(I add some onion skins because I like the rich brown colour, but leave out if you prefer)
Water
Oil – olive, sunflower, etc. (optional), enough to gently fry the veg
Additional veg, chopped
2 onions or leeks
2 carrots (leave out if you have a lot of carrot peelings in the mix)
2 celery stalks (leave out if you have a lot of celery in the mix)
2 cloves garlic (more if you really like it)
2 bay leaves
½tsp whole peppercorns

'Sweating' brings out the flavour of the vegetables. Pour some oil into the stock pan, add the vegetables and cook over a low heat with the lid on, stirring regularly for 30 minutes or so. Then add enough hot water to completely cover the vegetables (with about 1cm (0.5in) water above the veg), bring to the boil, reduce the heat and simmer for an hour, stirring occasionally. Allow to cool and strain through a sieve.

Alternatively, put all of the vegetables and herbs in the stockpot, add enough hot water to completely cover the vegetables (with about 1cm (0.5in) water above the veg), bring to the boil, reduce the heat and simmer for an hour, stirring occasionally. Allow to cool and strain through a sieve.

Divide into pint containers, label and freeze. Or use right away to make your dinner.

CRISPY POTATO PEELINGS

These are stunningly delicious, full of fibre and make good use of potato, parsnip and sweet potato peelings.

Preheat the oven to 200°C/400°F/gas mark 6.

Put the peelings in a large bowl, drizzle on some oil (olive, sunflower, canola, etc.) and season with salt and pepper. You can also add finely chopped garlic, paprika, or sprinkle on your favourite seasoning mix.

Spread on a large baking tray and put in the oven for 15-20 minutes until crispy – stir once or twice whilst cooking.

Serve with your favourite dip.

rainbow veg

Favourite versatile recipes

HOMEACRES SOURDOUGH STARTER

This harnesses beneficial wild yeast to create a sourdough starter that is unique to your home.

Mix equal quantities of warm water and wholemeal flour (or spelt, rye) into a paste in a pot; we find 1 cup flour and 1 cup warm water works well for a family. Leave for about 5 days in a warm place (average temperature 20°C/70°F) until you see bubbles. Check daily to make sure it doesn't dry out. Add a little more flour or water each day to feed it. When it is very bubbly and frothy, you know it is ready. Keep covered in a cool place.

Two day old sourdough starter, bubbling with life

CHARLES' NO NEED TO KNEAD BREAD

Makes two loaves of 870g/1.9lb

- 1kg/2.2lb fresh ground rye flour
- 250g/0.5lb week-old starter dough
- 0.4 litres/0.7 pints warm water altogether
- 1-2tbsp oil, and seeds/nuts to taste

1. In the evening, add 2-3tbsp flour to the starter dough, and enough warm water to mix it into a paste. Leave overnight at room temperature.

2. In the morning, add this fermenting dough to the rest of the flour and water, mixing all together with a wooden spoon.

3. Spoon 250g/0.5lb of dough into the (washed and clean) starter pot, and put in the fridge (new starter).

4. The dough should be soft and smooth, not dry or stiff. Add more water if it is stiff because the wholemeal flour takes time to soak up moisture which dires the dough.

5. Add the oil (this helps prevent the dough from sticking).

1 Flour and water is added to the bowl

2 Rye flour and sourdough which needs activating

3 Mixing the dough

4 Some of the dough is reserved to start the next batch, the rest is shared between the tins

5 Dough has risen and is ready to bake

Two loaves of freshly baked sourdough bread

6. Spoon it into the tins; in this case there was 2kg dough, half in each tin (900g/2lb tins).

7. Leave to rise for 3-8 hours, depending on temperature and vigour of the starter.

8. When the dough volume has increased by more than a third, put in the oven at 175°C/350°F for 55-60 minutes.

9. Tap out of the tins. The bread is moist and is good to eat for a week or more, when kept cool.

This recipe works well with spelt, whole wheat and other flours, too. Ratios of flour to water vary according to different flours, you may need to add a little more warm water.

Remember to always set aside a cup of starter to keep until you bake again.

Dishes for all seasons –
meals using key seasonal fruit, vegetables and herbs

HUMMUS

Hummus is incredibly versatile. It is quick, easy and very nutritious providing fibre, protein, healthy fats, vitamins, minerals and nutrient dense calories. We usually think of hummus as a tahini and chickpea dish from the Middle East, but it lends itself to a wide variety of seasonal adaptations. As well as trying these recipes as dips and sandwich fillings, use them in salad dressings, to thicken soup, stuff mushrooms and squash, layer through nut roasts, as an alternative to tomato sauce on pizza and stirred through pasta and rice.

As an alternative to chickpeas, replace with the same weight of cooked homegrown Czar or borlotti beans or broad (fava) beans.

The basic hummus recipe:

330g/12oz/2cups cooked chickpeas
The chickpea cooking liquid (if you don't have it, a small jug of water or liquid left from boiling vegetables)
4tsp tahini
2 or 3 cloves of garlic, chopped
Juice of 1 lemon (3.5tsp)
½tsp freshly ground cumin seed
4tbsp olive oil
Salt and pepper to taste (optional)

Place all of the ingredients except the cooking liquid or water in a food processor and blend. Carefully add the liquid as it is processing until the hummus is the thickness you desire.

Seasonal hummus variations: add to the above ingredients in the processor before blending

Parsnip – 240g/8oz/2cups cooked (boiled or roasted)
Beetroot (yellow, red or pink) – 240g/8oz/2cups cooked (boiled or roasted)

Colourful hummus with vegetables

Hummus topped with home dehydrated tomatoes

Roast tomato – 200g/7oz/1cup diced tomatoes, roasted with 1 bulb garlic. Add to processor with 1tbsp chopped fresh basil
Roast onion and garlic – 100g/3.5oz/1cup onions roasted with 1 bulb garlic
Roasted squash – 240g/8oz/2cups diced roasted squash
Spiced roast carrot – 240g/8oz/2cups diced roasted carrot with 1tsp ground cumin, ½tsp ginger, ½tsp cinnamon
Roasted tomatillo – 6 large tomatillo roasted, blended with juice of 1 lime (instead of lemon) 2tbsp fresh chopped coriander and 1-2 fresh chillies (according to taste)
Raw courgette – 240g/8oz/2 cups sliced courgette with 2tbsp fresh chopped seasonal herbs
Chard – 100g/3.50z/1cup diced stalks and 120g/4.5/2cups chopped leaves, steamed.
Raw kale – 240g/8oz/2cups raw kale leaves, stem removed, chopped
Cucumber – 240g/8oz/2cups diced raw cucumber, 2tbsp fresh mint or dill
Mixed roast veg – any seasonal vegetables work well for this: roots, aubergine, peppers, etc. 240g/8oz/2cups roasted seasonal vegetables

HERB AND VEGETABLE PESTO

Delicious, adaptable pesto is a quick way of using seasonal herbs, vegetables and leftovers. Add your choice of vegetable, fruit, herbs (or a combination) to the basic recipe. The nuts can be raw if you prefer or replaced with seeds (sunflower, pumpkin, etc.). Experiment with the quantities to suit your taste and meal. Add a chilli or two for a spicy variation.

For example: beetroot tops, kale leaves, spinach, basil, parsley, dill, tarragon, mint, cooked broadbeans, tomatoes, watercress, roasted pepper, coriander, cooked or raw broccoli, nettles, apples, pears. Or herb flowers: sage, chive, rosemary, basil.

- 240g/8oz/2 cups chopped leaves or fruit
- 60g/2oz/½cup toasted nuts – walnuts, pinenuts, hazelnuts, cashew, almonds etc.
- 2 tablespoons lemon juice
- 2 or 3 cloves of garlic (to taste)
- 4tbsp oil plus more if you want – olive, walnut, sunflower, sesame (or a mixture of oils)
- Salt and pepper if desired

Put all of the ingredients in a food processor and whizz until fully blended. Add more oil to make a thinner consistency if required.

Keeps for a few days in the fridge or process in a canner for a longer shelf life.

SOUP FOR ALL SEASONS

Filling, cheap and a wonderful way to use up leftovers and seasonal gluts, it freezes well too. This recipe serves four hungry people with seconds and can easily be increased to feed a crowd.

- 450g/1lb/4 cups onions and leeks, chopped
- 450-900g/1-2lb/4-8 cups mixed vegetables, chopped
- 2-4 cloves of garlic, finely chopped
- 3tbsp fresh herbs, finely chopped(1.5tbsp dried)
- 1 or two finely chopped chillies if desired
- Vegetable stock, left over water from cooking veg or plain water
- Salt and pepper to taste
- Olive or sunflower oil

Drizzle the oil into a large soup pan until it covers the bottom and add the onions, leeks, garlic and chillies (if using). Turn on the heat until the oil is sizzling, then reduce heat, replace the lid and leave the vegetables to sauté, stirring regularly for 10-15 minutes. Add the diced vegetables, stir and allow to 'sweat' on a low heat for 15-30 minutes, stirring regularly. You may need to add a little of the liquid to prevent sticking.

Add the herbs, stir and season (if desired) then pour over the water until the vegetables are completely submerged and there's 2.5cm/1in liquid above the ingredients. Bring to the boil, reduce heat, cover and simmer for 20 minutes until all of the vegetables are cooked.

Taste and add more seasoning if you wish. Either serve as it is, or blend using a stick blender for a smoother soup.

We eat this with homemade sourdough bread and a bowl of seasonal leaves.

versatile recipes

Homegrown raw summer salad

ROASTED VEGETABLES FOR MAIN COURSES AND SALADS

Another dish that is completely influenced by the seasons, trays of roasted vegetables make tasty main courses, cold as salads, lasagne filling, a quick soup simmered with stock or as a base for the pesto and hummus recipes here. Roasted veg freeze well too.

Suggested ingredients:

> Potatoes, parsnips, carrots, squash, onions, leeks, apple, beetroot, celeriac, kohlrabi, cabbage (cut into 1in/2.5cm slices), oca, yacon, tomatoes, aubergines, sweet peppers, courgette, tomatillo.

The method could not be simpler.

Dice the vegetables, put into roasting pans with two whole bulbs of garlic, drizzle with olive oil and roast approximately equal quantities of everything for 25-30 minutes at 180°C/350°F/gas mark 4, until everything is cooked.

Serve with the roasted garlic squeezed from its papery case mixed through and seasoning according to your taste.

RAW GRATED SEASONAL SALAD

A food processor or mandolin speeds up making this salad, however I have used a regular cheese grater many times to grate even parsnip and beetroot; just be careful with your knuckles.

Use whatever vegetables you have in the garden: parsnip, celeriac, carrot, beetroot, kohlrabi, radish, apple, shredded kale or cabbage, courgette.

Optional extras: dried fruit, toasted seeds, nuts, cooked broad beans.

Here I use an American cup measure which has a 236ml capacity.

> Choose three vegetables and grate 1 cup of each (use more vegetables if you wish; just make the total quantity about 3 cups). Put into a bowl and mix with 1tbsp finely chopped seasonal herbs.

Make the salad dressing:

> 4tbsp cider vinegar (or sherry, balsamic, wine)
> 2tbsp olive oil
> 2tbsp lemon or lime juice (include the grated zest if you wish)
> 2tsp Dijon or wholegrain mustard
> Salt and pepper to taste, if wanted

Put everything in a jar, replace the lid and shake until mixed.

Gradually drizzle onto the grated salad, stirring until the food looks glossy and well coated. You may not need all of the dressing, which will keep in the jar in a fridge for a week or so.

Summer roasted aubergine and seasonal vegetable salad

Roasted squash salad

Recipes using stevia, yacon and oca

MAKING LIQUID STEVIA EXTRACT

Use in drinks and cooking, 1-2 drops sweetens a hot drink, in fruit smoothies, lemonade and cocktails.

You will need:

- 1 glass jar with a lid
- Stevia leaves – either dried or fresh, crumbled, chopped or ground into small pieces
- Vodka
- Fine mesh strainer, coffee filter or muslin

Put the stevia in the jar. The ratio is 2 parts stevia to 3 parts vodka, so for example for 2 cups of stevia leaf, add 3 cups of vodka. Put the lid on tightly, shake and put the jar somewhere where you will remember it as it needs shaking regularly – near the kettle is a good place in my house.

Leave in the jar, shaking when you pass it, for 36 hours.

Strain through muslin or a paper coffee filter into a jug; compost the leaves. Pour into a dark coloured bottle if you are happy to use it in its more alcoholic form. Alternatively, to reduce the alcohol, pour the extract into a small pan, bring to a simmer (do not boil) and let it simmer on a very low heat without a lid for 10 minutes. As it needs regular stirring it is best to do this when you are already cooking something else.

When cool, pour into a jar or bottle, label and store in a fridge or other cool place – it will last for about 3 months. I use brown glass ones with droppers.

Alternatively, you can make liquid stevia using just water – ¼ cup stevia to one cup of hot water in a jar. Stir and leave for 24 hours, shaking occasionally. Strain as for the vodka stevia extract and store in the fridge.

Store the stevia extract in a dark bottle

Dried stevia leaves and some vodka

Dried stevia leaves mixed with vodka, left to infuse

Filter the infused stevia into a jug

HOW TO SUBSTITUTE STEVIA LEAVES FOR SUGAR

1tsp ground stevia = 1 cup/ 200g sugar

1tsp stevia liquid = 1 cup/ 200g sugar

6 drops stevia liquid = 1tbsp sugar

2 drops stevia liquid = 1tsp sugar

A pinch of ground stevia = 1tsp sugar

PARSNIP AND APPLE MUFFINS WITH STEVIA

These are a denser, more chewy muffin, great to provide an energy boost when gardening! This recipe makes 12 big muffins. If you don't have stevia, substitute with 200g/1cup soft brown sugar.

- 2 cups grated parsnips
- 125g/4oz/1 cup grated apple
- 80g/3oz/½ cup raisins
- 1tsp ground stevia
- 250g/9oz/2 cups brown self raising flour
- ½tsp baking powder
- 1tsp mixed spice
- 1tsp ground cinnamon
- ½tsp vanilla extract
- 120ml/4floz/½ cup apple sauce (I use homemade unsweetened)
- 120ml/4floz/½ cup sunflower oil or melted butter
- 120ml/4floz/½ cup milk or non-dairy alternative

Pre heat the oven to 180°C/350°F/gas mark 4.

Whisk together the vanilla, apple sauce, oil or butter and milk in a large bowl. In another, mix together the dry ingredients, sprinkle on the stevia powder and add the apple, parsnip and raisins. Mix together, then fold the liquid mixture into the dry until just mixed. Put into the muffin tins and cook for 20-25 minutes until golden.

Fruitcake and muffins, sweetened with stevia

FRUITCAKE

The sweetness in this fruitcake comes from stevia and dried fruits.

- 400g/14oz/2½ cups dried fruit, whatever you have in the cupboard chopped – raisins, figs, apricots, dates, cranberries, etc.
- 185g/6.5oz/1½ cups chopped nuts – I used walnuts
- 185g/6.5oz/1½ cups plain flour
- 1tsp baking powder
- 240ml/8floz/1 cup apple sauce
- 120ml/4floz/½ cup orange or apple juice
- Grated zest of an orange and lemon
- 1tsp mixed spice
- 1tsp cinnamon
- 1tsp ground stevia

Mix everything in a large bowl and leave for about 15 minutes. Then, pour into a greased or lined loaf tin and bake in the oven at 180°C/350°F/gas mark 4 for about 45 minutes.

Lemonade sweetened with stevia extract

LEMONADE

The green stevia extract adds sweetness and colour to this drink.

- The juice of 2-3 lemons
- 600ml/1 pint water
- ½/1tsp stevia liquid – taste as you add; you may want more

Mix the ingredients together in a jug. Taste and add a few more drops of stevia if you prefer it sweeter.

For a beautiful summery drink, add your choice of mint, lemon balm and borage flowers, whatever you have in your garden.

Clockwise from top left: yacon salsa, boiled oca, yacon coleslaw with mustard dressing, roasted oca

YACON SALSA

This is a very crisp, fresh tasting salsa in which the crunch of the yacon really shines through.

- 125g/4oz/I cup yacon, peeled and diced quite small
- 65g/2.5oz/½ cup finely chopped onion or shallots; spring onions taste good too
- 1 red pepper, finely chopped
- 6tbsp coriander leaves (cilantro)
- 2 fat cloves of garlic, minced
- Juice of ½ lemon
- Juice of 1 lime
- 3tbsp olive oil
- Salt and pepper to taste

Mix the yacon and the lemon juice to prevent it from discolouring (it goes a bit brown without lemon juice but still tastes good). Add the rest of the chopped vegetables.

In a jug mix together the olive oil, lime juice and finely chopped coriander. Pour over the vegetables and mix thoroughly. Adjust seasoning to taste.

HOT BOILED OCA

Simple and surprisingly delicious, the oca gives this dish a light, lemony taste.

Bring a pan of water to the boil and add the oca. Simmer for 10-15 minutes until soft and strain.

Stir in some olive oil or a knob of butter, add salt and pepper to taste. It is delicious with minced garlic too.

YACON COLESLAW WITH MUSTARD DRESSING

A simple, crunchy salad which can be changed seasonally. If you don't have any yacon, apple is a delicious substitute.

- 125g/4oz/1 cup of yacon, grated
- 250g/8oz/2 cups of vegetables – I used grated carrots, chopped onions and celery
- 1 clove finely chopped garlic
- 1tsp Dijon mustard
- ½ cup olive oil
- 2tbsp cider vinegar
- Salt and pepper to taste

Whisk the dressing ingredients together in a jug. Mix the vegetables in a bowl, pour on the dressing and mix thoroughly.

ROASTED OCA AND YACON

- 2 good handfuls of oca
- 2 medium sized yacon, cut into 7mm/4in slices
- 1 bulb of fat garlic, broken into cloves and peeled
- 2 good handfuls of shallots, onions or leeks peeled and cut into oca sized pieces
- Olive or sunflower oil

Pre heat the oven to 180°C/350°F/gas mark 4.

Prepare the vegetables and place in an oven dish, drizzle with oil and mix thoroughly. Roast on the middle shelf for about 30 minutes until the oca is tender and the vegetables cooked.

Chapter 13

Top Perennial Vegetables

The most productive, for least time needed

Perennial vegetables need looking after, in different ways to annual vegetables. Soil preparation is similar, starting with thorough mulching of weeds, especially perennial weeds, so there are none of their roots to grow among the vegetables and become a permanent demand on your time.

Cropping periods

Most of these plants need a year or more between planting and the first harvest, and then have a defined cropping period. Often this is during the hungry gap in spring, when many annual vegetables are not ready to eat, which makes the harvests of perennials more valuable.

Yield and quality

The yield figures are one year's harvests from plants in healthy, fertile soil, mulched every autumn with compost of variable quality. Mulches can be more lumpy and imperfect than for annual vegetables, because established perennial plants are not bothered by the fineness of mulch. Wood-based mulches are possible too.

Possibly the food from perennial plants is more nutritious than from annuals, because their well-established root systems can explore further into the soil. This also helps soil structure to stay open, all year round.

Summer view of perennials corner

Asparagus in its fourth spring, first harvests in early May

Annual plant maintenance

For each vegetable it's different but generally there is one period of the year when you need to cut back stalks and stems, or to thin and replant. Be timely with these interventions to keep your perennials healthy. Apart from that, the main time needed is for harvesting, and occasional weeding.

Before planting

For weedy areas, mulch thoroughly to eradicate perennial weeds before planting: using polythene at the pre-planting stage means less compost needed; see Chapter 3 page 15. When the initial weeds are mostly annual rather than perennial – for example, where there is only a little or no couch grass and bindweed – you can spread a 10-15cm (4-6in) mulch of compost on top of weeds, and plant straightaway.

Thenceforward, patrol the area and remove any shoots of perennial weeds before they re-establish, until you see no more. They may stop growing within three months, or continue for a year, depending on the weed.

Weeds

In theory you can allow weeds to grow between established perennial vegetables, without them suffering too much competition, at least for a while. However it's a difficult balance to maintain, and weeds still need cutting back. Having no weeds at all is actually quicker, because there are none dropping seeds or spreading roots, which results in you needing to do very little weeding or ground maintenance.

At Homeacres, for example, we spend almost zero time weeding between and around asparagus, even though it's usually reckoned a difficult crop to maintain weed free.

Planting plan

Many perennial plants grow large, develop extensive root runs, and may also grow leaf cover that harbours pests such as slugs. Therefore, where possible it's good to group them together rather than have them dotted around the garden.

Respect the spacings given, because when setting out small plants of rhubarb, kale and artichoke, they look too far apart initially. Soon, however, they fill the space and need all that soil and light to keep growing.

asparagus

Clockwise from top left:

Asparagus midwinter, mulched and planting crowns

Mulching regrowth of weeds with cardboard & then fabric on top

Fabric removed late summer; asparagus establishing but slow

Mustard green manure sown early autumn on asparagus bed, this view early winter

Creation of two narrow beds with rockdust then extra mulch, in second spring

Midsummer third year growth strong and even

Skirret is a valuable winter root

When planting small perennials, you can take a catch crop of say onions from the space between, planted at the same time.

Sea kale just planted, late spring

Sea kale flowering shoots in late spring

Perennial veg for big harvests and harvests in the hungry gap

This selection is based on the size of harvest, its timing, and frequency. The quickest and easiest is perennial kale, while asparagus takes much longer to be productive. But it crops when few other vegetables are ready to pick, and every harvest is a celebration.

Artichoke, Chinese (*Stachys affinis*)

Growing Soil can be any type except very stony, but harvesting is easier in drier, free draining soil. Spacing 45cm (18in).

Varieties None offered, just plant tubers.

Yield per plant 0.5kg (1lb) = 2.1kg/m^2 (0.4lb/ft^2).

Propagation Sow tubers in pots undercover early spring, or direct in soil after last frost.

Pests and diseases Nothing major, some slug damage.

First harvests In mid autumn, and harvest all winter in mild areas, otherwise take last harvest before frost -7°C (20°F) and store in sacks, cool and damp.

Years of harvest There may be many, although you have healthier crops from new plantings after about four years.

Annual maintenance Thin new growth in spring, from crosnes (tubers) left in soil: it's always likely that some are missed at harvest. Mulch soil before spring growth appears.

Summary **UPSIDES** are nutty flavour and creamy texture. **DOWNSIDES** are time needed to clean the small, ribbed crosnes.

Artichoke, globe
(*Cynara cardunculus (Scolymus)*)

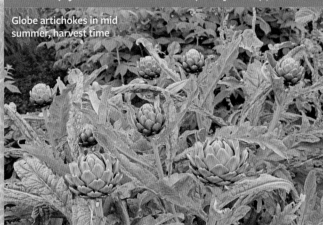

Globe artichokes in mid summer, harvest time

Growing Tolerant of most soil. Spacing 90cm (36in).

Varieties Commonly Green Globe and Purple Globe; the latter is less productive; buy either seeds or plants.

Yield per plant Up to 5 chokes = $6/m^2$ ($0.6/ft^2$).

Propagation Either sow in autumn or early spring; beware mice eating seed. Best results are from sowing undercover in modules, to plant mid spring. Or cut a piece of root from the edge of an established plant in autumn, plant it directly in soil, or in a pot undercover to plant out in spring.

Pests and diseases There are few, mainly aphids inside chokes in dry weather, they can be rinsed out before cooking.

First harvests These are small, in mid to late summer of the first year, thereafter regularly in early summer every year.

Years of harvest Sometimes more than 10, as long as winters are not below -8°C (18°F) too often, in which case you can mulch with a thick layer of straw before hard frosts.

Annual maintenance Mostly in summer, chop or twist finished stems at ground level to make room for new growth, then twist out any smaller new growing points to leave an average three new growths per each plant at the 36in spacing. In winter, any mulch is possible.

Summary **UPSIDES** are easy and quick harvests, and plants live for years if there are few frosts below -8 to -10°C (18 to 14°F). **DOWNSIDES** are plants' susceptibility to low temperatures, and the space needed for a relatively small amount of food.

Other Cardoons. *Cynara cardunculus* look similar but have small chokes of little culinary use; for food, you need to blanch some young stems. Only grow these if you have lots of space to fill!

Artichoke, Jerusalem
(*Helianthus tuberosus*)

Jerusalem artichokes in August

Growing Soil can be any type except very stony, but harvest is easier in free draining soil. Spacing 60cm (24in). Care while growing can include pulling surface soil/compost around stems in early summer to support them.

Varieties There are many; best yields and easier harvest are from varieties with large, smooth tubers such as Fuseau.

Yield per plant 2kg (4.5lb) = $5.3kg/m^2$ ($1.1lb/ft^2$).

Propagation Sow in early spring; use a trowel to slot tubers 10-15cm (4-6in) below the surface.

Pests and diseases Mainly slugs eating tubers in wet winter weather, rodents too.

First harvests In mid autumn as leaves turn yellow. Harvest period is until early spring when tubers regrow.

Years of harvest There can be 10 or more but quality and size become less.

Annual maintenance Thin new plants in spring, by using a trowel to lever out the unwanted tubers, and mulch with any organic matter after final harvest.

Summary **UPSIDES** are how well they compete with weeds, the small yellow 'sunflowers' in autumn, and that you can keep your own seed. **DOWNSIDES** are flatulence from eating, shading of nearby plants, and the difficulty of clearing ground for other crops, hence their 'perennial' quality.

Jerusalem artichoke harvest from one plant: over 5 kg (11 lb)

Asparagus
(Asparagus officinalis)

Growing Soil must be pH 6.5 or higher. This is a seaside vegetable: adding a seaweed mulch in winter, say 5-7.5cm (2-3in) thick, enhances growth considerably. Spacing 60cm (24in). Always weed thoroughly and do not allow perennial weeds ever to establish. From the second year, stems need support by tying to stakes, then from year three you can simply run a wire or two held by stakes around/along the edges, to keep the abundant summer growth upright – the ferns can be 2m (6-7ft high).

Varieties It's worth planting all male hybrids for significantly higher yield, such as Gijnlim, Guelph Millennium, Mondeo; purple varieties are sweet but lower yielding.

Yield per plant Up to 25 spears per plant, say 1.2kg (2.8lb) = 3.4kg/m^2 (0.7lb/ft^2).

Propagation Either sow seeds late winter in modules, then move to 10cm (4in) pots for summer planting. Or plant crowns in late autumn to early spring; the latter works better because it allows more time to mulch weeds, and crowns are at less risk of rotting in a wet winter, before they can establish.

An option is to plant on ridges where drainage is poor, otherwise level ground is good.

Pests and diseases Mainly the asparagus beetle, *Crioceris asparagi*. Squash them regularly when seen: in organic gardens the beetle *Tetrastichus asparagi* may be present and parasitises the Crioceris eggs. You may need to fence against rabbits, and beware of slugs eating new spears in spring.

First harvests From two to three years after planting, and harvests increase for the first few years. The harvest period is mid spring to summer solstice, say eight weeks, after which you allow ferns to grow and feed the roots.

Years of harvest Up to 20, sometimes longer.

Annual maintenance Cut off all stems before winter, mulch with compost, and keep the area weed free.

Summary UPSIDES are continuous harvests all through the hungry gap, and a wonderful flavour. **DOWNSIDES** are an average three years to first harvest, and the lack of weed-shading in spring.

Chilli pepper
(Capsicum annuum)

Growing You can grow chillies as perennial plants, as long as they are undercover in winter and never subjected to frost. Over the years they become like small trees with a woody trunk and branches, fruiting earlier in the summer than chilli plants grown from seed.

Varieties and propagation Sow seeds of a chilli variety you like, in a seed tray of compost, and grow as for container tomatoes or peppers, except to water and feed less.

Converting to perennial In the autumn and after last harvest, cut off all long stems to leave the main one, which becomes a small trunk, together with a few short branches. Prune hard, so that next year's plant is more compact.

Overwintering Overwinter in a frost free place; light is not important until early spring when new shoots grow. Roots want to be slightly damp but absolutely not wet in winter; one method is to soak compost after pruning, then give no water until new growth appears.

Keep plants on a sunny windowsill through early spring, when shoots are growing. At this stage, occasional and light watering is good.

Summer care As soon as the last frost has occurred, move plants to a sunny and sheltered spot, or into a polytunnel or greenhouse. Pot on into a slightly larger container, and enjoy a harvest by late summer.

Years of harvest Repeat this cycle in the following autumn, with another hard prune, leaving a little more stem and branch than the previous year. Plants therefore stay manageable. In summer, water as little as you dare, sometimes letting the leaves wilt before watering, and do not feed except for the additional compost when potting on. At Homeacres a four-year-old Habanero grew three feet high, sturdy and not staked.

Horseradish
(Amoracia rusticana)

Growing Horseradish is invasive and persistent, so think carefully before planting. A large pot of horseradish on a paved area (to stop the root 'escaping' into the soil) works well.

Propagation Horseradish is easy to grow from thongs or by sowing in early spring. Put 2-3 thongs in a pot of rich compost with their tops 5cm/2in below the surface.

Annual maintenance and harvests Plants are simple to maintain and suffer few pests, except for small damage from cabbage white butterfly caterpillars. The foliage dies back in autumn, then harvest roots after the first frost; even if you remove large pieces, some will remain and regrow.

Qualities The powerfully spicy root adds a zing to sauces, preserves and condiments. It has medicinal qualities too. (See recipe for fire cider on page 62.)

Kale
(*Brassica oleracea* var. *ramosa*)

Three-year-old Taunton Deane kale in spring, when other kales are flowering

Growing Fast and willing, tolerant of most soils though preferring heavy soil, more alkaline than acid. Spacing 24in (60cm).

Varieties They include Taunton Deane 2m (6ft), whose height means it's inclined to suffer wind damage, or to lean over; Daubentons 1m (3ft) whose stems may snap off as they recline on the surface; Asturian Tree Cabbage 1.2m (4ft) on a single stem, whereas the first two grow multi-stemmed.

Yield per plant 8kg (17lb) = 4.4kg/m^2 (0.9lb/ft^2), of Taunton Deane.

Propagation Place small stems in soil or compost. They initially wilt, then make new roots within 3-5 weeks, depending on the season. Or put the stems in a glass of water on the windowsill, then transfer to pots of compost when you see first roots, after about two weeks. Plant rooted stems at any time from spring to early autumn.

Pests and diseases These are mainly summer caterpillars but plants survive their ravages. Also the usual brassica pests such as pigeons and rabbits.

First harvests Two to three months after planting. The harvest period is from early spring and through the hungry gap to late autumn, then some leaves in mild winters.

Years of harvest Often five or longer, during which time plants are multiplying their stems, while sometimes they die for no obvious reason. So it's good to always have a spare or two.

Annual maintenance Remove side shoots and yellowing leaves, to have easier picking of larger leaves on remaining stems. Maintain a surface mulch, and stake plants if you do not have space for them to recline.

Summary **UPSIDES** are high yields of nutritious leaves, over an exceptionally long period of many months each year, and for several years.
DOWNSIDE can be that tall plants are difficult to net against birds.

Leek
(*Allium ampeloprasum* var. *sectivum*)

Perennial leeks, mid spring

Growing Easy to grow and multiply. They grow and look like other alliums: most perennial leeks have swollen bulbs akin to garlic, and their flowerheads look like walking onion. Spacing 30cm (12in).

Varieties They include Babbingtons, and elephant garlic which is also in this family, and sometimes perennial leeks are called pearl onions.

Yield per plant Variable, up to 0.68kg (1.5lb) = 7.3kg/m^2 (1.5lb/ft^2).

Propagation Sowing is a rare event as they grow so well from bulbs or shoots. Plant at any time, the young shoots from the base of parent plants; dib a hole and water in.

In dry weather give some water, but mostly they look after themselves.

Pests and diseases Leek moth and rust, rarely severe.

First harvests Three to four months after planting in spring or summer. The harvest period is mostly spring and then late autumn into mild winters.

Years of harvest Plants keep producing for a decade or more, when looked after.

Annual maintenance Repeatedly thin and replant after you harvest a parent leek, and mulch at any time, being sure to weed little and often.

Summary **UPSIDE** is harvests over a long period.
DOWNSIDE is a need to replant, usually at harvest time.

Nine star perennial
(*Brassica oleracea botrytis asparagoides*)

Nine star perennial, early spring

Growing Lovely broccoli harvests in the hungry gap are offset by a tendency for plants to lose vigour, and the need to protect them from pigeon damage for a long time between cropping. This is not a vigorous perennial; for large harvests it's best grown as an annual.

Propagation Sow in late spring and space at 45-60cm (18-24in). Yields vary enormously and decline after the first year. When harvests finish in late spring there are small flowering shoots that need cutting off to keep the plants' energy for new growth.

Pests and diseases Pests are the same as kale.

First harvests In the spring, about nine months after planting, and the harvest period is six to eight weeks.

Onion
Allium, many

Chives, with coriander behind, mid spring

Growing Easy to grow, from root division, and in any soil, but weed regularly. Spacing 30cm (12in).

Varieties It's more about types, and they include:

Egyptian ('walking', 'tree') onion (*Allium cepa proliferum*) which sows itself by flowerheads falling at random – also it produces edible bulbs on some stems.

Potato ('multiplier', 'hill') onion for harvests of all bulbs in autumn and you replant in spring, with similar growth pattern to shallots.

Welsh onion (*Allium cepa fistulosum*) which is for continual growth of new leaves with only small bulbs.

Chives (*Allium schoenoprasum*) and garlic chives (*Allium tuberosum*).

Yield per plant This is not applicable; there are so many types and methods of harvest, little and often.

Propagation Sowing is best left to self seeding, then transplant seedlings. However allium seedlings grow like weeds: chives for example are best cut to ground level after flowering and before seeding, also this encourages new leaves.

Plant bulbs (for example potato onion) in spring, or small divisions of seedlings at any time.

Pests and diseases The same as annual onions; see Chapter 14.

First harvests of leaf onions are soon after planting. Of bulbs in summer to early autumn depending on type.

Annual maintenance This is weeding, thinning and replanting, and spread 3cm (1in) compost or other mulch in winter.

Years of harvest There are many, depending on types grown.

Summary UPSIDE is regular harvests for much of the season, mostly of leaves. **DOWNSIDES** are few, mainly the different harvesting methods according to which type you grow.

Rhubarb
(Rheum rharbarbarum)

Rhubarb loving some damp weather in midsummer

Growing Water new plants if spring is dry to help establishment; watering increases both yield and stem quality in dry weather, so rhubarb grows best in heavy soil, away from moisture-competing trees. Remove any flower stalks as soon as seen, because they weaken stem growth. Spacing 90cm (36in).

Varieties They include Timperley Early for harvests from early spring, the Sutton for top flavour.

Yield per plant It can be high, up to 3-4kg (6.5-9lb) per plant = approximately 4.8kg/m^2 (1lb/ft^2).

Propagation Either sow in spring to plant in summer. Or plant root trimmings/potted plants in autumn to spring.

Pests and diseases Usually none.

First harvests A few stalks in the first summer, after which the harvest period is from early spring (depends on variety) to early summer. Then stop picking so that new growth can feed the roots. Forcing in late winter weakens plants, but gives sweeter, blanched stems.

Years of harvest There are many, perhaps 10-20.

Annual maintenance Just a small amount of weeding, and mulch in early winter after leaves die down.

Summary **UPSIDE** is the earliness and ease of harvest. **DOWNSIDE** may be the plants' need for moisture, and space occupied.

Rhubarb planted into compost on ground full of creeping buttercup and dandelion, late winter

Sea kale
(Crambe maritima)

Sea kale in midsummer, now regenerating after harvest period

Growing Soil must be free draining, but well structured clay is possible. A mulch of seaweed gives superb results; sometimes that one thing makes all the difference. Spacing 40cm (15in).

Varieties Lilywhite is the only named variety.

Yield per plant Around 0.2kg (0.5lb) = 1.5kg/m^2 (0.3lb/ft^2).

Propagation Either sow in spring, with germination usually slow and uneven. Or the better option is to plant roots (thongs) in early spring, in pots under-cover, then plant early summer.

Pests and diseases Pigeons eat some leaves, rabbits gnaw the tops of plants in early spring and can kill them, cover plants with mesh or netting.

First harvests From year two, leaves and then perhaps a broccoli stem. The harvest period is throughout spring, and there is an option to force, but it weakens plants.

Years of harvest They may crop for decades, especially when fed with seaweed.

Annual maintenance Tidy older leaves at season's end mostly, mulch with 3cm (1in) compost and/or seaweed in winter.

Summary **UPSIDES** are great flavour, green leaves in the hungry gap and delicious flowering stems in late spring, the white flowers smelling of honey. **DOWNSIDE** is the low yields.

Skirret
(*Sium sisarum*)

Skirret, after using a spade to lever the whole clump upwards

Growing Skirret was a more popular root crop in Europe before the introduction of potatoes from the Americas. It's an umbellifer so the thin, white roots have sweet tastes of carrot and parsnip, with a dense texture. Soil can be any but light soils make it easier to harvest and clean. Spacing 50-60cm (20-24in).

Varieties None named.

Yield per plant Around 0.5-1kg (1-2lb).

Propagation Plant, in spring, any shoots with little roots that you see emerging from existing crowns.

Sowing seed is possible but the first harvest is small.

Harvest period Lever out the roots anytime in winter.

Annual maintenance Plants flower in late summer and flower stems are best cut off in autumn before they shed hundreds of seeds. The rhythm is harvesting and then replanting of shoots.

Summary **UPSIDES**, it's a perennial root crop for winter harvest, and withstands cold to about zone 6. **DOWNSIDE** is thin roots that are fiddly to clean.

One skirret plant cleaned gave 1.23kg (2.7lb)

Sorrel
(*Rumex*)

Clump of buckler leaved sorrel, summer

Perennial sorrel (Profusion) has darker green leaves than broad leaved sorrel

Growing An easy and vigorous plant, tolerant of shade and of moist soils. Spacing 25-40cm (10-15in); use the wider spacing for large leaves.

Varieties Broad leaved *Rumex acetosa*, buckler leaved *Rumex scutatus* for small, round leaves which are wonderful in salads and omelettes, also there is Profusion *Rumex acetosa* 'TM683', a large leaved cultivar that does not flower in spring.

Yield per plant 0.9kg (2lb) = 9.7kg/m^2 (2lb/ft^2) for broad leaved, and one fifth this amount for buckler leaved.

Propagation Either sow at any time to plant in any season but spring works best. Or plant root trimmings or divisions at any time, preferably early spring or autumn, then water well if planting in dry conditions.

Pests and diseases Slugs like sorrel leaves, and the shiny dock beetle Gastrophysa viridula makes leaf holes all season, together with its hungry larvae.

First harvests From one to two months after planting, with a long harvest period from mid spring to autumn, the biggest and healthiest harvests in spring.

Years of harvest Plants may crop for 5-10 years, but this varies with soil and climate.

Annual maintenance Cut flowering stems in early summer, then tidy/cut back in autumn, and spread 3cm (1in) compost.

Summary **UPSIDES** are lemon flavours, harvests over long periods, also you may be able to forage wild or sheep's sorrel *Rumex acetosella*. **DOWNSIDES** are slow picking of buckler leaves, and repeated flowering in summer.

Chapter 14

Top Vegetables for Roots & Leaves

Essential info for some key vegetables

In this and the next chapter, we explain how to grow and pick vegetables that repay you massively for the care they need to grow well. With the tips given here, we imagine you succeeding, without too much difficulty, in making a serious amount of harvests.

Yield figures are to give an idea of what you may achieve and are from undug beds at Homeacres, with annual dressings of 5cm (2in) compost. They are equivalent to or higher than the yields from dug soil with similar dressings of compost.

Preparing ground

It's normal practice to detail a variation of soil preparation for each different vegetable, such as, "carrots are light feeders and add no compost because it makes them fork", and "take out a trench for climbing beans", and so forth.

Not only does this make it complex to learn about growing a range of vegetables, it often involves extra work. Also you need a precise plan before preparing ground, of what is to plant where. Instead, this method of mulching all soil allows flexibility and last minute changes, for example if a friend gives you some unexpected plants.

You will be delighted to read that in the next two chapters, soil preparation is the same for all vegetables. No dig growing is easier! Plus you have higher yields, for example from adding compost to the carrot bed, and less weeds from not disturbing soil to make a bean trench.

So that is the soil question sorted; let's grow some food.

Chard picked and kept tidy, very pretty

Beetroot

A special tip for beetroot is that if you struggle with direct sowing (pests like the seedlings!), sow undercover in a module tray, because beetroot grows well from transplanting. Your first harvests are earlier, then raise more plants in early summer and pop them between garlic, shallots and onions, up to a month before their harvest.

From this comes a harvesting tip: rather than pulling a whole clump of module-sown roots, rotate the largest of each clump until it comes free and leave others to grow; this extends the harvest period and gives roots of even size to cook or grate.

Growing Beetroot in early summer is a special treat and the variety Boltardy makes this possible, because it does not flower from being sown in late winter and early spring; plus it gives good and tasty harvests in all seasons. Sow other varieties from mid spring. Spacing 25-37cm (10-15in) for clumps, 7×30cm (3×12in) for direct sowing.

Varieties Boltardy for all early sowings, Touchstone Gold for yellow beets, Marina di Chioggia for pink and white rings, Cylindra for long beetroots.

Yield From a 1.5m (5ft) row there can be 4.5kg (10lb) in early summer, up to 9kg (20lb) by autumn.

Propagation Sowing options are undercover from late winter in modules, 4 seeds in each thinned to 4-5 plants; or direct in drills from mid spring, probably needing a fleece or net cover against birds.

Latest sowing date is early summer for normal roots, or a month later for harvests of baby beets.

Plant from mid spring, covered with fleece if cold or windy, and last plantings are in late summer for mild areas.

Pests Sparrows and deer eat leaves, leaf miners tunnel in leaves and make yellow patches of mostly little significance, and if slug populations are high they damage roots. Rodents eat roots from below, so damage is hidden at first; the only remedy is to harvest early.

Diseases Normally few; beetroot are one of the easier vegetables.

First and last harvests In early summer the first harvests possess great flavour, especially the earliest harvests of small beets. Last harvests are in late autumn, before moderate frost, and roots store until spring.

Follow with After summer harvests, plant any salads, fennel, leeks, chard, kale and broccoli.

Boltardy beetroot, the largest are ready for first harvest, 1st June

Boldor beetroot, second crop after garlic, September

Last beetroot harvest, early winter, to store

Carrots

Sometimes difficult to grow, always worth it for the amazing flavour of fresh harvests. Give yourself a pat on the back when you grow good carrots because they are slow to get underway: and the tiny seedlings are vulnerable to pests such as slugs and rabbits.

Growing Carrots thrive in a 5-7cm (2-3in) layer of compost on top of undug soil, and superb results come from growing them in a bed of 6in (15cm) compost, and they grow well in containers of compost too. Don't believe the myth that compost makes carrots fork. Spacing 1×22cm (0.5×9in) for early sowings and harvests of small roots, 3×30cm (1×12in) for harvests to store.

Watering in dry weather helps growth, say twice a week, while any big watering of carrots may cause them to split. On heavy soils, water less so that roots are sweeter.

Varieties Early Nantes and Amsterdam Forcing for early harvests, Berlicum and Oxhella for autumn harvests and to store; Nantes varieties have perhaps the best flavour.

Yield From a 1.5m (5ft) row you can harvest 2.3kg (5lb) in early summer, rising to 5kg (11lb) in autumn from sowing in early summer.

Propagation Sowing is best direct, in drills 1cm (0.5in) deep, and if the surface is dry, water the drill-bottom only, then sow, cover with dry soil and tamp the drill lightly with your foot or a rake; sow a few radish in the same drills to mark the lines and for an extra harvest. Latest sowing date is early summer for large carrots, midsummer for smaller harvests by late autumn.

Pests Some eat leaves, some eat the carrots: Slugs can quickly gobble a long line of tiny seedling leaves, so in damp areas, sow carrots as far away as possible from slug habitats, and in damp weather check and cut or collect slugs at dusk with a torch.

If you are visited by rabbits or deer, a cover of fleece/mesh/net is necessary, especially for seedlings, as they love the leaves.

The main pest is carrot fly larvae eating roots, however Oxhella are dense enough to stay mostly uneaten, as with parsnips. See Chapter 5 for more on carrot fly and how to exclude them.

Diseases Not too common and rotation keeps them at bay; they include violet root rot and cavity spot (both dark disfigurements of roots) while aster yellows, and motley dwarf (or red leaf) virus transmitted by aphids in late spring, cause yellowing of leaves and stunted growth – best remove affected plants.

First and last harvests It's a joyful moment in late spring, the first small carrots with that special flavour, a sign of summer arriving. Harvesting in spring and summer is best done by pulling just the larger roots, leaving others to grow. If soil is dry and hard, use a trowel vertically next to the carrot(s), to lever gently while you pull the leaves. Last harvests are before moderate frost in mid to late autumn, or earlier if carrot fly damage is happening, best harvest a few weekly to check this.

Follow with Depending on timing of harvests, any of chard, leeks, kale and broccoli, salads, fennel.

Sowing carrots in March, fine compost and no slug habitats nearby

Comparing harvests from a dug bed, top, no dig below; notice soil on the dug carrots

Kale

(For perennial kale see Chapter 13)

We grow annual and perennial kale. Both types have excellent flavour and can be used in the same way, though leaves of annual kale are more tender. Kale grows easily, is available year round and is delicious cooked, raw in salads and in smoothies.

Growing Sow in early summer and seedlings grow fast, most reliably when undercover. Outdoor sowings may require a mesh or fleece cover, depending on pest numbers. Spacing 45×45cm (18×18in).

Varieties Cavolo Nero is less prolific than other kales, but the long dark green leaves are particularly flavoursome, and some small side shoots are tasty in salads. Red Russian has pretty pink-green leaves with frilly edges; Sutherland kale and Red Ursa produce delicious leaves and tasty shoots in the spring.

Yield From a 1.5m (5ft) row 3.5-9kg (7-20lb), depending on weather, soil, variety.

Propagation Sow June/July for autumn and winter harvests. If you sow in April, plants grow larger but suffer more caterpillar damage in midsummer. A late summer sowing, to plant in a polytunnel, gives small plants which then provide an abundance of tender leaves in the 'hungry gap'.

Pests Protect with mesh/butterfly netting against caterpillars, although kale are tough plants and can recover. Remove yellowing leaves at the base, to avoid slugs establishing there.

Diseases Kale are generally resistant to disease, even clubroot to some extent, more so than cabbage.

First and last harvests These merge because kale crops in almost every month, three months or so after sowing. Pick the leaves small as salad leaves, larger for cooking, and remove from the bottom upwards. Winter harvests are small and special, then by spring there is plenty again, with flowering shoots to eat broccoli, until they become thin and stringy.

Follow with Any vegetable that you sow or plant in early summer, such as summer beans, carrots and leeks.

Cavolo Nero kale in an autumn frost. It survives to -8°C (18°F), sometimes colder

Many kale varieties in August, planted after carrot harvest; in front are Darkbor and Redbor

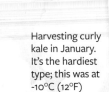

Harvesting curly kale in January. It's the hardiest type; this was at -10°C (12°F)

Onions and shallots for bulbs

These special vegetables have been devalued, money-wise, by the ease of growing them in industrial fields, making them cheap to buy. They are a fine staple and store well, with extra flavour from being homegrown: a box or rope of your own is a warming prospect for winter. Also there is time for another crop after harvest.

Growing Onion leaves are gorgeously upright and look fantastic throughout spring, however they do not shade weeds. Hence diggers space them wide, so they can run a hoe between. But with no dig, weeds germinate less and hand weeding is viable, so onions are easier and more high yielding. Space either in rows 5×39cm (2×15in) or equidistant clumps at 30-39cm (12-15in).

Varieties include Sturon and Stuttgart for yellow onions, Red Baron for red onions, Longor and Red Sun for shallots.

Yield From a 1.5m (5ft) row, can be 3kg (6.6lb) for shallots and 5kg (11lb) for onions.

Propagation Sow seeds late winter undercover, outside early spring, or plant sets/bulbs early spring. Latest sowing date is early spring because onions need a long growing time before the summer solstice, in order to make decent sized bulbs in summer. Tips for propagation are similar to beetroot, 3-6 plants per module depending how large you want them to grow, and 15-20°C warmth helps germination.

Pests These vary according to region; onion fly is perhaps the worst. Rabbits like seedlings and a fleece cover after planting is worthwhile, for a month.

Diseases These depend on the weather in late spring and early summer, when mildew in damp weather can almost destroy a crop, though Santero F1 has some resistance. If mildew has been a problem before, give more space and do not water except in arid conditions. White rot lingers in some soils, see Chapter 5 page 45.

First and last harvests Onions from sets ripen first, their stems folding over in mid summer; start eating at this stage and fold the rest down, just above the bulbs, to hasten ripening. Either leave another two to three weeks, or pull within a week when the tops are still half green. Either leave bulbs on the ground if it's dry weather, or in damp conditions you need space undercover to finish drying the bulbs. Once dry, leave in trays undercover or hang in bunches/ropes.

Follow with Turnips, spinach, autumn and winter salads, Florence fennel, spring broccoli; also you can interplant (as plants) beetroot and kale in mid summer, between the allium plants.

14 onion modules Red Baron (7 modules) and Balaton (7 modules), in August

Multi sown onion plants in module of compost, ready to plant

Red onion harvest, August, was interplanted with beetroot and chicory four weeks earlier

Spring (salad) onions are grown the same way except for doubling up on spacing. Harvest before bulbs swell much: sow varieties such as White Lisbon, which tends to bulb, and Ishikura, which is bred for extra leaf and longer stems, but is prone to rust.

Parsnips

Parsnips give huge yields when grown for the whole season and the dig/no dig experiments show how well they grow in undisturbed, composted soil, despite most advice saying the opposite. The roots are high in dry matter, denser than potatoes, and they become sweeter after frost.

Growing Germination is often mentioned as a problem but sowing into surface compost definitely encourages seedlings to establish. Most gardeners sow parsnips into dug soil whose structure they have recently damaged so it's lying cold and wet. If you are still worried, it is possible to pre-germinate parsnip seeds on damp paper towel in the kitchen, then sow once chitting. But it's easier to sow direct, into the compost on top.

Space in rows, 10×40cm (4×16in) for large roots or 3×30cm (1×12in) for small parsnips.

Varieties White Gem for broader shoulders and Gladiator F1 for longer roots; both offer some resistance to canker, and Gladiator gives very high yields.

Yield From a 1.5m (5ft) row is up to 13.6kg (30lb) in a good year, from spring sowing.

Propagation Sow from early spring, and soil in the drill needs to stay damp for a fortnight so that the slow-germinating seeds can send roots down into moisture: a compost mulch helps this. Latest sowing date is early summer, when you may need to water drills thoroughly before sowing, and harvests are smaller.

Pests The main pest is carrot fly, but damage is less severe than for carrots because the affected root edges can be trimmed off. Slugs may eat seedlings in spring and rats sometimes devour parsnips in winter; if you notice that, it's best to harvest and store in sacks.

Diseases Canker (brown rotting) around the shoulders in damp soil increases through late autumn and winter. Best harvest to store if it is spreading, and trim off any damage when preparing roots to eat.

First and last harvests Start in autumn when parsnips are the size you like, and continue until early spring and before there are too many new leaves. Or if your winters are severe, harvest them all in late autumn and store in sacks. With a spade or strong fork, push in vertically near the roots and wiggle while pulling on the stem and root, gently lever them out with minimal disturbance to soil structure, then re-firm the soil with your foot.

Follow with Any spring sowings and plantings can follow parsnips, including potatoes.

No dig parsnip seedlings, and spinach planted, few weeds growing

6.5kg (14.3lb) parsnips in late autumn from 1.2m² (13ft2), Gladiator

In soils/compost with many weed seeds, slow germination of parsnips makes it worth waiting a month before sowing. This allows time for germination of the first flush of weed seedlings; hoe them once or even twice when barely visible, then sow into a cleaner surface. Or sow at the normal time, and with a few radish (one seed per 2cm/1in) in the drill with parsnip seeds: the fast-germinating radish reveal the line of sowing within a week, allowing you to hoe tiny weed seedlings before they smother the parsnips.

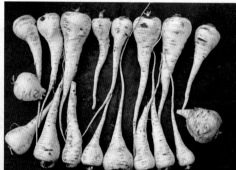

Aromata parsnips gave 2.9kg (6.4lb) from the dug bed, and 3.2kg (7.1lb) from no dig with cleaner and longer roots

Potatoes

There are three main types, defined by speed of growth and maturity date:

- First earlies grow rapidly in spring and finish by early summer. Harvest as soon as leaves start to yellow; flavour is 'newest' at this moment, with a slightly smaller harvest
- Second earlies mature in mid summer and can give high yields, also there is time to grow many other vegetables after harvest
- Maincrops mature late summer to early autumn, with high yields as long as blight (see Chapter 5) has not prevailed, therefore where summers are often damp, grow second earlies rather than maincrop
- Also you can keep a few second early seed in a windowsill (they grow sprouts slowly) for planting in late summer, to harvest new potatoes in late autumn; leaves are at risk of blight but we found that Maris Peer resist well.

Growing Potatoes send roots into undisturbed soil for food and moisture, while you 'earth up' around stems with organic matter, to exclude light from developing tubers. In damp areas with slugs, compost is the best mulch, otherwise straw, hay, grass clippings and even cardboard are possible. Another method is to lay 5-10cm (2-4in) compost and then black polythene over weeds, and cut small holes to plant seed into the soil and compost below.

Space first earlies at 30cm (12in), second earlies at 45cm (18in) and maincrop at 50-60cm (20-24in).

To keep light off developing tubers so they stay white, you can either pull surface soil and compost around stems, or add more compost or other mulches on top of the growing tubers, before they are visible above surface level.

Varieties are many, so try some of each type to see which grow well in your soil and climate, and whether you like their flavour. A special mention for Sarpo varieties whose resistance to blight is allied to good flavours, as long as harvests are taken before autumn, otherwise the potatoes become very dry.

Yield From a 1.5m (5ft) row expect around 3.6kg (8lb) for first earlies and double that for later varieties.

Propagation Seed can be your own tubers, even green ones of small to medium size. It's safest to keep seed for one year only and then buy new seed, to avoid the risk of viruses increasing; see diseases below. Sow from late winter to early spring, around four weeks before last frost for first earlies, a little later for maincrop. Latest sowing date is mid spring, with the risk of late sowings running out of time to mature before blight perhaps arrives.

Late summer harvest of Sarpo Kifli planted in compost on pasture weeds, through polythene

Tip for propagation: early potato seeds are often chitted before planting, by placing upright on a windowsill to encourage sturdy green shoots. However this makes only a small increase of harvest and it's also fine to plant un-chitted seed.

A frost in late spring, potatoes earthed up with surface compost

Pests These are all of developing tubers:

- If slugs are present, best avoid mulches that encourage dampness
- Wireworm occurs after long-term pasture then lessens over time
- There are other burrowing larvae such as eelworm, but best check local knowledge

Diseases It's almost all blight, (see Chapter 5), also blackleg (stems rot at base) and viruses which show as bright yellowing/curling/veining of leaves; fortunately most soils grow healthy potato plants.

First and last harvests Harvest by pulling the stems rather than digging, to reveal clusters of tubers in the soft, surface mulches; some varieties grow tubers further out, and in sandy soils they develop downwards, so a trowel is helpful. Even while leaves are green you can pull first early plants in late spring, for a few small and sweet tubers, quality not quantity.

Last harvests are maincrop varieties in early autumn, and since potatoes store so well in 3 ply paper sacks with a little soil on the tubers, there is no advantage to leaving them in the ground where pests may eat them, also potatoes turn to mush when frozen so they must be harvested before first frost.*

Follow with First earlies are like a catch crop and you can follow them with almost any vegetable. After second earlies there is time to plant calabrese and other brassicas, beetroot, leeks, fennel, chard, spinach and many salads.

---

* www.youtube.com/watch?v=EBV_ri1_XSQ

Spinach and leaf beet/chard

For the longest season of picking true spinach, sow late summer or early spring, so that it crops for months before the summer flowering season. Leaves grow profusely during autumn and spring, when they are sweeter than in hot weather.

Chard and leaf beet are prolific and tasty in summer, so their season of cropping complements spinach.

Growing Check the seed packet to be sure which you are growing, of true spinach or leaf beet/chard. Chard is pretty in salads but less delicious than true spinach. Spinach loves starting life in a surface mulch of compost, and is very hardy to cold, so you can plant (plants) early, outside and under fleece (row cover).

Space according to the leaf size you want, from 10-25cm (4-10in); the closer spacing is for salad leaves.

Varieties Medania is the top recommendation for true spinach. Grow chard of the stem colour(s) you like such as white, ruby, yellow, or rainbow chard of many colours.

Yield From a 1.5m (5ft) row of spinach you can pick 4.1kg (9lb) over six weeks from an early sowing, and more from sowing in late summer to pick in both autumn and spring. A 1.5m/5ft row of chard can yield 5.5-8.2kg (12-18lb) of stems and leaves, through summer and autumn mostly.

Propagation Sowing can be direct into soil or three seeds in modules, or you can prick seedlings from trays into modules. Sow spinach in the last month of summer to plant three weeks later, after last harvests of carrots, lettuce, French beans, onions. Module sowing adds three weeks to the growing season, from the overlap of both first and second crops growing at the same time, one finishing and the other starting.

Best sowing dates are early spring and late summer for spinach, and mid spring to mid summer for chard. The latest sowing date for both is early autumn, to grow undercover through winter and early spring.

Pests Slugs cause problems so take the usual precautions, minimise habitat etc., also remove any while picking – we always find some under older leaves. Leaf miners damage some leaves but should be only a minor problem.

Diseases Mildew on older leaves is the main problem, so remove them to compost. Sowing at the best time and growing in fertile, no dig soil ensures healthier harvests and less disease.

First and last harvests Spinach grows in cool conditions, so from August sowings you can pick new leaves in mild winters, then in spring pick weekly at least so that new, tender leaves keep growing.

Ruby chard roots dug out before frost, here having spent six weeks on a windowsill

Medania spinach, two weeks in the ground here, was sown August and planted after lettuce

Same spinach in spring under fleece, and it cropped until early summer

Once plants make a stem to flower, they will not go back to producing any large amount of leaves, but small leaves of flowering chard can be picked for about a month before they become too bitter.

When picking leaves, twist or cut off their stems as well: they are edible (and colourful in the case of chard), and having no old stems on plants makes the next picking easier; likewise remove yellowing leaves to compost, and this reduces pest habitats.

Last harvests outside are in autumn before the first significant frost.

Follow with Any vegetable; sometimes we even grow beetroot which is the same family.

Chapter 15
Top Vegetables for Pods & Fruits

Chosen for high yields over a long period

Late Sungold, mid autumn

Broad (fava) bean

The weight of edible food is not high because around 70% of harvested weight is pods. However they are a filling and tasty vegetable, and of great value in the kitchen when ready before so many other vegetables. Broad beans are hardy to frost, unlike French and runner (pole) beans.

Growing The last sowing date is late spring, because although you can sow in summer, this leads plants to mature when they are not in season, giving low yields and more chance of disease.

Special care is to support varieties that grow over 1.2m (4ft) tall, in exposed locations, for example run a stout string along either side of beds or rows, tied to stakes at the corners.

Spacing is 15×45cm (6×18in) single rows across beds, or a double row with 30cm (12in) between each row and 60cm (24in) between each double row. Do not sow too thickly or you have more leaf than pod: each seed makes three or more stems.

Varieties We recommend Aquadulce Claudia for sowing in late autumn and early spring, De Monica for early crops from sowing early spring and a top flavour too, Robin Hood for dwarf plants and Green Windsor for top tasting, green beans in summer.

Yield From a 1.5m (5ft) double row in summer, according to weather, expect from 8-12kg (18-27lb) of pods, giving approximately 2-3kg (5-7lb) of beans.

Propagation Sowing options:

- Either direct into dibbed holes 5cm (2in) deep, in late (not mid) autumn if winters are not too severe, otherwise in early spring
- Or sow in 5cm (2in) modules in late winter, to plant early spring.

Pests Mainly blackfly aphids (*Aphis fabae*) which appear mid to late spring and suck the sap, possibly spreading viruses too. Three ways to reduce damage are:

- Sow before winter, so that plants are older and with tougher leaves when aphids arrive, so that less harm is done
- Pinch out the tips (delicious to eat as 'broad bean greens') when plants are in full flower, so that aphids lose their main landing places
- Keep plants well watered in any dry spring weather, so that they make new growth while aphids are grazing

Diseases The fungus 'chocolate spot' *Botrytis fabae* arrives late spring in wet weather and if soil fertility is low; avoid spacing too close, and compost-fed soil results in less damage to plants, see also Chapter 5 page 44.

First and last harvests Begin in late spring from autumn sowings. Harvesting is with a downward push and starts with pods at the bottom:

- Either pick pods when soft and with beans the size of peas
- Or leave two to three weeks longer, until pods are showing a hint of brown and contain fat beans, which give a larger amount of food.

Last harvests are in late summer, and don't be tempted by supposed 'autumn cropping' varieties, which generally produce little to eat.

Follow with Plant any of cabbage, beetroot, carrots, leeks, kale, broccoli, swede, chard, radicchio and other salads, depending when you take the last bean harvest.

Tips for propagation: the strong tap root needs a deeper module or pot than other vegetables, but transplants are successful even after the main root is stopped at the bottom; preferably set out plants while they are small, say 5cm (2in) high. Broad beans are almost immune to cold, but fleece helps early transplants to establish.

Broad beans in February from November sowing, netted against birds

Same beans in June

Climbing and dwarf beans

These beans are warmth loving, and the climbing varieties need sturdy supports; in windy spots a wigwam structure, rather than a line, diffuses the wind around plants. Climbing beans are a whole-season crop, while dwarf beans crop and mature more quickly, so are useful for a later planting after early carrots, garlic, cabbage and salads.

Growing Runner (pole) beans are perennial in mild winters and when soil drains freely, but not every plant survives and spring sowings give a higher yield. Watering in dry summers helps to maintain the rapid growth.

Space climbing beans at 30cm (12in) between plants in a double row 50cm (20in) apart, either along or across bed, or wigwams, 30cm (12in) between plants. Space dwarf beans at 40cm (15in).

Varieties Climbing varieties include Czar for white butterbeans, borlotti (which like Czar can be harvested in summer as green pods), Cobra for green pods of French beans and two yellow climbers:

- Golden Gate has wide, stringless, golden yellow pods of up to 25cm (10in), with a sweet flavour raw and a crisp texture even after cooking
- Cornetti Meraviglia di Venezia grows similar beans to Golden Gate but they crop three weeks later, useful for continuity of supply

For dwarf beans we like Cupidon (green pods), Orinoco (yellow pods) and Purple Teepee (purple pods).

Yield You may expect, from a 1.5m (5ft) row:

- Green pods of climbing French beans 7kg (16lb)
- Green pods of dwarf French beans 2.9kg (6.4lb)
- Dry Czar shelled 1.2kg (2.5-3lb)
- Dry borlotti shelled 1.4kg (3lb)

Propagation Sow no earlier than mid spring undercover or late spring in dibbed holes outside. There is no rush to sow because plants set out too early suffer stunted growth in cool conditions. Latest sowing date is early summer, and up to the solstice for dwarf beans.

Plant two to three weeks after sowing, and if the weather is cool a fleece cover for two weeks will help. Then for climbing beans, push supports in once plants are established.

Pests There are few and they are annoying: slugs eat leaves of weak seedlings (plant later in warmth), and deer graze on the leaves (deer fence).

Diseases None of significance, perhaps a little botrytis on bean pods in wet, cold weather.

Golden Gate climbing French beans are tender-podded even when swollen

DRY BEANS

Leave pods unpicked in summer and instead, pick dry or drying pods in autumn, to shell out the beans for homegrown protein. After shelling, the beans often need further drying on a tray in a sunny windowsill, until fully dry, then store in jars. They give food in all seasons, have noticeably more flavour than bought beans, and although their yields are not eye-catching because it's a dry harvest, the food value per area is impressive.

Climbing beans four weeks after planting out

First and last harvests The first pods are ready long after broad beans, in mid summer at the earliest, but then there may be an avalanche of more than you can eat. Unpicked pods quickly swell their beans, giving another harvest option. Last pickings are as weather cools in mid autumn, until first frost.

Follow with Garlic, or if beans finish earlier there is time for winter salads.

Courgette / zucchini

In summer warmth you can have plentiful harvests from just one or two plants, and a bonus is the large flowers, to dip in batter, and fry. However each plant needs at least 60cm (24in) to grow and keep cropping, also their roots travel outwards in search of moisture.

Growing Set out plants after all risk of frost has passed, and lay fleece over them if winds are still cool, for up to three weeks. Special care is to water generously in dry conditions, otherwise plants go semi-dormant and crop less. Apart from that, the main job is picking.

Varieties There are so many that it's simplest to mention the types of fruit: long or round, green or striped or yellow fruits, while highest yields are often green, long fruits of F1 varieties.

Yield From a 1.5m (5ft) row of 2 plants and with 60cm (2ft) on either side, you could pick 40-80 fruits, say 5-10kg (11-22lb) – or you could pick 6-10 marrows over the season, each of 1-2kg (2-4lb).

Propagation Sow in mid spring undercover and give warmth, or from early summer outside. Latest sowing date is midsummer, for harvests in autumn. Propagation of early sowings involves repotting after only 2-3 weeks, thanks to the speed of growth; later sowings can go out as small plants.

Pests Slugs nibble young leaves of weak plants, so avoid sowing/planting too early in cold conditions.

Diseases There is always powdery mildew on older leaves from late summer, bright white and with the leaves yellowing. It looks bad but is normal and does not prevent new growth. There is no need to remove these leaves, which are not infecting younger ones; see Chapter 5. A few courgette varieties have grey patterns on their leaves as part of their normal colouring.

First and last harvests The first, precious fruits in early summer soon become a glut in any hot weather, when it's worth picking fruits smaller to reduce the yield. Look carefully for all fruits because missed ones soon become marrows, and slow the production of new courgettes. Harvest either small or larger fruits up to 20cm/8in; it's your choice. Gloves and long sleeves are an option because the plants' spikes can cause an allergic reaction. Harvests diminish through autumn, until plants are killed by the first frost.

Follow with Garlic, broad beans or spring sowings.

Silver veining is normal healthy growth, and courgette roots under the path are robbing from the nearby beetroot

Midsummer courgettes through polythene mulch

Courgette to plant in hole through polythene, after removing bindweed shoots

Cucumber

Fast growing cucumbers are a versatile fruit: raw in salads and smoothies, made into pickles and chutneys, fermented, cooked for soup, baked, sautéed, they make a delicious gin and a refreshing treatment for the skin.

Growing Outdoor ridge cucumbers grow like squash plants with long trailing stems, and undercover cucumbers can be grown vertically. We usually grow all female (F1) varieties undercover and remove all side shoots, and baby cucumbers too, for the first 60cm (2ft) of growth. When the plant has reached your desired height, pinch out the growing tip and allow a side shoot to trail down. Spacing is 60cm (2ft) between each plant.

Varieties F1 varieties Passandra, La Diva and Burpless Tasty Green can grow undercover or outside, for sweet fruits of medium length 20cm (8in). Femspot and Flamingo grow longer cucumbers undercover, 30cm (12in) and slightly ribbed skin.

Open pollinated cucumbers include Tanja (equivalent to La Diva), and Wautoma which is a lightly striped spiny fruit for undercover and outside.

Yield From a 1.5m (5ft) row you may pick up to 4kg (9lb) over 10 weeks, depending on summer warmth.

Propagation Sow indoors in early to mid spring (outdoor varieties in early summer) on heat. The seed can be expensive so if rodents are a problem protect with a propagating lid until germinated (we once lost a whole tray to mice). Do not over water, or plants may keel over with rotten stems, and keep as warm as possible. The young plants are fragile so be gentle when potting on.

Plant undercover in late spring, after the danger of frost has passed. We grow them up strings in the polytunnel with the knotted end under the rootball at planting time. Plant outdoor varieties in the warm weather of early summer.

Pests Red spider mite may kill mature cucumbers, while young plants are susceptible to woodlice and slugs. Red spiders are reduced by high humidity but this can encourage downy mildew! Buying predators *Phytoseiulus persimilis* is an option against red spider mites but is expensive, and they need introducing in early summer, before you see red spider damage of yellowing leaves.

Diseases In late summer and autumn, powdery mildew covers the underside of older leaves, but these can be removed (or not, it's up to you) and the mildew does not harm plants. Downy mildew is becoming more prevalent and is a damaging disease; it may even kill cucumbers (and melons) in late summer. The only control we know is to keep leaves dry, which contradicts the control of red spider mite, so it's difficult; see also Chapter 5 page 44.

Carmen cucumbers, midsummer in the polytunnel, stems twisted around strings

Cucumber plants on a hotbed of fresh manure, were sown in modules three weeks earlier, then potted on

First and last harvests Check plants daily in warm weather, to pick ripe fruit, with usually very abundant pickings through summer, and much less in autumn when it cools.

Follow with Autumn salads outdoors, and salads or other over wintered vegetables in the polytunnel.

Peas

Flavour is what you notice with fresh picked peas; perhaps they do not even reach the kitchen. For the healthiest plants and biggest harvests, follow peas' natural growth cycle by sowing in early spring, to crop in early and mid summer before mildew and pea moth are prevalent; see Chapter 5 page 44. After clearing plants, there is time to grow many other vegetables.

Growing Peas like a moist, mild climate, not too hot, another reason to sow early. Browse a catalogue to see the choice of types to grow, from small and early cropping plants to abundant tall varieties that need support: some grow pods to shell, others grow mangetout pods to eat almost empty, while snap peas are mangetout with peas in them as well. Support with branches, poles and netting to keep plants upright and make picking easier. Spacing ranges from 10×45cm (4×18in) for shorter varieties to 10×120cm (4×48in) for tall peas.

Varieties For 2m (6ft) plants, Alderman for shelling peas and Tall Sugar Pea for snap pods, cropping in mid-summer. For dwarf early peas, Kelvedon Wonder and Hurst Greenshaft. For mangetout, Oregon Sugar Pod. For mildew resistance in summer, Terrain.

Yield From a 1.5m (5ft) row you may pick 2.7-4kg (6-9lb) from tall plants, 1.3-2.3kg (3-5lb) from bush varieties, over about four weeks in early to mid summer.

Propagation Sow from late winter undercover, to early/mid spring outside. The latest sowing date can be in early summer, but must be a mildew-resistant variety, and the harvests in early autumn are much smaller than in summer.

Pea plants establish well from sowing in modules, to transplant after three to four weeks, then a fleece cover for a fortnight can help them establish, even though they are frost hardy.

Pests Rodents eat the seed which is another reason to sow in modules, with a mousetrap nearby; pigeons eat leaves so fleece and netting help. Moths may lay eggs inside pods from early summer, then their larvae tunnel into peas, out of sight. Reduce damage by early sowing.

Diseases Mildew on leaves is the main one, only from early summer; sowing in early spring reduces damage.

First and last harvests Small, tender pods are super special in late spring. Harvesting depends how you like to eat them: young pods have sweet 'petit pois' (little peas and bright green) and you need to pick regularly for these, while older pods give high yields of initially sweet peas, which become starchy as pods change from pea green to a paler colour. Last harvests may be less sweet, because of mildew on leaves reducing photosynthesis.

Follow with Choices include leeks, brassicas, beetroot, carrots, chard, salads.

Sugar snap peas picked midsummer. Peas crop well before beans; see immature climbing bean plants in background

Midsummer's day, Oregon Sugar Pod mangetout peas

Summer squash

Colourful, prolific, delicious raw, cooked and pickled, best eaten when young and tender and used like courgettes. Summer squash are also tasty stuffed and baked. As with courgettes, the flowers are edible and delicious stuffed, or in tempura batter. Harvested squash will keep for a few weeks in a cool place, while large summer squash that have a thick skin will keep for many months, not to eat but as really beautiful autumnal decorations for the home.

Growing Growth is similar to courgettes, and by regularly picking the small squash, more growth is encouraged. During dry spells, water generously. Space at minimum 60cm (2ft).

Varieties Patty pan types are circular with scalloped edges, and include Pattison Blanc (white), Bennings Green Tint (green) and Sunbeam (yellow). These are best picked at 7-8cm/3in diameter but are still usable larger, although the skin is tougher. Summer Crookneck is a knobbly, firm-fleshed and curved fruit with a lovely nutty flavour, best at 12-15cm (4-5in).

Yield From a 1.5m (5ft) row, around 3.5-5kg (7-11lb).

Propagation, pests and diseases As for courgettes above.

First and last harvests From early summer, cut the fruit stems carefully with a knife – see 'courgettes' for information about possible allergic reactions. Harvests are perhaps weekly, then reduce during autumn until the plants are killed by frosts.

Follow with Garlic or broad beans, then spring sowings.

Summer squash Crookneck: at this stage the skins and flesh are tender

Squash planted too early in cold, wet weather, with slug damage to leaves; we replaced this one!

Summer squash under a five-year-old apple tree; this combination needs a wet summer

Tomatoes

Few vegetables have so much vigour and give so many exciting harvests over such a long period, with a choice of fruits of such varied colours and sizes. They are not difficult to grow, but here are some tips:

- Choose varieties according to your space and time available. Cordon/indeterminate varieties grow tall, at least 2m (6ft), and need support and regular removal of side shoots from their stems. Bush/determinate varieties sprawl out as much as up, need little pruning but take longer to harvest, and grow nicely when hanging over tall pots or baskets
- In climates with damp summers, blight disease makes it difficult to keep plants alive when tomatoes are ripening outside, so undercover growing is more worthwhile, and tomato plants' high yield should repay the cost and effort
- Tomatoes in containers and grobags need daily watering in summer, and weekly or fortnightly feeding
- Tomatoes in soil undercover need watering every 2-4 days according to the weather, and they do not need feeding when grown in surface composted, heavy soils.

Growing Tomatoes are demanding plants, repay you for the time and effort. Space at 45-60cm (18-24in), no closer or picking is difficult and diseases increase. Avoid overwatering at fruiting stage, which gives watery flavour.

Special care undercover is removal of lower leaves and finished truss stems, to improve ventilation and reduce blight habitat. Keep all leaves above fruiting trusses, to help tomatoes mature with good flavours and sweetness.

Varieties Our suggestions from hundreds of good ones include Sungold F1 orange cherry, Rosella pink cherry, Resi red medium, Yellow Brandywine beefsteak, Pantanu Romanesco plum tomato – all cordon varieties. For bush plants, Maskotka and Montello red cherry for containers, and Red Alert for outside.

Yield One undercover plant in soil, depending on variety, can produce from 2.3-5.5kg (5-12lb), and you can harvest over 4.5kg (10lb) tomatoes from one well tended grobag.

Propagation Sow undercover in 20-25°C (68-77°F) warmth in early spring, not too early because tomatoes grow fast, and plants quickly become potbound and leggy. The latest sowing date is mid spring, for tomatoes to grow outdoors.

Plant when confident that the last frost has happened, or perhaps a week before that if planting undercover, then cover plants with fleece at night if there is a slight frost.

Pests There are many:

Whitefly (aphids) on young plants in spring, until predators arrive to maintain a balance. If aphids are bad you can spray water on plants to keep them in check.

Root nematodes which you rarely see but can increase when tomatoes are grown in the same soil every year. Nonetheless some gardeners manage this and an annual 5-7cm (2-3in) compost on no dig soil maintains health and vigour, plus the roots of grafted plants resist the soil pests, but are expensive.

In warmer areas, caterpillars eat leaves and fruits: have a look, find and squash or remove them.

Diseases Chiefly blight (*Phytopthera infestans*); see Chapter 5. After mid summer never water leaves and keep plants as dry as possible; for outdoor tomatoes in damp areas, grow blight resistant varieties such as Resi and Mountain Magic, but they are not immune.

First and last harvests It's after midsummer before fruits ripen in zones 8/9: cherries first, beef later. Harvesting is a matter of choice, how ripe you like your tomatoes, but they soften and lose acidity if left on the plant after reaching full colour.

Last harvests are just before first frost, or earlier if you need space for planting winter vegetables undercover. Pick any mature fruits that are still green; they will slowly ripen in the house at room temperature, even until the winter solstice, but with less flavour than in summer.

Follow with Undercover: salads, spinach and brassica greens to crop through winter and spring, in zones 5 or warmer, also in zones 7-9 sow carrots mid autumn to crop in the spring. Next summer you can grow tomatoes in the same soil, with the new compost on top.

Tomato varieties
Sungold, Matina,
Sungella, Big Boy, and
Black Russian in middle

Hybrid tomato varieties, over-wintered side shoots in conservatory (frost free)

Tomatoes in the greenhouse growing from side shoots, hybrid but no seeds for 3 years

Last tomatoes ripening, late September

Orange Wellington, Black Russian, Super Marmande, Purple Ukraine, MpF, Summer Salsa, Orange Kiss peppers

Maskotka bush tomato plants, trailing stems from container plants on shelves; in distance are cordon Yellow Brandywine

TIPS FOR PROPAGATION

Before plants grow too long in the stem (leggy), pot them into a larger container and bury the stem as much as you can, with adequate light all around to keep growth sturdy.

You may need to pot them on a second time, about seven weeks from sowing, usually planting is eight or nine weeks after sowing.

The most important thing is never to allow any frost on them, or they singe and die very quickly.

Winter squash

Plants grow rapidly through the summer, producing beautiful ripe fruit in the autumn. Although they take up much space, they are easy to grow and give delicious winter food over many months.

Growing Timings and spacings are the same as for summer squash. The difference is leaving all fruits to mature on the plants, until either they have hard skin and a shrivelled neck, or before an autumn frost can damage them.

Varieties There are so many great varieties, including our favourite Uchiki Kuri (also known as Red Kuri, Onion Squash) whose fruits are onion shaped with orange-red skin, and a delicious sweet chestnut flavour. It ripens early and stores until spring. The skin is edible too; just deseed the fruits and chop. Crown Prince is larger, with dense flesh, creamy like sweet potato. Galeux d'Eysines has amazing warty skin and is best made into soup, while for something different grow Pumpkin Nut for its green, edible seeds.

Yield From a 1.5m (5ft) row you may pick up to 5kg (11lb) depending how much space and soil the sprawling stems can grab.

Propagation Sow undercover in mid April into modules, ignoring seed packets which suggest earlier sowing time, to avoid having huge plants when it is too cold to put them out. Or sow in late May if not on heat, then as for courgettes above.

Pests Slugs as for other squash, and rats sometimes chew out the insides and eat the seeds too.

Diseases Powdery mildew after late summer and into early autumn is a normal part of ageing plants, and does not affect fruiting, in fact it encourages plants to ripen the fruits.

First and last harvests It all happens in autumn, sometimes just before a first frost. Cut the stems and leaves away from fruits, which should be hard. Store in a warm place, up to 27°C (80°F) for a week or two after harvest, to cure the skin. We keep them in the house, where they look beautiful as decorations and last a long time.

Follow with Garlic or broad beans, then spring sowings.

Uchiki Kuri squash plants trailing over a pallet partition, growing in a compost heap

Decorating the windowsill with winter vegetables, including chillies, yacon, Monkeynut pumpkin on left and Marina di Chioggia squash on right

Winter squash plants recently set out, climbing beans on right and broad beans on left

Chapter 16

Salad Leaves all Year

Leaves and flavours change with the season

Home-produced salad leaves have wide ranging flavours, different in every season. In most climates you can harvest leaves for most of the year, in good amounts from a small area. Top tips are:

- Wider spacing, careful picking
- Sow seeds at the best time
- Keep soil fertile.

How much can you harvest from one bed?

I grew salad for a whole year, with successional plantings in an outdoor bed of 4×8ft (1.2×2.4m). There were bowlfuls every week from mid spring to mid autumn, and a total harvest of 156lb (71kg) leaves, with a peak of 10lb (4.6kg) weekly in early summer, good to give away or cook with.

Early summer salad harvest from the 2.4x1.2m (8x4ft) bed, lettuce just picked

Picking leaves

How you pick is as important as how you grow. Choose the method you like in order to harvest leaves quickly, consistently and for many weeks from each sowing.

Pick and come again

This method suits all larger salad plants, and is especially effective for lettuce. A gentle twist and push downwards on lettuces' outer leaves detaches them quickly and without harm to the plant, which repays you with rapid growth for 10-12 weeks. I created this method in 2003 when orders for salad bags increased unexpectedly, and I needed to keep the lettuce productive for longer than usual.

The benefits:

- Plants regrow more quickly when their baby leaves have not been cut
- You need less seed and plants, from wider spacings and longer life
- Time saved thanks to less clearing and replanting, because plants live for longer
- When picking leaf by leaf, it's easy to grade out old and yellowing ones
- Yield of leaves is higher than from cutting baby leaves, because leaves are larger and the ground is producing almost all the time.

At the same time as picking leaves to eat, remove to compost any old leaves, pests and weeds that you see. This does not take long and is justified by results:

- Less pest damage because as well as removing them, you have removed the decaying leaves that are otherwise attractive to slugs, for instance
- Beds or rows of salad look appealingly full of vibrant plants, and are quicker to pick next time.

See opposite page for more on this method.

In times of glut, continue picking at least weekly, so that plants stay youthful and productive.

From early spring to early autumn, sow new seeds of salads just before they come into their main season of growth, for healthier harvests over a long period from each sowing. This means you enjoy different flavours through the year.

Microleaf method: Dill, coriander and sorrel close sown for 2-3 cuts in the winter greenhouse

A variation for mizuna and mibuna is to grow plants at 22cm (9in) until leaves are touching, then cut across the top, 5-7cm (2-3in) above ground level. Regrowth is rapid, especially in autumn from sowings in late summer, with three or more cuts possible at 10 day intervals.

Cut and come again

This gains a little time at harvest only, and gives small, tender leaves from sowings every three to four weeks. Sow 2-3 seeds per cm (½in) in rows about 15cm (6in) apart, and make a first cut with knife or sharp scissors when leaves are 7-10cm (3-4in) high, cutting above the height of smallest leaves. Should you cut into stems, plants cannot regrow.

Two more cuts are often possible, after 7-10 days depending on weather and seedling type. From each harvest you need to grade out diseased leaves, because there is usually mildew and some yellowing as a result of the close spacing.

Flavour is different to the first method; these small leaves taste milder.

Hearts

Growing plants to the stage where they make hearts needs an extra 6-10 weeks compared to leaf harvests, and hearting plants mostly need more space and water; see page 156.

Heart leaves are sweeter, so it's an ideal way to grow endive and radicchio whose leaves are otherwise bitter. There are many leaves in a heart, you need only a few plants from each sowing.

1 Lettuce in June, before its third weekly pick, late June

2 Same lettuce 40 minutes later after being picked of outer leaves

3 Same lettuce mid August, after 10 weeks of harvests

4 Same bed late August, new planting of salad rocket and Red Fills mustard

5 Same bed on 19th September with one side of outer leaves of rocket and mustard already picked

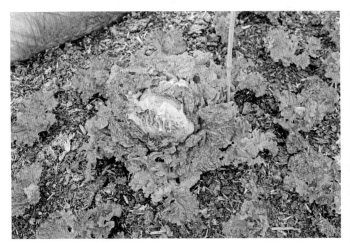

Clockwise from top left:

Grenoble Red hearting for seed tunnel, was the same size as surrounding plants just five weeks before

Amorina and Dazzle lettuce 10 days after planting at 23-25cm (9-10in)

Pea shoots in modules can be picked before planting, when this large

Sowing, planting, spacing

The two choices are sow direct, or raise plants (usually) undercover.

For direct sowing, draw a drill in the surface compost, 1cm (½in) deep; in dry weather water the drill before sowing, then (unless it rains) water every four days. This leads to the cutting method of harvest and you need to sow again every month.

To propagate plants, sow a small amount of seed in either a tray, to prick out, or into the compost of modules or small pots, two to four seeds per module. Plant the modules 3-4 weeks later, depending on the weather. Sowing in Chapter 4 has more on this.

Spacings for leaf or heart, pick or cut

When picking rather than cutting, there is simplicity of spacing at 22cm (9in) for all plants, from mustards to lettuce to pea shoots to coriander. You can raise a tray of different seedlings and pop them in quickly, without needing to work out different spacings. Hearting plants mostly need more space, from 25-30cm (10-12in) for lettuce to 35cm (14in) for radicchio and Chinese cabbage.

When cutting rather than picking, space more closely as in the table, and for picking salad chard and spinach leaves, space as close as 10cm (4in).

Two methods	Seed amount	Spacing cm/in	Picking method	Advantages	Disadvantages
Sow direct	More	2×15/1×6	Cut every 7-10 days	Small leaves, quick sow; first cut is soon ready and is quick	More time clearing/ resowing, more yellow leaves, needs more seed
Sow in trays/ modules	Less	9×9/22×22	Pick weekly	Less pests eat seedlings, harvests over a longer period	1-3 weeks longer before harvest

Slugs always bother pak choi

Lettuce root aphids arrive in late summer, after overwintering on poplar trees especially. Often they are present and you barely notice their eating, especially when moist, fertile soil helps plants to grow through the root damage. However in dry summers, lettuce may suddenly go limp, and die within a week. If your garden is prone to this, consider endives as an alternative green salad because they are not susceptible, and grow abundantly during summer and autumn.

Plant care

Watering

Salads need more watering than other vegetables, because they keep growing leaves full of moisture, and root easily into surface mulches which are moist.

Watering varies with the season and in a winter polytunnel, we water salad plants every three or four weeks, allowing the surface to dry between each wetting. This reduces slug activity, leaf mildews and germination of weed seeds.

Only in dry, summer heat, and for plants in containers, is it necessary to water every day. Our normal watering regime of summer salad, in dry weather only, is twice weekly. Check after watering that you have done more than wet the surface, because dry soil and compost need a surprising amount of water to re-moisten them.

Pests

Have less pests by offering them minimum food and shelter, in four ways:

- Sow seeds in the best season for each kind of salad plant, for strong growth and few pests; see box overleaf
- Tidy plants while picking – it's quick when you make it a habit – to reduce pest habitats and feeding possibilities
- Space wider to reduce hiding places, for example slugs do not like the drier, unshaded zones between plants
- Maintain soil in a fertile state because strong, healthy growth is less interesting to pests.

If flying pests are causing bad damage, mesh or fleece covers can be laid over plants to prevent their entry, for example to protect developing hearts of Chinese cabbage from butterflies.

See also Chapter 5.

Diseases

Use the same methods as for pests, to reduce the likelihood of diseases such as mildew, which otherwise increases in closely spaced plants and on older leaves. The variety of plant families for salad leaves enables a two year rotation and this helps to keep diseases at bay, allied to conscientious picking and tidying.

Spring lettuce for leaves; Homeacre's first commercial salad, May 2013

Spring sowings, direct or modules	Sowing dates months 3-5	First-last harvest, weeks from sowing
Lettuce for leaves	All spring	8-20
Spinach	Early spring	8-14
Peas for shoots	Early-mid spring	7-18
Coriander, dill, parsley	Early spring	8-14
Chard, salad beets	Mid spring onwards	7-26
Salad onion	Any time	10-13
Basil	Mid spring undercover	12-20, or 10-23 undercover

Lettuce planted early spring, 29th March

Spring season

Spring is exciting for salad because increasing daylight makes leaves chunkier and more colourful with every passing week. Lettuce thrives in its natural season of leaf growth, before a switch towards flowering in late summer and seeding in autumn. You can still grow lettuce leaves in those times, but they are less glowing than in spring and early summer.

Seasonal harvests

In early spring, continue picking from overwintered plants such as lambs lettuce, land cress, mustards, kale and spinach. New sowings can crop by mid to late spring; for quantity grow lettuce, for flavour grow pea shoots and the herbs, also pick wild (wall) rocket from sowings made in autumn.

As a catch crop, sow rocket, mustards and mizuna in early spring, for quick cut and come again harvests of small leaves. It's only a short harvest period from brassica salads in spring because it's their flowering season, plus there are many flea beetles on young brassica leaves at this time; see Chapter 5.

Lettuce

Three main types are upright cos, crunchy Batavians and ground-hugging butterheads, all in a range of colours. Seed availability varies: look for Bijou red cos and Sweetheart green cos, Navara red oakleaf, Saragossa, and Maravilla di Verano bronze Batavian: the latter is especially high yielding and long lived, but is prone to root aphid in late summer.

For hearts space at 30cm (12in), or half that for Little Gem varieties. For leaves, a 22cm (9in) space allows plants to grow for 12-16 weeks after planting, with regular picking of outer leaves, starting when leaves of each plant are just touching their neighbours' leaves.

Pick and come again

The first pick, when leaves have filled the space to their neighbours, is slower and more difficult because young leaves are at ground level, making them harder to twist off. Hold the plant with one hand while twisting each leaf with the other, pushing slightly downward. Aim to break leaf stems at the point where they meet the plant's main stem, which after a few weeks of picking becomes a small trunk.

Removing all leaf stalks means less hiding places for pests, and makes it easier to pick leaves the next time. Cos and Batavians are easier to pick than butterheads, and each subsequent picking is faster, when you can pick with two hands.

After about 10 weeks in spring, flavour becomes bitter when plants start to make a flowering stem. Some varieties do this rapidly, such as Salad Bowl, and bolting is also likely if soil is too dry or infertile.

For a continuous supply of lettuce leaves all season outside, make a first sowing in early spring, a second three months after that, then a third six weeks later in mid summer.

The glory of spring 1, pea shoots

Lettuce is for bulk, while pea shoots and wild rocket give strong flavour.

Pea shoots are possible from any variety, but tall varieties which would otherwise grow to 2m (6ft) give long, tender shoots every few days or weekly. Tall Sugar and Alderman give tender harvests over a long period, with minimum tendrils. This is the method:

- First pick when plants are 25-30cm (10-12in) high; pinch off 5cm (2in) of the main stem to eat
- New shoots appear from the base and stem, second pick after 10-14 days
- Harvests increase every week until early summer, then plants switch to flowering mode and new shoots become thinner and fibrous.

The glory of spring 2, wild rocket (*Diplotaxis tenuifolia*)

Wild rocket for spring harvests can be sown early autumn, to overwinter with a few ragged leaves. Or if winter temperatures are below -8°C (18°F), overwinter small plants undercover in pots, to plant in spring. They surge to life for regular cuts or picks of increasingly pungent leaves until early or mid summer, when they flower. Flea beetles make small holes but the leaves are still good to eat.

After flowering, wild rocket becomes a weed from shedding so many seeds. To prevent this:

- Either cut flower stems every three weeks, which leads to more leaf harvests in autumn
- Or pull out plants in summer and resow in early autumn.

You can sow wild rocket in spring but harvests are only small before flowering begins, and flea beetle damage is worse on young plants.

See also salad rocket below, glory of autumn page 163.

Other spring leaves

- Pinch the tips off broad (fava) beans when plants are in full flower; they are tasty but less tender than pea shoots, and they cook well.
- Brassica shoots are sweet, such as the flowering stems of kale, Brussels sprouts and brassica salads such as mizuna.
- Sorrel is prolific from perennial clumps of broad leaved, while the smaller leaves of buckler leaved offer a lemon-surprise effect to salads.
- Spinach and chard continue from overwintered plants, or start in mid to late spring from plants sown early spring.
- Coriander and dill from early sowings crop for longer than when sown in late spring.
- Parsley (flat leaved) adds flavour and vitamin C.

Early pea shoots in May, already picked, more to follow for several weeks on same plants

Wild rocket cut at different times and regrowing in stages

Orache and dill, June harvest

- Mint offers a zest to spring salads, a few tender shoots.
- Salad alliums include perennials (Chapter 13), chives, and spring onions sown late summer or early spring.
- Red Orache leaves, picked small from early sowings, give colour more than flavour.

Spring flowers

Cowslips, pansies such as heartsease, flowers of herbs such as chives and coriander, and flowers of brassica vegetables, peas and broad beans all have good flavours. It's the colours that stand out, so vibrant; see Chapter 18..

Grenoble Red lettuce in July from a February sowing, picked for 12 weeks, finally rising

Early-mid summer sowings	Sowing dates months 6-7	First-last harvest, weeks from sowing
Lettuce for leaves	Early summer, also mid summer for autumn picking	6-17
Endive	Throughout summer, all types	10-14 hearts, 7-20 leaves
Summer purslane	Any time in dry weather	5-8
Chicory	From solstice onwards	10-16 hearts, 7-20+ leaves
Chard, salad beets	Early to mid summer	6-40
Chinese cabbage	End of mid summer (7)	9-15 hearts

Early to mid summer season

This period offers a glut of lettuce from spring sowings, and is a key time to make second sowings. Psychologically this is difficult when you are dealing with leafy abundance, as demonstrated every year when Homeacres salad sales dip in early summer, then increase after mid summer, because local gardeners' lettuce are running to seed and they have no replacements. Often by mid summer there is a general shortage.

Seasonal harvests

Many leaves are the same as in spring and lettuce is still the main leaf: keep picking regularly so that young growth comes through. Herb leaves lift the lettuce flavour and once basil plants are ready to pick, salad days have surely arrived.

Endive

Endive is easy and abundant, its bitterness mitigated by the flavours of other leaf types, also by using a sweet dressing. Plus when you grow endive hearts in autumn, from mid summer sowings, their blanched leaves are sweeter.

Endives need even more moisture than lettuce, especially the large leaved scarole types which are best sown in late summer, to crop through autumn's damper conditions. Keep them watered, to reduce bitter flavours and browning of leaf tips.

Late summer linum (red flax) in front of oca, agretti and sorrel, flowering lettuce on left, for seed

The glory of summer 1, basil

For a regular abundance of mild but attention-grabbing flavour, grow Sweet Genovese, the standard sweet basil. Its yield, taste, robust growth and longevity make it a winner every year, but in our zone 8/9 climate where summers are often damp, it's best grown undercover to avoid brown spots on outdoor leaves. Basil likes dry, warm air and moist roots.

Some other basils to try, in order of how many harvests they give, are lemon, Thai, cinnamon, large lettuce (prone to slug damage) and lime.

To keep plants producing all summer:

- First, harvest (pinch or cut) the main stem (shoot) when plants are 20-25cm (8-10in), similar to pea shoots
- Pick new shoots of basil every week until autumn, always before flowering
- In damp climates, water only at soil level to keep leaves dry, and remove yellow leaves weekly.

The glory of summer 2, purslane

Summer purslane, *Portulaca oleracea* (pigweed), is a succulent that thrives in dry conditions, and it sets seed to become a weed in warm, dry climates. Harvest shoots as soon as you can pick a small length and keep picking or cutting new shoots and leaves, for three to four weeks.

As soon as you see or feel seed pods, which are bitter to eat and barely noticeable, pull plants before they flower. Golden purslane is extra pretty but flowers more quickly.

Other summer leaves

- Pea shoots become less prolific during this time, unless you sow in early summer, but that runs the risk of mildew on leaves, with a shorter period of harvest.
- Sorrel is flowering in summer: remove flower stems to encourage new leaves
- Salad onions are abundant
- Wild rocket flowers from mid summer, reducing the amount of new leaves which also become pungent
- Chard and young leaves of any beet plants are prolific
- Agretti (*Salsola soda*) is 'land seaweed' with spiky leaves, to pick young and tender, or cut across the top: sow by mid spring as seeds lie dormant in warm soil
- Coriander and dill are heading to flower in summer: sow a few seeds every month
- Flat leaved parsley gives many pickings, as from Gigante d'Italia sown in spring.

Summer flowers

Summer flowers are nasturtiums, calendula marigolds, phlox and lavatera, among others. Add small flowers of borage for intense colour, wild rocket flowers for peppery flavour, and herb flowers such as rosemary and Tangerine sage.

Endive (right) was picked, above was cut, both a week earlier, shows strong regrowth from picking of outer leaves

Maravilla and Lollo Rossa lettuce in August, picked twice already

Last outdoor Marzatica chicory, a loose and colourful heart for Christmas

Late summer sowings	Sowing dates month 8	First-last harvest, weeks from sowing
Endive and chicory	Early	7-38, winter harvests small and intense flavour
Salad rocket	All month	6-36, later sowings overwinter best
Land cress	All month	8-38, with new leaves in mild winters
Orientals – mustard, pak choi, mizuna, leaf radish	All month	6-36, many losses in winter frosts
Spinach	Early for autumn harvests, otherwise all month	7-45, plants may look ragged in winter but are frost hardy
Lettuce	Late month, to overwinter	For spring harvests, 25-35
Chervil, coriander, dill, parsley	All month	7-38, dill is the least frost hardy, and coriander survives to -3°C (27°F)
Wild rocket	Late month and early autumn	6-52, but little in winter

Late summer season

Brassicas' period of flowering is recently finished, so the new sowings grow leaves for a long period through autumn mostly. Furthermore, leaves are cleaner because flea beetles are less numerous now.

Sowing dates

As days shorten and temperatures decline, sowing dates become more precise, because later sowings cannot regain lost time. It's the opposite of spring when there are better growing conditions ahead, enabling later sowings to catch up. These sowing dates are based on a first frost and dark days by mid autumn; check local knowledge for your best timings.

Seasonal harvests

Lettuce is still plentiful, from sowings in early summer, but leaves are more inclined to suffer mildew, and growth is reduced by aphid damage to roots (see above). In contrast, endive is highly productive, and chards and basil continue. New flavours are chervil, salad rocket and leaves of oriental vegetables.

Chicory

Around mid summer is the best time to sow chicories. The time at which you want harvests, and the warmth of your autumn, determine exact sowing dates. To harvest leaves in summer and autumn, we sow any time after the solstice, and for hearts in autumn we sow Palla Rossa types from solstice and through the month following.

Hearts (radicchios) come ready at different times from the same sowing, and tend to rot after firming, so harvest their hearts as soon as they firm up.

There are varieties for long or round leaves, and with colours from white to yellow, pink and red. Another option is to harvest roots in late autumn to pot and then force in a dark place. Classically this is done with Witloof to produce yellow chicons in winter and spring, and with Treviso for pink chicons.

Autumn season

Autumn is a mirror image of spring in terms of growth patterns, except that the soil is warmer and harvests are bigger at first. Many plants have established root systems from earlier growth, so be prepared for some gluts in the first half of autumn.

Seasonal harvests

Sow in late summer and enjoy your salads becoming more varied by the week. Coming into season of harvest are rockets, orientals, endive, chicory, land cress, claytonia, lambs lettuce, spinach, chard, chervil and coriander. Lettuce has a secondary role by late autumn.

Autumn sowings to grow outside	Sowing dates month 9	First-last harvest, weeks from sowing
Salad rocket, mustard, pak choi, mizuna, leaf radish	First two weeks	6-32
Lambs lettuce, Claytonia winter purslane	First three weeks	10-32

Autumn salad leaves, still with basil and the first chicory and endive

Chervil

The flavour of this herb brings appreciative comments from customers. Leaves are of similar shape to parsley but finer, more tender and with a taste of aniseed.

Sowing in summer is key, and Charles learnt the hard way in the 1980s, every year obeying seed packets' instructions to sow chervil in spring. Each sowing produced few leaves before turning into a mass of little white flowers. Then an experimental summer sowing revealed the wonderful harvests of autumn, and beyond winter if it's mild.

The glory of autumn 1, salad rocket (arugula)

Salad rocket, *Eruca sativa*, grows differently to wild (Wall-) rocket, *Diplotaxis tenuifolia*: both are of the brassicaceae family, but in different genera. *Eruca* rocket is annual, quick to make a flowering stem in spring and summer, while *Diplotaxis* is perennial.

The best period of cropping is autumn for *Eruca*, spring to early summer for *Diplotaxis*.

If you normally find rocket leaves too peppery, check out the milder leaves of young plants in autumn, from sowings 6-8 weeks earlier: rapid growth on a small root run gives mild-tasting leaves. Flavours strengthen as brassicas age, and cutting the small leaves of young plants is a way to have less pungency.

The glory of autumn 2, oriental leaves *Brassicacea* family

Mostly bred in Asia, these offer a pantheon of flavour, colour and form. The themes are fast growth, sappy and tender leaves, sometimes crunchy stems, with a wide spectrum of bright colours, and spicy, mustard flavours.

- Leaf radish is the fastest, a mooli with hairless leaves tasting of radish: best variety is Sai Sai; Red Stemmed is pretty.
- Mizuna (serrated) and mibuna (smooth edged) have long, thin leaves on long, pale stems; they are rapid growers, and there are red mizuna varieties too.
- Mustards come in all shapes and colours: Red Frills (similar to Ruby Streaks) and Red Lace look wonderful in both garden and salads, milder flavoured than Green in the Snow's taste of horseradish.
- Pak choi and tatsoi are prolific in cooler conditions: their crunchy stems of small leaves add a bite to salads, with many types available.

Pest warning – these tender brassicas are loved by slugs, caterpillars and other pests. We find pak choi in particular is holed by slugs when nearby lettuce and spinach are slug free; possibly it needs a drier climate.

Other autumn leaves

Winter purslane, *Claytonia perfoliata*, offers succulent and mild-tasting leaves, at a time when most others are pungent or bitter. Plants respond well to cutting across the top. In spring the leaves themselves grow white flowers and look great in salads.

Land cress, *Barbarea verna*, is in the cabbage family, but like the rockets is in a different genus to most brassicas. Its leaves taste similar to water cress and plants can be cut over, or picked of outer leaves, a few at a time in mild winters.

Lambs lettuce (corn salad) is in season from mid autumn to early spring; see below.

Chervil outdoors in early winter which has been picked all autumn

Salad rocket with mustard Red Frills in front, late autumn

Mustard Red Dragon, tatsoi, mustard Pizzo, komatsuna – all oriental leaves in September, from August sowing

autumn

Winter season outdoors

Winter's salad bowl has little leaves and big flavours. Leaves in high latitudes and continental climates are especially small and infrequent, even with protection. Lambs lettuce resists severe frost, land cress to a lesser extent.

Seasonal sowings

There are none outdoors, with sowing for winter harvests completed in autumn.

Outdoor lambs lettuce (corn salad – *Valerianella locusta*)

The word 'lettuce' is a misnomer: at mature size after two to three months, plants are barely 10cm (4in) across and weigh less than 28g (1oz). Rather than growing larger, plants make side shoots, and the result is fiddly harvests in cold conditions. It's fortunate that a buttery flavour and deep green colour recompense this.

Early growth is slow so a weed-free soil helps, or you can sow in modules to transplant. Lambs lettuce does not thrive in dry soil, because its mat of roots is at the surface, so water more regularly than other salads. Dry soil causes mildew on leaves, often a problem if it's sown in summer.

Winter season undercover

Undercover allows a wide range of salad plants that grow slowly in cool conditions, and tolerate freezing. Some damage occurs below -8 to -10°C (18-14°F) and if these temperatures are common, lay fleece (row covers) over plants in a greenhouse or polytunnel, for extra insulation, as described in Eliot Coleman's *Winter Harvest Handbook* (see Bibliography).

Small, precious harvests in the depth of winter turn into regular feasts by late winter and early spring, off the same plants. One sowing in early autumn can give leaves until mid spring, so make notes to remind you of these sowing dates in autumn.*

Sowing method

Undercover spaces are often cropping tomatoes and other summer crops in early autumn, when these salads need sowing. Therefore sow in modules to have plants after four weeks, by which time the summer crops are finishing and can be removed.

Tatsoi, pak choi

They thrive in mild winters and resist frost, but are susceptible to slug damage. Tatsoi grows new leaves in even cooler conditions than pak choi, with a downside that it flowers earlier. The Savoy-leaved, larger varieties of tatsoi are easy to pick of their outer leaves, and a productive pak choi variety is Joi Choi F1.

* See *Charles Dowding's Vegetable Garden Diary*

Steph with her chicories from outside, and Homeacres' greenhouse salads in December

SOWING DATES ARE KEY

By comparison with winter sowings, seeds sown early autumn give plants a well developed root structure before it's too cold and dark. This allows them to translate favourable winter weather into new growth.

Sowing dates for winter salads are precise. They allow enough time for plants to establish to a medium size, even to give some leaves before winter, without growing so large that they become vulnerable to frost.

Land cress in February snow

winter

The glory of winter 1, mustards

Mustards for salad thrive in temperatures of 5-12°C (40-55°F), and in warmer weather their leaves often grow quickly to a size for cooking. In mild winters, you can pick regularly and for hot leaves, grow Green in the Snow.

Mustards flower in late spring, so an early autumn sowing gives leaves for five months off the same plants. In early spring the leaves are large and tender, before growing smaller as plants rise to flower. The yellow flowers and shoots are edible, with a spicy flavour.

The glory of winter 2, spinach

Like the two rockets, true spinach, *Spinacia oleracea*, and leaf beet spinach, *Beta vulgaris*, share the same English name, but grow and taste differently. The Latin names inform us that leaf beet and chard are beetroots, while true spinach is in a different subfamily *Chenopodiaceae*, therefore related even to fat hen/lambs quarters *Chenopodium album*.

For salads I recommend true (*Spinacia*) spinach which grows well in cool conditions, when the leaves also become sweet, even sugary: so although not abundant in midwinter, every leaf is a treat. In mild winters there can be a few outdoor spinach leaves, but they are often damaged by weather and for salad quality it's best to give protection.

Lambs lettuce was sown between fennel, late autumn

Tunnel salads in late autumn, planted five weeks earlier, sown four weeks before that

Midwinter salad with spinach on left; Steph finishing our pick

Protecting winter salad leaves

(see also Chapter 8)

Cloche and fleece

This is a minimum level of protection. Sow in late summer so that plants are well established by winter, then cover with the cloche before the first deep frosts or stormy weather.

Fleece covers, although simpler and cheaper, are more likely to suffer wind damage. Winter's lack of sunlight means they generate little warmth, so new growth is small and weak, but the fleece is a survival aid. Or, when uncovered plants such as spinach survive winter, cover them in late winter, to convert the increasing daylight into warmth.

Greenhouse/polytunnel

These give great results, both for plants and people because gardening and picking are easier and more pleasant undercover. Salad plants are helped by the protection from wind and precipitation, although nights in winter greenhouses and tunnels can be as cold as outside.

Give a little ventilation most of the time, to keep leaves reasonably dry and discourage fungal diseases. Plants are healthier in dry cold than in damp cold.

Salad in boxes

If your greenhouse has empty staging in winter, you can grow leaves in old crates, such as plastic boxes that are thrown out by stores. Line them with newspaper, fill with any compost and press it in firmly, then sow or plant salads, 10-15cm (4-6in) apart. Leaves are smaller than the same plants grown in soil, but are easy to pick from the boxes at waist height.

Greenhouse grown container salad plants in a wheelbarrow, February

Winter salad leaves undercover

Vegetable (no. of plants per clump)	Space cm/in	Harvest period*	Comments
Chard (2-3)	7-15/3-6	10-5	The closer spacing for salad leaves
Chervil (1-2)	20-25/8-10	10-4	Flavour complements other leaves
Chicory (1)	15-20/6-8	11-5	Colourful, bitter
Coriander (1-3)	20-25/8-18	11-4	Flavour, few leaves
Frizzy endive (1)	22-25/9-10	11-5	Productive when picked regularly
Kale (2-3)	20-35	11-5	Salad and/or cooking
Komatsuna (2-3)	20-22/8-9	11-4	Fast, but often slug damage
Lambs lettuce (1)	20/8	2-4	From sowing mid autumn
Land cress (1)	22-25/9-10	11-4	Productive in cold weather
Lettuce, leaf (1)	20-25/8-10	11-6	Grenoble Red is reliable
Lettuce, heart (1)	22-27/9-11	4-5	Aphid risk in early spring
Mibuna (2-3)	20/8	11-4	Thin leaves, and slug risk
Mizuna (1-2)	20-25/8-10	11-4	Fast, productive, can sow late
Mustards (2-3)	20-25/8-10	11-4	Huge variety and they love winter
Onion, salad (5-8)	20-25/8-10	3-5	Multi-sown modules
Pak choi (1-2)	20/8	11-4	Attracts slugs
Parsley (1)	20-25/8-10	11-5	Sow late summer
Pea for shoots (2-3)	20-30/8-10	3-6	Sow late winter, crops in spring
Radish, leaf (2-3)	20/8	11-4	Roots damaged by severe frost
Rocket, salad (2)	20/8	11-4	Keep picking flowering stems
Rocket, wild (1)	25/10	mainly 3-6	Dormant in winter unless v mild
Sorrel, broad (1-2)	20-25/8-10	11-5	Productive, sow late summer
Spinach (1-2)	10-25/4-10	11-5	Salad and cooking, sow late summer
Tatsoi (1)	20-25/8-10	11-4	Early to crop, and to flower
Winter purslane (1-3)	25/10	11-4	Many leaves, delicious flowers

* Months: 9 early autumn, 10 mid, 11 late then 12, 1, 2 are winter and 3, 4, 5 are spring

Salad from tunnel and greenhouse in January, three weeks since the previous pick

Chapter 17
Growing and Using Herbs

Versatile, useful and lovely plants, herbs enhance the garden with their beautiful leaf shape, textures, fragrances, colours, flowers and taste. Our modern diets can have too little variety, and herbs add an energetic dimension to meals, drinks, health and home. Herbs increase the biodiversity of your plot, providing forage and habitat for wildlife. As well as using herbs to enhance our food, we also grow herbs to create a medicine chest and home cleaning kit.

Herbs have been valued for their culinary and medicinal qualities for thousands of years. They can provide you with a supply of fresh and home preserved, chemical free herbs. Preserving herbs yourself, you will know exactly how they have been dried, stored and how fresh they are. It saves you money and reduces waste because you can pick just what you need for a recipe and store gluts. Growing an assortment of herbs encourages experimentation, exploring new flavours

Potted herb garden (left to right): Rear pots both lavender; middle row mint, thyme, southernwood; front row thyme and sage

and combinations. You can experience the multifarious varieties (there are over 50 different kinds of basil, 30 of thyme, hundreds of mint) or try unusual or exotic herbs which are not usually available in shops.

Herbs are good for your health, containing vitamins, antioxidants and minerals. Many also have healing, therapeutic and other beneficial properties. Throughout history they have been vital for helping to keep people well; a source of treatment for and prevention of illness and disease, to fragrance the home and keep pests and illness at bay. They are extensively used in rituals and religious ceremonies.

Growing your own herbs opens up the possibilities of using much more of the plant, not just the leaves but also flowers, seeds and even the roots of some (coriander root is delicious).

Herb plants fit beautifully into different garden designs, equally at home in an ornamental border as the veg patch, in a specific herb garden or in pots indoors and outside. They work well as catch crops, to fill in gaps and are so abundant, if

picked regularly to promote growth, that they make full use of smaller spaces. They can be excellent companion plants; some varieties repel unwanted insects or attract beneficial ones, as well as providing forage for bees and other benefits for wildlife. Many herbs thrive growing indoors on windowsills, creating a useful and beautiful indoor garden during cold months or year round for people without any outdoors space

We mostly grow herbs in a polyculture with the vegetables and flowers, allowing space so that plants can thrive and reducing habitat for pests. We plant module tray raised herbs out using a dibber.

Growing herbs in the garden close to the house makes it easy to pick fresh for cooking if possible, rather than at the allotment. We mostly grow in the ground but also some in pots to brighten up paved areas and contain invasive species. During the cooler months, annual herbs and potted tender perennials grow in the greenhouse, polytunnel and on windowsills indoors. This is also a time that we make the most of home preserved herbs.

Extending the season

Many useful culinary herbs – coriander, chervil, dill – bolt in the late spring, just when you may be wanting to use them in summer salads, salsas and vinaigrettes. This is an ideal time to experiment with other herbs and explore new flavours but if you really want a little coriander for your curry, try sowing them as micro-leaves.

Take a seed tray, spread 2cm (1in) of compost at the bottom and water. Sprinkle the seeds on top, sprinkle on a thin layer

Planting dill and basil in April. These herbs will be used as leaves for salad bags and cooking.

Wasabi rocket, coriander and dill growing with outdoor tomatoes; here, the rocket and coriander have been allowed to 'bolt' so we can harvest the seeds

of vermiculite or compost, just to cover the seeds, and protect with a propagating lid if the weather is cool. If you are growing them in your house it might be easier to use smaller trays (perhaps upcycled plastic tubs from shop bought veg) or plant pots so that they fit easily on a windowsill. A propagating tray with several individual rectangular pots is ideal for this.

Keep the tray moist (but don't overwater) and on a low heat if the weather is cold. Cut the herbs carefully when they are about 6cm (2.5in) tall and have several true leaves, leaving about 1cm (0.5in) of stalk so that the cut herbs are free of compost. Often you can get another crop from this seed tray before composting.

This method also works well for growing some summer herbs in the winter, for example basil, which would require heat. A foil-covered reflector (see page 77) is ideal to ensure indoor grown herbs get enough light and don't become too leggy.

Angelica (*Angelica archangelica*)

Angelica is an impressive, statuesque herb growing to 2.5m (8ft) with large white or creamy green umbels in the summer which attract bees and hoverflies. It is a perennial herbaceous plant which produces flower stalks after three years and can die after setting seed. Cut off the flowers before they seed to prolong the life of the plant or cut it to ground level and mulch in the autumn. Angelica self seeds freely: new plants can be propagated from sowing the seeds (as fresh as possible) or from side shoots. Just cover the seeds and prick out to pots as soon as they are large enough before planting out. It grows in full sun or partial shade and, although tolerant of most conditions, prefers a damp soil. My best angelica plants chose their own position, self seeding close to the garden tap.

Microleaves emerging in seed trays sprinkled with vermiculite

All parts of angelica are edible – roots, leaves, stems, seeds, flowers. Harvest the stems in April or May, the leaves in May and June, the roots and seeds in autumn.

Angelica has a long history of medicinal uses, including as an aphrodisiac, a cure for alcoholism and the Bubonic plague, and is used as a botanical in alcoholic drinks: vermouth, Benedictine, some sweet wines. Crushed leaves in the car are said to help with motion sickness. Angelica root tea is a general tonic. It also makes a refreshing skin splash and can be added to water for a reviving bath. The herb is an ingredient in toiletries including soaps and shampoos.

Angelica leaves can be boiled like spinach and used to flavour soups, stews and fruit dishes. Add the aromatic seeds, which can be used as a substitute for juniper berries, to drinks, cakes and sweets or crush to use as a spice (in Middle Eastern recipes). Add the young lightly aniseed flavoured leaves and fresh flowers to salads.

Boil or blanch the stems, from plants in their second year or older, like celery. It cuts through acidity when cooked with rhubarb and apple or chopped in preserves (chutney, jams). Candied angelica is used in cakes and other confectionery. In Iceland, angelica stewed in salted water is served as a side dish.

CANDIED ANGELICA

Fresh green angelica stems, cut before the plant starts to flower in 10-20cm (4-8in) lengths, whatever size you prefer.

- Water
- Sugar
- Icing sugar for dusting
- An earthernware lidded pot (or a bowl with a plate on top)
- A pan

Fill a large pan with water (enough to boil the angelica), bring to the boil and add the stems. Reduce the heat and simmer for 6 minutes or so until the stems are tender. Drain. Rinse the stems in cold water and when cool enough to handle safely, peel off the skin and weigh. Next measure an equal weight of sugar.

Put the stems in the pot and sprinkle with the sugar. Put in a cool place for two days.

Empty the contents into a pan, bring to the boil and simmer for 10 minutes. Cool for a few minutes and then drain off the liquid and pour the angelica into a colander to drain further. When the angelica stems are cool enough to handle, dry in an electric or solar dehydrator at its lowest setting, or spread on racks in a low oven until they are dry. Alternatively spread on cooling racks and leave somewhere warm to dry.

Dust with icing sugar then store in an airtight container, such as a large glass jar, out of direct sunlight.

Basil (*Ocimum basilicum*)

Basil is best sown in April and May as it requires plenty of light to grow well. Sow on gentle heat, either in seed trays to prick out or directly into module trays. Do not overwater, especially if it is a cool spring. Basil grows best in a greenhouse or polytunnel in the UK; I plant most of mine alongside the tomatoes as a beneficial companion plant as well as valued crop.

There are many incredible varieties of basil to explore. Sweet basil, the one we are most familiar with, has an excellent flavour, abundant leaves, grows well and is delicious in pesto, tomato sauces, raw in salads, etc. Lettuce leaf basils have a milder flavour and huge leaves: I grow it to use the leaves as plant based mini wraps. Lemon and lime basil has smaller leaves with a wonderful strong citrus flavour – use the leaves in salads, it makes a delicious pesto on its own or mixed with sweet basil, it is fantastic in salad dressings and tastes gorgeous made into basil syrup for alcoholic and non-alcoholic drinks. Thai basil is a valuable ingredient for many Thai recipes; I like to use it too instead of coriander in tomato and tomatillo salsas and other summer dishes. Cinnamon basil tastes amazing in spicy dishes. Red or purple basil looks beautiful but has a slightly bitter flavour; I grow two or three

Thai basil (left) and sweet basil flowering in the polytunnel

Below:
Dried herbs (left to right): Basil flowers, calendula petals, sage, chamomile, lemon verbena

Basil flower oil infusing

Tip...

if you sow basil into a seed tray, after pricking out keep any remaining seedlings in the seed tray and grow on for a few weeks as micro leaves, for an early taste of summer.

plants mainly for the colour in summer salads and to use in curries and a spicy purple (or red) pesto sauce.

To encourage abundant leaf production, remove the flowers and add to salad, compost or use to make basil flower infused vinegar or oil. The flowers are very pretty and beneficial for wildlife, so I grow a few plants specifically to flower as food for insects.

HOW TO DRY BASIL FLOWERS

Gather into small bunches, tie with string and hang in an airy place, or dry on a herb drying rack, somewhere out of direct sunlight, such as the airing cupboard, a dark room or under the stairs, or inside brown paper bags hanging in the kitchen. When dry, crush between your fingers or in a pestle and mortar

to use as a culinary herb, then store in a labelled jar. For pot-pourri, add to other dried flowers and herbs and pour into little fabric bags to fragrance drawers or in bowls around your home.

BASIL FLOWER OIL

Pick fresh flowers and loosely fill a lidded glass jar. Pour in enough olive oil to completely submerge the flowers. Push the flowers down if necessary. Replace the lid and leave in a cool place for 2-4 weeks, depending how strongly flavoured you wish the oil to be. Check the oil daily to make sure the flowers are still submerged, so that they don't go mouldy.

When ready, drain through a fine sieve or muslin (compost the flowers) and store in a clean jar or bottle. It makes delicious dressings and marinades.

Basil flower vinegar, basil flowers behind ready to dry on the bamboo tray

BASIL SYRUP

Use to make cocktails, add sparkling or still water for a refreshing drink, drizzle over fresh fruit, add to sorbets, add to iced tea. You can use any kind of basil but I especially like the citrus of lime and lemon basil, the zing of Thai and red or purple basil makes a beautiful coloured syrup.

> 1 cup sugar, ½ cup water, ½ cup basil leaves
>
> Put the ingredients in a pan on a low heat and simmer, stirring, until the sugar is dissolved. Remove the pan from the heat and leave to cool.
>
> When the syrup has cooled, strain through muslin and pour into a glass jar with a lid. The syrup keeps for 2 weeks in the fridge.

BASIL INFUSED VODKA

This recipe does not contain any sugar.

> 2 cups of vodka, 1 cup of basil, a large glass jar with a lid
>
> Put the ingredients in the jar, replace the lid and leave somewhere dark for 3-4 days, shaking every day. If you prefer a less strong flavour, leave for 2 days only before straining.
>
> Strain through muslin and store in a glass bottle.
>
> Use to make cocktails.

Bay (*Laurus nobilis*)

Bay is an evergreen tree with hard, shiny, spicy, aromatic leaves. It is one of the few herbs that doesn't lose its flavour when dried: in fact, drying the leaves increases the flavour. Bay trees can grow very tall, to around 12m (39ft), so I grow mine in a 30cm (12in) pot to keep it small. The compost I used is a mixture of 50/50 shop bought potting compost and homemade compost with a small handful each of rock dust and seaweed meal (this is optional). Bay likes full or partial sun and doe not enjoy being waterlogged. Prune to keep it to your preferred size and shape.

Cooking bay releases warm, complex aromas so add it at the start of cooking, but remember to remove it before serving as it is not pleasant to eat. Bay is used in vinegars, classic bouquet garni, pickling, pates, marinades, soup, risotto, making stocks, infused bay oil, Indian recipes and in poaching liquid.

Traditionally, bunches of dried bay are hung in the kitchen to deter flies. It has many uses as a herbal remedy, including as a hair rinse for a healthy scalp – steep in hot water for 15 minutes and when cool enough, use as a final rinse when washing hair.

BASIL FLOWER VINEGAR

This is similar to making basil flower oil. Here I also added leaves that had come off when I picked the flowers – mostly from lemon and lime scented basils.

Add flowers to the jar and pour on white wine vinegar. Push the flowers down a bit and add more vinegar until it fully covers the basil. Put the lid on and leave in a cool place, checking regularly, for a week or two (depending how strong you want the flavour to be), making sure that the petals are always below the surface of the vinegar. Strain as above and bottle.

BOUQUET GARNI

This traditional combination of three herbs adds flavour to many dishes. I add it to the water when boiling home dried and shop bought beans after rehydrating. It is great added to many stews, soups and other liquid based dishes.

Simply tie together, using unwaxed string:

- 3 stalks of parsley (you can use parsley stalks with leaves or just the stalks, left over from using the leaves in something else)
- 2 sprigs of thyme (about 10-12cm/4-5in long)
- 1 bay leaf

Add to the cooking as you heat the liquid and remove when everything is cooked.

Chamomile (*Matricaria chamomilla*)

Sow chamomile in the spring into modules for planting out in May. I usually grow it in clumps in different parts of the garden. Chamomile is very beneficial for wildlife but like many herbs self seeds freely if allowed. Fortunately the emerging seedlings are easy to spot and hoe off the following year if they pop up where you don't want them.

We mainly use chamomile to make a relaxing tea, using the fresh and dried flowers and chamomile salve.

CHAMOMILE TEA

2tsp dried/4tsp fresh flowers per 8fl.oz cup – pour on hot water and brew for 5-10 minutes, depending how strong you like it.

Chervil (*Anthriscus cerefolium*)

Chervil has sweet, lightly aniseed flavoured feathery leaves. As it bolts in the spring, so sow in August and again in the autumn for leaves undercover all through the winter. Chervil loses its flavour quickly in cooking so add at the end of the dish (it is delicious sprinkled on top of carrot soup). I mostly use it raw in salads, beetroot dishes and vinaigrettes. Chervil is a key ingredient of fines herbes.

FINES HERBES

Finely chop equal quantities of chervil, parsley, chives and French tarragon. Add to the end of cooking to keep the flavours or use in raw dishes.

Chives (*Allium schoenoprasum*)

Chives are propagated by splitting an existing clump or sown from seed in the spring – I sow into pots so they can be planted out as clumps. Undercover, chives can be harvested right through the winter, where they grow happily on a windowsill. The purple edible flowers are loved by bees. Remove them before they go to seed to stop them spreading (I have some which have self seeded happily in cracks in some concrete)

and use in salads or to make chive flower vinegar.

We grow garlic chives too, which have an edible white flower, flatter leaves and a delicious garlicky flavour. Use as you would chives and also in stir fries and many Asian recipes.

CHIVE FLOWER VINEGAR

A pretty pale purple lightly onion flavoured vinegar.

- 1½ cups white wine or cider vinegar
- 1 cup chive flowers

Clean the flowers to remove any insects by swishing several times in cold water, then either drain and dry using towels or give them a whizz in a salad spinner. Snip off the stalk and put in a glass jar with a glass lid (the vinegar will damage a metal lid).

Warm the vinegar and pour over the flowers.

Replace the lid and leave to infuse for 2 weeks before straining.

Coriander (*Coriandrum sativum*)

Coriander leaves are mostly used in cooking but all parts of coriander are edible. It tolerates lower temperatures so can be grown with protection through the winter. (See Chapter 16 for propagation.) I use coriander widely in curries, stir fries, salads and salsas. It makes a delicious pesto too.

Coriander root is finely chopped and used in Thai cooking, you can use the stems too although the flavour is not as delicate. It is best to harvest the plants at 5-6 weeks for tender roots. Soak the roots and clean with an old toothbrush to remove any dirt. The root can be frozen as it is or made into curry pastes before freezing (ice cube trays are good for freezing the pastes).

I grow some coriander specifically for the seeds, which are delicious eaten green. They have a spicy, citrus flavour sprinkled whole on top of hummus or crush to use in cooking (they are widely used in Indian dishes). The seeds make a delicious syrup for drinks (see method above) using 1 tablespoon of crushed seeds to 1 cup water and 1 cup sugar.

PICKLED GREEN CORIANDER SEEDS

Use as you would fresh seeds, crushed before use.

- ½tbsp salt
- ⅓ cup water
- ¼ cup white wine or cider vinegar
- 1 cup fresh seeds

Simmer the salt, water and vinegar until the salt has dissolved. Pour the seeds into a preserving jar (approx 250ml/8floz) and add the vinegar liquid. Replace the lid and process in a water bath canner for 10 minutes. Allow to cool before storing. Once opened, keep in the fridge.

Dry seeds too for use year round. The flavour of freshly ground coriander far surpasses that of shop bought ground coriander and is so easy to store. When the seeds are dry, remove from the plant, pick out any twiggy bits and store in glass jars in a cool, dark place. To use, crush in a pestle and mortar or electric grinder.

Cumin (*Cuminum cyminum*)

Cumin is a little more complicated to grow than the annual herbs but worth the effort for the incredible spicy flavour of truly fresh ground dried seed.

- Sow between April and July, to have bushy plants by late autumn. Their leaves resemble carrot foliage with shorter stems and need 22-30cm (9-12in) space between them. You can sow direct, or in modules to transplant.

- If winters are cold with common frosts below -5°C (23°F), you need to harvest the roots before it freezes hard, to store in sacks or boxes of moist compost, say in a shed where it's cool but not freezing.

- Then replant these roots in early spring, at 30cm (12in). Or if your winters are mild, wait for the overwintered roots to regrow. They send up flowering stems of 60-90cm (2-3ft) which need staking in early summer when the small white flowers are appearing.

- By mid summer these flowers turn into cumin seeds. Check for the seeds changing from green to brown: when about half are brown, gently pull up each plant, leaving some soil on the roots, and hang upside down in an airy space undercover.

- Within two to four weeks, the seeds are mostly dry and you can either rub them out by hand, or lay plants on a sheet over concrete, then walk over to separate seeds from the stems.

- Finally, transfer the seeds and chaff to a bucket, and winnow in a breeze.

We use cumin extensively in the kitchen. It is much more fragrant than shop bought seed. Use in hummus, curries, spice mixes, cakes and breads and infusions in vodka for spicy cocktails. It is widely respected for its medicinal properties. Cumin tea is used as a treatment for colds and to revitalise the mind and body. Make in the same way as fennel seed tea.

CUMIN SYRUP

- 1tsp toasted cumin seeds, crushed
- 2 cups of simple syrup*

Simmer in a pan for 15 minutes or so until the flavour has been extracted. Cool and strain through muslin into a clean jar – replace lid and label.

Use the syrup to make spicy refreshing non-alcoholic drinks: add soda water or homemade lemonade.

For cocktails, try it with ginger beer, lemon juice and vodka, (1tbsp syrup to each ounce/2tbsp vodka)

* Simple syrup is made with a 1:1 ratio of water and sugar, heated in a pan and stirred until all of the sugar is dissolved. Keep in a glass lidded jar in the fridge for up to 4 weeks. Experiment with flavourings for this simple sweet liquid – e.g. edible flowers, chilli, lemongrass, rosemary, mint.

Dill (*Anethum graveolens*)

(See page 158 for growing directions)

Dill has a refreshing slightly aniseed flavour with spicy seeds. Fresh, it is lovely in salads, makes a delicious pesto and is used extensively in Scandinavian cooking. It grows best from sowings in spring and early summer, going to flower during the summer which is just around the time that I want to use a lot of it for preserving with beans, cucumbers and other summer vegetables, so I sow it every two weeks, popping it into any spaces I have as a catch crop, to make sure I have enough leaves. The picking season extends to October or November if it is mild. I have grown it all winter undercover. You need to grow three times as many plants as you would during the spring, as it does not like very cold temperatures.

Dill pickle vodka looks striking, infusing for seven days, before straining

The flower heads and seeds are very useful in preserving too. Dry the seeds on the flower heads for sowing and to use whole and crushed in soups, sauces, pickles, breads, salads.

DILL PICKLE VODKA

For something unusual and very spicy, try this Dill pickle vodka, delicious with tomato juice.

If you don't fancy the spiciness, just leave the chillies out.

- 1 cucumber, sliced
- 10 sprigs fresh dill
- 1tbsp whole peppercorns
- 1tbsp mustard seeds or celery seed
- 1 small clove garlic chopped, or more if you like
- 750 ml/26fl. oz vodka
- 2-4 chillies
- 1tsp/2oz finely chopped horseradish
- Zest of a lime or lemon

Put all of the ingredients into a large clean jar and replace the lid. Shake daily for seven days, strain and bottle.

Fennel (*Foeniculum vulgare*)

Green and bronze fennel are hardy perennials which grow to about 1.5m (5ft). It has strong aniseed flavoured leaves and seeds. I enjoy nibbling on the fresh leaves but mainly grow fennel to dry the seeds to use in cooking and preserving. They can be ground and mixed with other spices to form the base of many dishes, infused with vinegar for salad dressings, with alcohol for liquorice flavoured cocktails, chewed on to freshen the breath, and make a delicious herbal tea. Ground fennel seeds may be added to homemade toothpowder and make a lovely homemade mouth wash.

Store dried fennel seeds in glass jars in a cool, dark place.

The tall flowers are beneficial for wildlife but unless you want a lot of fennel plants popping up everywhere, remove the seed heads to dry them indoors.

FENNEL SEED TEA

- 1tsp fennel seeds per cup
- water

Gently crush the fennel seeds in a pestle and mortar, then put into a teapot. Pour in the hot water (enough for the number of cups of tea you want) and steep for 10 minutes.

Pour into cups through a tea strainer.

Fennel tea tastes delicious and has many attributed health benefits including aiding digestion, easing menopausal symptoms and improving memory.

Lavender (*Lavandula*)

A highly scented evergreen shrub, lavender has green or silver-grey foliage and abundant purple flowers in the summer. Lavender is propagated from soft wood cuttings in the early summer and hardwood cuttings in the autumn. Plant in the spring. It grows to around 1m (3ft), preferring a sunny position in free draining, poor soil and grows well in a pot. Prune lavender every year to keep a compact shape. The edible flowers are simple to dry in bunches.

Lavender's beautiful flavour can be overpowering so use sparingly. It lends itself to many dishes including lemon curd, desserts, bread, cakes, infused in alcohol (especially gin and wine), in salt, in sugar, salad dressings, oil, vinegar, lemonade, in chocolate, chutney, jams, jellies and herb blends.

I use it around the home in fragrant bunches and powerful cleaning potions.

HERBES DE PROVENCE BLEND

There are many variations for herbes de Provence which include, in differing quantities, dried thyme, marjoram, summer savoury, rosemary, basil, bay leaf, mint, fennel seeds, orange peel, tarragon, chervil, oregano and lavender flowers – experiment with what you have, substituting and adjust the quantities according to taste, however I would moderate the amount of dried lavender used so as to not overpower the mix.

All herbs should be dried and the larger leafed ones crushed in a spice mill or pestle and mortar before mixing.

- 2tsp thyme
- 2tsp rosemary
- 2tsp oregano (or marjoram)
- 2tsp mint
- 2tsp basil
- 2tsp summer savoury
- 1tsp fennel seeds
- 1tsp lavender flowers

Mix together and store in a lidded jar.

Potted herb garden (left to right): In the large planter lavender, southernwood, two thymes and sage; mint in front, beside lemon balm

Lemongrass (*Cymbopogon*)

Lemongrass leaves grow to around 1m/3ft long. The bulbous base of the stem is chopped and used in curries and soups, and the leaves added to dishes for the lemon flavour and removed before eating (they are too fibrous.) Lemongrass oil is highly prized in perfumes and flavourings. It contains citronellal and can be used as a homemade insect repellent. With anti bacterial and antifungal properties, it is a helpful treatment for bites and good in homemade cleaning products. Lemongrass tea, using the stalks and leaves, is said to benefit the digestion.

Grow from a stalk:

- Buy some fresh lemongrass from an Asian supermarket. Trim the leaves off 2-3 stalks (use these in cooking) and put in a jar of water, just enough to cover the base of the stalk and place somewhere warm. Leave for a few days, checking to make sure the water hasn't evaporated. After 3-4 days, roots should have started to develop. When the roots are looking strong (around 2 weeks) plant into pots or the garden.

Grow from seed:

- I sprinkle the seed on top of a small tray of potting compost in March in a propagator. Germination can be slow (21-40 days) so do not give up hope if nothing happens for a while! Prick out when they are big enough into 4 cm (1.5in) modules and grow on, again on heat. When they resemble small clumps of grass and danger of frost has passed, plant into their growing position either in the ground (I grow mine in the polytunnel) or in pots.

- In the late autumn, bring potted lemongrass indoors to a frost free environment to overwinter. For lemongrass which is growing in the ground, dig up some and pot on to overwinter (as above) and harvest some to preserve.

Lemongrass freezes well: discard the leaves (you can dry these to use in cooking for flavouring, see above or to make tea) and place the clean dry stems into a blender and puree or finely chop with a knife. Freeze in small portions using an ice cube tray – you'll need 1 or 2 cubes for most dishes. Alternatively, freeze the stems as they are in labelled freezer bags or freezer proof containers.

Lemongrass stems can also be dried in a dehydrator or air dried.

Line steamers with fresh lemongrass leaves before steaming vegetables or fish to impart their delicious lemon flavour.

Lemongrass growing in the polytunnel as part of the summer polyculture (the copper stakes are there to guide the hose when watering and prevent plants from getting damaged)

FRESH LEMONGRASS TEA

> 2 stalks of lemongrass, leaves discarded
> 500ml boiling water
>
> Use a wooden rolling pin or meat tenderiser to carefully smash the stalks on a wooden board. Place in the teapot with ½ litre of freshly boiled water and brew for 5-10 minutes, depending how strong you like it, before pouring into cups.

I drink it without sugar, but you can sweeten with sugar, honey or agave syrup if you wish.

Lemon balm (*Melissa officinalis*)

An invasive perennial, lemon balm is started from seed in the spring or bought as an established plant. As it is very invasive, it is worth asking around to see whether anyone has a spare plant (or six!) to re-home.

Use lemon balm to add a bright, lemon flavour to salads, fruit salads, baking, drinks (syrups, cordials, infused alcohol), infused vinegar and cooking. It makes a delicious tea.

Lemon balm is easy to dry; just hang for a few weeks in bunches in a cool, dry place until brittle. Then crumble into jars and store.

LEMON BALM VINAIGRETTE RECIPE

> 2tsp lemon balm, finely chopped
> 1tsp minced shallot or spring onion
> ¼ cup olive oil
> 2tsp cider vinegar
> Salt and pepper to taste

Lemon verbena (*Aloysia citrodora*)

Lemon verbena is a perennial, sparkly tasting herb, like lemon sherbet and utterly delicious. It is well worth growing to make a delightful herb tea. Buy it as an established plant and grow in a pot because it does not like harsh winters – I overwinter mine in the polytunnel, bringing it into the house if it gets particularly cold; I value this herb so much!

Like lemon balm, use it to make delicious citrus flavoured syrups, cordials, infused vinegar, salad dressings. Warm gently in coconut milk or dairy cream to extract the flavour and use in savoury and sweet recipes, or make the lemon verbena sugar below to use in baking.

Both lemon balm and lemon verbena are useful for adding a citrus flavour to dishes and, with some creativity and experimentation; can be used to replace lemon and lime including sorbets and salad dressings.

Lemon verbena is a gorgeous homemade spa ingredient: it has been used for centuries to fragrance perfumes, soaps and other body products. It is worth drying lemon verbena just for the sheer pleasure of crushing the dried leaves and inhaling the fragrance on a gloomy January day.

LEMON VERBENA SUGAR

- ¼ cup crushed dried lemon verbena leaves
- 1 cup sugar

Blend in a food processor until ground together.

LEMON VERBENA LIQUEUR

- 4 cups vodka
- 10 sprigs of fresh lemon verbena

Place the herb and vodka in a large jar, replace the lid and leave for 2 weeks to infuse. Strain through a sieve with muslin and store in a clean bottle.

This tastes amazing in cocktails and with tonic water. You could also use gin or brandy.

Lovage (*Levisticum officinale*)

Lovage is a tall perennial herb (it can reach over 2m/7ft) that prefers sun or partial shade. Grow it where its height will not overshadow other plants. Its ornamental quality, statuesque with light green umbels, means it looks good in flower borders, as long as you have access to pick it. Be aware that it self seeds with enthusiasm, so remove the seedlings

Rosemary, lemon verbena sugar, Italian seasoning, herbs de Provence, bouquet garni

if you do not want it to take over. Cut the plant to just above ground level in the autumn and mulch. Large clumps can be divided in the spring.

Lovage tastes like a slightly aniseed scented celery, but it is stronger so do not use it to replace celery in recipes (I have made this mistake; the result wasn't very tasty). Lovage shoots can be blanched when young by covering ⅔ of the plant with light-excluding material, leaving the remaining ⅓ exposed at the top (steam the blanched stems as a vegetable). Pick the young leaves to use in the kitchen before the plant flowers.

Lovage is used in salad (young leaves only), soups, stews and stocks. Dried seeds are added to cakes, biscuits, chutney and pickles.

SUMMER LOVAGE SOUP

- Olive oil
- 1 cup onions, sliced
- 2 cups potatoes, diced
- 1 cup fresh or frozen peas
- 30g/1oz lovage, chopped
- Vegetable stock or water

Drizzle some olive oil into a large pan and soften the onions on a low heat stirring occasionally, for 5 minutes. Add the rest of the ingredients except the water and stir for a further 5 minutes. Pour on the stock, enough to cover the vegetables by 2.5cm (1in). Bring to the boil, reduce heat and simmer for 20 minutes. Remover from heat, season with salt and pepper if you wish and puree using a hand blender.

Marjoram (*Origanum majorana*) and Oregano (*Origanum vulgare*)

Although they are different herbs, marjoram and oregano are close relatives and are grown in the same way. They prefer full sun and a well drained soil, so grow well in pots. Both plants self seed enthusiastically. The best oregano plant I have is a self seeded one that has grown in a crack in some paving slabs in my front garden.

Oregano and marjoram can be grown from seed (start in the spring) or from dividing existing plants. There are several different varieties including sweet marjoram, golden marjoram (bright yellowish leaves) and slightly furry Greek oregano.

Sweet marjoram has a lighter, milder flavour than oregano, which is more peppery. Both herbs are in season from spring to late autumn and are easy to dry for year round use. Use the fresh leaves in raw dishes or towards the end of cooking, and put dried leaves in at the start of cooking.

They are both good with summer vegetables, soup, salad, infused oils and vinegars and roasted dishes. Stronger flavoured oregano lends itself better to spreads, dips, tomato sauces, pizza, pesto and Mexican dishes.

HOMEMADE ITALIAN SEASONING

This recipe uses the dried leaves of 5 different homegrown herbs including both oregano and marjoram. Store in glass jars in a cool dark place. The blend will last for at least a year. Use during the winter in pasta and other sauces, as a rub, and in marinades.

- ½ cup basil
- ½ cup marjoram
- ½ cup oregano
- ¼ cup rosemary (chopped)
- ¼ cup thyme
- Put all of the herbs in a jar and shake.

Mint (*Lamiaceae*)

Mint is an invasive perennial plant so, with the exception of water mint which grows in a pond, all our mints are grown in pots, regularly watered to ensure a good supply of leaves and fed monthly in the summer with comfrey feed (or topped annually with a mulch of compost). Mint divides easily to create new plants. It is more reliable to buy small plants rather than grow from seed. The leaves can be used fresh or dried. Apple mint, ginger mint, spearmint, chocolate mint, banana mint and water mint are just some of the varieties we grow – the choice is huge.

Mint starts to emerge in March, or earlier in a polytunnel, and by summer is producing many scented edible flowers which are loved by beneficial insects; removing these encourages more leaf growth.

Well known as an aid to digestion, we use mint as a beverage (refreshing hot and cold), when cooking new potatoes, beans and peas, in salads, as a syrup and cordial and to make various herbal potions (see Chapter 6). To extend the season, bring a pot into the kitchen for the winter.

Add a bunch of mint to warm water for a refreshing, scented bath or soak sore feet in a washing up bowl of warm water for 10 minutes (with ½ cup of Epsom salts, if desired).

One of the more unusual mints, Pineapple Mint
(*Mentha suaveolens* 'Variegata')

Parsley (*Petroselinum crispum*)

Both flat leaved and curly parsley can be grown year round with protection. Parsley is one of the key ingredients in many of my homemade cleaning products and skin treatments, see Chapter 6, page 46.

PARSLEY FACE PACK

- 8 sprigs fresh parsley – curly or plain leaf
- 2tsp apple cider vinegar
- Whizz together in a blender.

Apply to your face (avoiding the tender area around the eyes), massage and leave for 5-10 minutes. Use homemade reusable cloths to clean the mask from your face and splash your skin with water. This is good for blemishes and acne.

Rosemary (*Rosmarinus officinalis*)

Rosemary is usually bought as a young plant, but can be propagated from cuttings (make some new plants when the herb is getting old and woody) or from seed, but this takes some time. Sow in the spring for a bushy plant the following year. It is a hardy perennial evergreen from the Mediterranean and once established can be picked year round. Rosemary prefers a well drained sandy soil but will tolerate most soil conditions except waterlogged (mine grows well in heavy clay). Rosemary is very easy to look after, requiring very little attention except some pruning in the autumn to keep it at your desired size and shape. Rosemary has blue or white small edible flowers. It is easy to pick: cut off a few inches of stem with scissors or secateurs.

An aromatic, pungent herb, rosemary is widely used in cooking in soups, stews, tomato dishes, meat, pizza and focaccia. It is also a key ingredient in many of my cleaning potions. Simmered in water on the woodburner in winter, it freshens rooms and the scent of freshly crushed rosemary is said to enhance the power of the brain when studying.

ROSEMARY BAKED POTATOES

A delicious side dish, although I am happy just eating these with a large pile of seasonal fresh vegetables.

For each 500g (1lb) potatoes (chopped into 3cm cubes or sliced to resemble chunky chips) you will need:

- 3tbsp olive oil
- ¼tsp salt
- ¼tsp black pepper
- ¼tsp rosemary, chopped
- 2 garlic cloves, finely chopped (optional)
- Preheat the oven to 200°C/400°F/gas mark 6.
- Put the potatoes in the oven for 20 minutes, add oil mixture, toss and return for 20-30 minutes until crispy and cooked.

Sage flowering in the garden; you can use the leaves and flowers

Sage (*Salvia officinalis*)

Strongly flavoured sage requires similar growing conditions to rosemary and like rosemary, is best bought as a young plant. After 3-4 years it becomes woody and loses flavour, so take cuttings and propagate new plants. Sage enjoys plenty of sun and is happy in most conditions. Prune and mulch in the autumn.

In the kitchen, sage can withstand long cooking without spoiling the flavour and its slight bitterness is especially good at cutting through fatty dishes. Pick the leaves and use in stuffings, roast vegetable dishes, salad dressings, stirred through pasta, in risotto and drunk as a delicious herb tea.

To dry, either pick individual leaves (crumble into jars to store when dry – very useful for making stuffing in the winter) or gather 20cm/8in bunches and hang to dry. Bunches of dried sage, tightly bound together, make fragrant smudging sticks.

Sage is a valuable cleaning herb, with powerful cleansing and healing properties (see Chapter 6).

CRISPY FRIED SAGE LEAVES

Sprinkle on soups, stews, rice dishes, pasta, cheese dishes or simply eat as a snack. They will keep for up to two days when cool, in an airtight container in a cool cupboard.

- Sage, leaves removed from the stems
- Olive oil, enough to cover the base of the pan with 2.5cm (1in) oil
- Sea salt
- Some small pieces of bread to make sure the oil is hot
- A plate with kitchen roll or clean tea towel on, for draining

Heat the oil in a heavy pan, observing it carefully to ensure it doesn't get too hot. When you can see bubbles, carefully drop a small piece of bread in. It will rise to the surface and start to cook if the oil is hot enough.

Remove the bread with a slotted spoon and add the leaves, 6-8 at a time. Fry for 5 seconds, removed with a slotted spoon and put on the prepared plate to drain.

When dry and crisp, sprinkle with freshly ground salt.

Shiso (*Perilla*) – green and red

Sow green and red perilla shiso in the spring on gentle heat, at the same time as basil. Keep the compost moist without over-watering until the seeds germinate. When large enough, prick out into small pots and plant out after the last frost. I grow most of my shiso in the polytunnel, it will grow outside in temperate climates too. Shiso is grown for its edible leaves, flower buds, seed pods and seeds. It is an annual herb, but in temperate climates with mild winters, shiso can self seed freely.

Green shiso has large, jagged, crinkled leaves with an interesting, strong flavour that is quite difficult to describe – hints of mint, basil, cinnamon, citrus, even coriander. It is used widely in Japanese and Korean cookery. The seed pods are salted and preserved, the seeds added to recipes or ground as a spice. The large leaves are used to make wraps, pesto, shredded (as a green vegetable), in salads, tempura, sushi, sashimi, rice and noodle dishes, salted, made into Shiso sugar and used in desserts, cocktails and mocktails. Experiment by using in place of mint, basil or coriander in recipes.

Red or purple shiso has large, colourful crinkly leaves with a less spicy and more bitter flavour than green shiso. It is mainly used in some pickles, in particular umeboshi pickled plums and pickled ginger, and to make a shiso juice.

RAW SHISO WRAPS

- Shiso leaves
- Julienned raw vegetables – carrot, cabbage, tomato, courgette, cucumber, sweet pepper, etc.
- A dip made from 3tsp soy sauce and 1tsp sesame oil
- Or use some of your homemade ketchups and sauces

Place strips of vegetables into the centre of the leaf, root up, and dip into the sauce before eating.

Sorrel (*Rumex acetosa*)

See page 166 for growing tips.

Sorrel's tart, lemony flavour is delicious raw and cooked in soups, sauces, dips, hummus, pulse dishes, pasta sauces, pesto and curries. We grow several different kinds of sorrel; all can be used in this recipe.

SPRING SMOOTHIE WITH SORREL

- 2 cups sorrel leaves
- ½ lemon, juice and zest
- 2 cups liquid – water or nut/seed/dairy milk
- 2 cups spring leaves – spinach, kale, lettuce, fresh nettle leaves (4-6 nettle tops in the mix)*
- 1 cup fruit – your frozen summer fruit or store bought banana, apple, cucumber, pineapple (whatever you fancy!)

Put everything in your smoothie blender and whizz.

* We harvest nettle tops from the nettles which grow in the wild edges of our gardens. We pick them carefully using bare hands but if you want to avoid stings, wear a pair of gloves, protect your arms and use garden scissors or shears. Make sure the nettles are fully blended before drinking to avoid stings – you really do need a powerful blender to make sure they are properly processed.

Summer savoury (*Satureja hortensis*)

Summer savoury is easy to grow from seed, undercover in March or outside in May. Prick out seedings into 2.5cm (1in) modules and plant out when they are 5cm (2in) high, 30cm (12in) apart or in pots. Growing to around 40cm (16in), the fresh leaves are harvested from May to November. Hang the whole plant upside down to dry in the autumn for dried leaves.

Known as the 'bean herb' in Germany, peppery summer savoury is delicious cooked with beans and other pulses. It is a good companion plant for beans, as it is said to deter black fly.

Fresh or dried, summer savoury is used in stuffings, herbal rubs and marinades, with mushrooms, tomatoes, courgettes and squashes.

Southernwood (*Artemisia abrotanum*)

Southern wood is a hardy deciduous plant which grows in full or partial sun and likes a well drained soil. I grow mine in a large pot. Southernwood grows to around 1m/3ft over 10 years. To prevent it from going straggly, cut back in the autumn. Propagate from seed or hardwood cuttings, or buy a young plant. The strong camphor scented leaves are used to deter moths and other insects.

See Chapter 6 page 56 for some potion recipes using southernwood.

Sweet cicely with green seed pods; chewing releases a delicious aniseed flavour

Sweet cicely (*Myrrhis odorata*)

Sweet cicely is an aromatic perennial herb with delicate fern like leaves and white umbel flowers which produce torpedo shaped green fruits. These are aniseed flavoured and nice to chew (spit out when chewed as they are not so pleasant to swallow). Cut it back after flowering in the summer and it will re-grow. It is traditionally grown near to the house so that it can easily be available to add sweetness to tart dishes. All parts of the plant are edible – leaf, seed, flowers, stalk and roots. It is not grown widely anymore, surprisingly, given its many uses.

It is one of the earliest plants in my garden to flower, providing valuable nectar for wild insects and bees.

Sweet cicely can be divided in the autumn to make more plants or to grow from seed, sow in situ or in pots in the autumn; the seed requires the cold of winter to germinate.

The fresh leaves are tasty in fruit salad and drinks or cooked like spinach. Make a tea from fresh or dried leaves (1tbsp fresh/1tsp dried leaves in a pot of water, 10-15 minutes). The stalks can be lightly cooked and the roots eaten raw (grated in salads) or cooked like parsnips.

Sweet cicely is well known for its ability to reduce acidity when cooked with fruits (in particular red, black and white currants, rhubarb and gooseberries) and therefore decrease the need for sugar. I rather like tart flavours and so can use this herb and leave out the sugar altogether, but this would not appeal to everyone. Use fresh or dried leaves and experiment with the amount of sugar you need when cooking or, alternatively, use no sugar and add maple syrup or honey to taste before eating.

You can use the herb to make wine and liqueurs – traditionally it is used to make Chartreuse and Akvavit.

In the home, use the leaves and seeds to polish wood simply by rubbing them on to release the oils and aroma and wiping with a damp cloth. Or pound, infuse in oil and use in the furniture polish recipe.

Tarragon, French (*Artemisia dracunculus* 'Sativa')

French tarragon is valued for its mild mint-anise flavour which adds a subtle depth to many dishes. In France it is called 'King of the Herbs'. A perennial, it is propagated from existing plants and grows to around 90cm (36in) in the summer. French tarragon prefers a free draining soil. As it is not hardy during harsh winters, I grow it in a pot with a sandy compost mix so that it can be brought under shelter if necessary. In the winter, cut the growth to ground level and mulch.

French tarragon is delicious added to potato salad, with roasted vegetables, in mushroom dishes, soup, ratatouille and even in some cakes.

Although it is best used fresh, the herb dries easily for winter use and can also be frozen. French tarragon chewed is said to ease toothache and is a mild sedative.

ROASTED SUMMER SQUASH WITH TARRAGON

This simple dish deliciously combines the bright flavours of French tarragon and summer squash.

- A selection of summer squash: courgette (zucchini), patty pan, crookneck, Tromoncino
- Olive oil
- A bunch of tarragon sprigs
- Juice of a freshly squeezed lemon
- Salt and pepper, to taste

Preheat the oven to 180°C/350°F/gas mark 4.

Cut the squashes in half, place a 5cm (2in) sprig of French tarragon on top of one half, drizzle both with olive oil and lemon juice and sprinkle on salt and pepper, if desired. Put one half on top of the other and place the squashes in a baking dish. Cut the squeezed lemon into quarters and tuck around the squash for an extra lemon flavour (or use in the lemon peel recipes in Chapter 12).

Put the lid on the baking dish and place in the centre of the oven. Bake for 30-45 minutes until tender (check using a skewer in the squash flesh). The overall cooking time will depend on the size of your squashes.

Remove from the baking dish and serve with any juices drizzled over with fresh salad leaves and new potatoes or crusty bread. The skin and seeds are edible.

If you do not have a lidded baking dish, either use a similarly sized ovenproof dish inverted on top or baking foil. Experiment with other seasonal herbs for different flavours.

Thyme (*Thymus*)

Another Mediterranean herb, thyme prefers to grow in dry conditions which prolong its life (it dies if too waterlogged) and intensify its aromatic flavour. It grows well in pots, and I also grow it along the edges of beds next to stone paths. Creeping thymes makes a good ground cover. There are many varieties to choose from with varied colours and scents (including orange, lemon, pine). I grow many different kinds of thyme for the beauty of their leaves, different fragrances and abundant small flowers which bees love.

Prune thyme in the summer and winter to stop it becoming too straggly. I put the prunings into large jars filled with vinegar to make thyme infused cleaners (see Chapter 10).

Thyme tea is excellent for sore throats and colds: gargle with it and drink (add honey if you desire as the taste can be too strong for some people). Thyme is a healing ingredient in home made mouth wash, sore muscle balms and as a natural disinfectant. Around the home it is one of the key ingredients in my homemade cleaners.

Use thyme with roasted vegetables (it is particularly good with roasted carrots, apples or onions), in sauces, savoury stuffings, infused oil and vinegar, savoury jams, chutneys (especially apple or tomato based chutneys) and infused vodkas.

Dried, the leaves make a lovely herb salt and mixed with other herbs, a variety of different herb mixes and rubs.

THYME AND ONION 'JAM'

I love slow cooked onions; they lift so many dishes. This is delicious as a condiment, spread on bread and pizza, stuffed inside vegetables (e.g. large mushrooms), added to burgers, stirred through rice.

This recipe works well with other pungent herbs – try it with sage, French tarragon, basil, rosemary.

- 4tbsp olive oil
- 4 cups chopped onions (or sliced, if you prefer)
- 2tbsp fresh thyme leaves (1tbsp dried)
- 2 garlic cloves (optional, or more if you prefer!)
- ¼ cup cider vinegar
- Salt
- Pepper

Pour the olive oil into the pan and add the onions, thyme and garlic. Simmer on a low heat, stirring often, until the onions are transparent (around 20 minutes.)

Add the cider vinegar, bring up the heat just to boiling point and then reduce to a simmer, stirring frequently for another 20 minutes or so, until the mixture has thickened.

This keeps for 3 days covered in the fridge. It also freezes well and can be canned in a water bath.

Picking mint and calendula

Chapter 18

Growing & Using
Edible Flowers

The colour, beauty and fragrance of flowers delight our senses. Serving them with your homegrown fruit and vegetables brings the whole garden to your plate, adding an extra sensual, colourful, uplifting dimension to meals. A culinary adventure of unique textures and flavours, they are food for the mind, body and the soul. Edible flowers are an important and pleasurable part of my garden, grown as companion plants and for wildlife as well as to harvesting to sell, for our meals and to make many different teas, oils, vinegars, cocktail ingredients and other wonderful homemade elixirs.

Edible flowers have been grown worldwide for centuries for ceremonial, nutritional and medicinal uses. In the UK the revival in the use of edible flowers is usually associated with the Victorians and their Language of Flowers, reflected by their use in main courses, salads and sweet dishes, however they were used widely in our rural communities long before then for valuable culinary and medicinal purposes and to flavour wines, beer, mead and liqueurs.

Valued as culinary ingredients for as long as there have been historical records, their use presumably predates documentation. Chrysanthemums and lilies were prized in Imperial China, they are widely mentioned in Greek and Roman texts, and the Persians steamed petals to extract the oils which were used to flavour dishes and beverages. They have a long historical use as part of religious ceremonies worldwide.

Edible flowers expand the possibilities and sustainability of your growing area, increasing biodiversity and maximising the productivity of your plot. They add welcome splashes of bright colour, complementing the vegetable and fruit crops. We grow them as part of stacking in our polytunnel polycultures, interplanting taller plants with the flowers. They are beneficial for wildlife, attracting bees and other pollinators which in turn of course help with the pollination of our vegetables. Some offer natural pest control by deterring, marigolds to repel black fly for example, or attracting predators – ladybird larvae or hoverflies.

This is particularly useful if you are growing in smaller spaces – such as allotments, urban gardens, balconies, rooftops, windowsills – where it is advantageous for every plant to have multiple uses. A good solution for those with smaller (or no) gardens, these versatile plants can be grown in pots, as ground cover, climbing up trellis or poles to make the most of vertical space, or indoors on windowsills. I use them widely in my potted forest garden. On a larger scale, they are an excellent useful ground layer for forest garden systems.

Another benefit of growing your own is that you know exactly what the plant is and can be confident it has been grown without chemicals. Always check that the variety you are growing is edible – not all marigolds are, for example. If you want to forage or use plants already established in a garden, do make sure you have accurately identified them before eating. Many toxic plants can resemble edible ones, so careful identification is very important.

Colourful violas decorating a spring salad

Some edible flowers are grown specifically for their blooms, others are picked from established perennials (daylilies, roses, angelica) or flowering herbs more often grown for their leaves (basil, chives, rosemary) or you can make use of the flowers of vegetables (peas, broadbeans, courgettes) or of 'bolting' vegetables such as brassicas. Forage for edible wild flowers (honeysuckle, elderflower, wild violet, dandelion) in many rural and urban locations, remembering to wash these especially well before using (try to avoid picking too close to heavy traffic).

The potential health benefits of edible flowers have been recognised in many cultures globally for centuries. They make you feel good just looking at them: the colours are uplifting, there is a sheer pleasure from enjoying eating the beautiful colours and shapes. Many are rich in valuable vitamins and minerals and can be a source of phytochemicals and antioxidants. Often herb flowers have the same properties as the leaves, usually tasting quite similar too.

Culinary uses of edible flowers include decorating food, fresh or crystalised with sugar, teas, tinctures, syrups, pickles, wines and other alcoholic drinks, jams and jellies, vinegars, stuffed and deep fried, and flavoured sugar. Many edible flowers in the permaculture garden have other uses too: to make herbal remedies, salves, beauty potions, ecological remedies for garden pests, in pot pourri and natural dyes.

Selling edible flowers

I sell them in 20g bags to local restaurants and in larger quantities on request, for example for weddings, parties and sometimes for special photoshoots. I pick the flowers early in the day when the dew has dried. They are supplied in plastic food grade bags, tied full of air to protect the contents or upcycled paper bags.

I charge around £250 per kilo for edible flowers, which sounds extraordinarily high but works out at an affordable £5 for a 20g bag containing usually 50-60 blooms and is a fair amount when one considers the time it takes to pick and pack fragile flowers carefully.

Dried and crystallised flowers are options for selling during the winter months. Dried calendula and cornflower petals add a splash of colour and flavour to rice and couscous dishes, sprinkled on fruit salads or soups. They make really lovely gifts too, packaged in recycled jars with recipe suggestions.

Polyculture of edible flowers (borage, calendula) with wild strawberries

Summer harvest of edible flowers

Blue butterfly peas growing in Chiang Mai, Thailand

Blue butterfly pea flower, growing in Steph's polytunnel

Growing

I start the flowers off in seed trays and modules, planting out as small plants. I grow most of my edible flowers along with the annual vegetables (most of these are also started off in modules) so having small plants makes it easier to design the garden and plant out. Also you should have plenty of little plants spare to fill in any gaps (should some die) and share with friends. Importantly, planting healthy small plants makes them less prone to destruction by pests such as slugs. They can of course be sown direct too.

Sow larger seeds e.g. borage, sunflower, nasturtium – into individual modules where they can grow into healthy little plants. Smaller seeds can be sown 2-3 seeds per module or into seed trays first and then pricked out into modules.

Blue butterfly pea flowers make the most incredible blue food colouring but are difficult to grow in the British climate (I am trying!), preferring somewhere sunnier, warmer and with a longer growing season. However the flower really is so extraordinarily versatile that I am persevering and exploring creating microclimates to extend the season for them and hopefully grow more flowers. They need to be started on heat indoors and kept frost free, so require a lot of nurturing and special treatment. I am growing them in my polytunnel where they have produced some stunning flowers but do grow quite slowly here compared with their exuberant growth in Thailand. In addition to their amazing blue and violet dyeing properties, tea made from the flowers is respected as a beneficial drink with many health giving properties. Just drinking something lapis lazulii blue can make a person feel cheerful! You only need 2-3 flowers per cup, steeped for 10 minutes; I use a glass teapot and tea cup to enjoy the full effect.

Adding lime or lemon juice changes the colour to an electric violet.

Most annual edible flowers grow well along with the vegetables. I usually grow them at the end of the beds, where they are easy to pick regularly and don't crowd the vegetables, or in between tall plants such as aubergines and tomatoes. Consider the eventual height and spread of the plant – nasturtiums in particular spread with great enthusiasm so if space is at a premium, choose a climbing variety and grow them up a trellis or similar structure. Plant tall sunflowers towards the back, borage in the middle, viola and marigolds at the front, for example.

It is best to pick in the morning, when the petals are dry, before the sun gets too strong or later in the day when temperatures cool. Sometimes this is not possible, particularly during a wet summer, when you just have to seize any opportunity to pick the flowers. Always pick carefully, ensuring that you do not damage the plant and check for insects, especially bees, before picking so that you do not accidentally squash them. It is alarming for both person and bee if they are accidentally picked! Regular picking encourages a longer growing season for the flowers.

Choose open flowers at their peak when their volatile oils are at their height, rejecting wilting or damaged flowers. Pick carefully with care for the plant; petals are easily crushed. If there are aphids, these can usually be shaken or blown off. For daily use in the kitchen, pick edible flowers when you want to eat them, so that they are fresh on your plate. They keep well in the fridge for a few days too.

To pick for storing, use a basket lined with a soft cloth, something with reasonably high sides (I also use small crates) so that the petals don't blow away, when it is as dry as possible because the flowers are easier to pick (wet petals tear easily and stick to your fingers) and store better.

Some edible flowers can be eaten whole – violas for example – whereas others you just eat the petals, so always check before eating. It is usually wise to move the green parts for most flowers which are eaten whole as often they are scratchy or bitter.

Always shake the flowers before using to remove any insects hiding within.

There are a huge number of edible flowers to chose from; here are some that we grow.

Annuals

Borage (*Borago officinalis*) – taste resembles cucumber

Traditionally in England it is used in summer drinks, particularly Pimms. The blue, white and sometimes pink flowers are pretty on salad and make beautiful ice cubes. Borage grows very easily from seed and self seeds voraciously. It will quickly take over so is best not grown alongside vegetable beds. Borage is an excellent forage plant for wildlife, in particular bees. Borage flower syrup (see recipe below) is used to make summer drinks, cocktails, in baking or drizzled on pancakes.

Basil (*Ocimum basilicum*) – delicious, fragrant flavour

Basil flowers come in a wide range of colours, from white and pale pink to deepest reds. Grow several varieties for a range of colours (see page 170 for growing tips). Basil flowers are tiny and need removing with care. I pinch off the whole flowerhead, which encourages the plant to continue producing leaves, and then remove the individual flowers and sprinkle on salads. Use the whole flower heads to make basil oil and vinegar, or dry to mix with pot pourri, make herbal tea or grind as a seasoning.

Calendula (*Calendula officinalis*) – slightly spicy, tangy, citrus flavour

Calendula is also known as pot marigold due to its use as an ingredient in soups and stews. It is easy to grow and quickly establishes and will continue to produce flowers until late winter, or right through the cooler months if the weather is mild and they have some protection (see Chapter 6, to explore recipes for potions using this powerful healing flower). Usually a sunshine yellow-orange, you can also find flowers with reds and multicoloured petals. To use as an edible flower in salads and cooking, harvest whole heads, which also encourages the plant to produce more flowers, and pick off individual petals composting the green part. Dry to use in the kitchen year round.

Chamomile (*Matricaria chamomilla*) – slight apple taste

Chamomile prefers growing in full sun in well drained soil but will tolerate most soils. Sow direct or into modules and plant out. The seeds are very small so sprinkle a few in each module, planting out using 6in (15cm) spacing for a dense planting of the herb. Chamomile will self seed with enthusiasm, popping up everywhere. It is a gentle herb, used in herbal medicine and is a useful herb to add to homemade cleaners, shampoos and other cosmetics. Use the flowers fresh or dried to make tea and add to puddings, cakes and other baking.

Cornflower (*Centaurea cyanus*) – sweet and spicy, like mild cloves

Sow cornflowers direct in mid April or in modules for planting at the end of April, two or three seeds per module. They prefer

Borage

Calendula

to grow in full sun and are tolerant of most soil conditions, self seeding freely once established. Cornflowers are known for their brilliant blue flowers, but you can also get them in shades of pink, lilac, red and white. Use the flowers fresh or dried in salads, stir through at the end of cooking to add a splash of colour, stir into cake batters, use as a garnish, to flavour vodka, make a flower herbal tea or to decorate iced confectionery. Add dry flowers to potpourri. Mixed with alum, the petals make a blue dye. Cornflower is used medicinally and in hair care products to benefit from their antifungal and antibacterial properties: add to the homemade shampoos and rinses in Chapter 6. A handful of petals, in an old sock or muslin bag to prevent the drain getting blocked, with a handful of Epsom salts added when running a bath, eases painful joints.

Courgette flowers (*Cucurbita*) – sweet, nutty taste

All courgette, summer squash and pumpkin flowers are edible (for growing advice see page 26). Shred and add to pasta, soups and salads, or stuff and deep fry in tempura batter: see recipe on page 194.

Left to right, from top

Drying calendula petals

Picking chamomile flowers to dry

Dried calendula and chamomile

Making calendula oil

Making calendula tincture

Polyculture in a summer polytunnel: marigolds and calendula growing with chilli peppers and sweet peppers

Nasturtium

Sunflower

Gem marigold (*Tagetes tenuifolia*) – taste of citrus

Sow gem marigolds direct or start in modules, two or three seeds to a module in April, to plant out when danger of frost has passed. Gem marigolds are excellent companion plants in the polytunnel and vegetable garden, attracting beneficial predators as well as providing forage for wild insects. Add the flowers to salads and cooked dishes, sprinkled into sandwiches and dried for winter use, when they can be used as a substitute for saffron and as cake decorations.

Nasturtium (*Tropaeolum*) – peppery taste, spicy like watercress

It is easy to grow annually from seed in mid spring: sow direct or individually into modules and plant out when 10cm (4in) or so tall. Climbing varieties can be trained to grow over trellises for vertical growing. The flowers are usually shades of orange, yellow and red; look out for the more unusual hues and spotted petals. As well as in salads, the flowers are delicious stuffed with roasted vegetables, fruit, tomatoes, nuts or cream cheese. Use the flowers to make flavoured vinegar and vodka. The flowers and leaves are edible, as are the seeds which when pickled make excellent homegrown substitutes for capers. Some seeds will survive the winter outdoors unless the weather is very cold, growing in the late spring.

Sunflower (*Helianthus annus*) – slightly nutty flavour

Sow sunflower seeds after the danger of frost has passed singularly in 3in (7.5cm pots) or large modules, or indoors a week or two before planting out. Protect the seeds from mice with a cloche or propagator lid if necessary. As their name suggests, sunflowers like to grow in full sun. Planting distances depend on the variety, from short dwarf varieties to plants of over 15ft (4.5m) with petals ranging from bright yellow through orange to deep burgandy. All sunflower varieties have edible petals, buds and seeds. The buds resemble artichokes in flavour and can be eaten steamed or boiled. Sunflower seeds are delicious roasted, spread on a baking tray in the oven at 200°C/400°F/gas mark 6 for 10-15 minutes, or hang the heads in the garden to feed appreciative wild birds in the winter. The dried petals are used in potpourri, soaps and candles and to make a yellow dye. Sprinkle fresh or dried petals on salads, stirred through rice and couscous or add to cake batter for a splash of colour.

Viola/eartsease (*Viola/Viola tricolor*) – tastes a little like lettuce

A very attractive flower, violas are easy to grow from seed in situ in the late spring or in modules: sow 2-3 seeds per module. They self seed and can form pretty banks of cheerful looking flowers. Violas have been used in herbal remedies for decades and this little flower is thought to be the 'love-in-idleness' mentioned by Shakespeare in *A Midsummer Night's*

Viola

Cake decorated with violas

Dream, used to make a magic love potion. Picked, they keep fresh for a week in the fridge and work particularly well as flower ice cubes and crystallised.

Perennials

Daylily (*Hemerocallis*) – light sweet melon taste

Grow daylilies in the ground or in containers in a sunny place; they are tolerant of most soils (except water logged). Keep well watered. Plant bare root daylilies direct in the spring or pot up and put out as strong plants. Alternatively, divide clumps and transplant. This is a good way to share different coloured flower types with friends, enabling each other to have a wide variety of free flowers with a long flowering season. Use the flowers fresh and dried in salads, soups, stirfried, steamed like a vegetable, in desserts, or stuffed with savoury or sweet fillings and held closed with a toothpick: ice cream, soft fruits, cream dairy or vegan cheeses, rice salad (mixed with dried fruits and colourful edible flower petals), and chocolate truffle mixture sprinkled with nuts.

Caution: some people cannot tolerate daylilies so try a small piece first. Other lilies are not edible so make sure you have a firm identification before consuming.

Honeysuckle (*Lonicera*) – sweet nectar

Climbing honeysuckle makes great use of vertical spaces using appropriate support: fences, scrambling over sheds, through hedges, up walls. There are also shrub varieties for pots or borders. Plant in the spring in fertile mulched soil in full sun or semi-shade. Different varieties require different pruning methods so do check the label that accompanies your plant. The flowers can be made into a tea, steamed like a vegetable, used to make a flower sugar syrup, wine or cordial or simply sucked for their sweet nectar.

Caution: honeysuckle berries are very poisonous, so do not eat them!

Lavender (*Lavandula*) – strong, fragrant, floral

Lavender enjoys sunshine and a well drained soil. There are a wide number of varieties to choose from. Plant the shrubs in April and May, 3ft (90cm) apart, 1ft (30cm) if growing as a lavender hedge, or in 12in (30cm) diameter pots. Prune every year in late summer to prevent them from becoming woody. Traditionally, laundry was spread on established lavender hedges in English gardens to dry and be infused with the scent. Lavender flowers have powerful healing properties and are beneficial in many homemade potions for the home and body. Use the flowers to make a spicy savoury gravy or red wine sauce for savoury dishes, or add to stews. Use lavender petals to make cordials, sugar, jellies, jams, wine, vinegar, ice cream, sorbet, custard, candies, cakes and biscuits.

Mint (*Mentha*) – strong, refreshing taste

See page 177 for growing advice. Add the small flowers to leaf and fruit salads, Middle Eastern dishes, chocolate desserts, cakes, ice creams, sorbets and to make vinegar, syrups, flower sugar and teas. Add to sauces and gravies for savoury dishes, stuffings, nut and dairy cheeses and vodka to make an infusion for cocktails.

Perennial alliums

e.g. Society garlic (*Tulbaghia violacea*); nodding onion (*Allium cernuum*); garlic chives (*Allium tuberosum*) – tastes of onions or garlic.

Perennial alliums are usually planted in a sunny spot in situ or in pots as bulbs in the spring. If they are grown in the ground, choose somewhere where they can regrow year after year. Society garlic has pale pink or white flowers, nodding onion (also known as Lady's leek) a deep pink, and garlic chives flowers are white. Sprinkle into salads, use to make a scented vinegar or stir fry the flower buds.

Primrose (*Primula vulgaris*) – delicate and sweet

Sow primroses in the autumn or early spring, in situ or in modules (2 seeds to a module) to plant out in spring, in fertile soil in a semi-shaded place. Alternatively, plant out established plants 20cm (8in) apart. Primroses can begin flowering in February: they are an early sign that spring is on the way and a useful food for early bees and other insects. Primroses make beautiful crystallised flowers; add fresh to salad and festive spring dishes or make into wine. The buds can be pickled (although this seems a shame for such an early flower).

Rose (*Rosa*) – sweet and fragrant: the more scented the rose, the stronger the flavour

Roses offer so much choice, whether you want to grow your roses in a border, scrambling over a wall or even through an old apple tree. Choose a strongly scented rose, (the older varieties are particularly lovely) and follow the growing directions for your chosen roses. Darker petals often have a stronger flavour. The petals have a lot of potential in culinary dishes from sprinkling in salads to making wine, syrups, jellies, vinegars, teas, crystallised and sauces as well as medicinal uses and also in cleaning products. Store dried petals in a dark container (a recycled brown glass jar is ideal) to keep their colour for a long time.

Rosemary (*Rosmarinus officinalis*) – spicy and savoury

See page 178 for growing advice. The tiny flowers are a little tricky to pull off but worth the effort. Sprinkle on salads and cooked dishes. Add to gravies and sauces, stuffings, pates, dumplings, nut and mushroom roasts, stuffed squash and winter stews. Stir into savoury biscuits or bread stick dough for a delicious spicy accompaniment to dairy and nut cheeses, homemade fruit cheeses (see Chapter 10) and hummus.

Sage (*Salvia officinalis*) – strong and savoury

See page 178 for growing methods. Sage flowers, like rosemary, are small and quite tricky to pick. Use in a similar way to the rosemary flowers. Try sautéed with onions and stirred through pasta or to make sage flower pesto (see page 120).

Thyme (*Thymus vulgaris*) – light and spicy

See page 181 for growing tips. These tiny flowers attract bees and other beneficial insects and make a pretty garnish for salads. Use in the same way as rosemary and sage flowers. Thyme flowers may also be used in the recipes for cleaning products in Chapter 6.

Thyme flowers make a delightful vinaigrette, can be added to ice cream and sorbets and make a delicious liqueur which is soothing for sore throats and coughs.

Thyme flowers

250ml vodka, whisky or brandy
⅓ cup soft brown sugar or honey
¼ cup boiling water
20g thyme flowers (or sprigs if you don't have enough flowers)

Place the flowers in a clean jar and pour on the spirits. Replace the lid and put in a cool dark place for 4-8 weeks; the longer it steeps, the stronger the flavour will be. Strain through muslin.

Mix the sugar or honey with hot water and stir until dissolved and allow to cool. Pour into the alcohol mixture and mix. Pour the liqueur into a clean bottle or jar and store in a cool dark place for 3 months before using.

Good for sore throats, it can also be used in cocktails.

Wild flowers

There are no growing instructions for these wild flowers as part of the pleasure is to explore your locality and find them, although most of us will have some of these growing wild in our gardens. Always make sure you correctly identify the plants before eating, using a good guide book and preferably double check with an experienced forager. It is best to avoid gathering wild plants which are growing close to roads and always forage responsibly, sharing with nature.

Cowslip (*Primula veris*) – light and delicate

The cowslip, related to the wild primrose, is an early spring flower. Sadly the population of cowslips in the UK has declined due to loss of habitat caused by agricultural changes, so this is one wild flower that you may need to introduce into your garden. The tubular deep yellow flowers provide beneficial early food for wildlife. Traditionally the flowers are used to make country wines and for scenting vinegars. Pickle the flower heads, sprinkle onto salads and make into tea. Mix the flowers (green parts removed) into the mixture for custard tarts or puddings.

Dandelion (*Taraxacum officinale*) – young flowers are sweet, mature ones are bitter

Dandelions are extremely common, well known and widespread wild flowers which grow in a wide variety of soil conditions. They are invasive, spreading freely by seed: the 'dandelion clocks' much loved in childhood as tellers of time. The leaves, root and flowers all have a wide range of uses in the kitchen and medicinally. Harvest dandelion flowers to use fresh and dried in salads, to make jelly and wine and a flower syrup. The refreshing tea is delicious with a slice of lemon and honey (or other sweetener) to taste. Sprinkle the flowers into fritter batters and cake mixtures.

Dog rose (*Rosa canina*) – light and sweet

The dog rose is a prickly, fast growing, scrambling wild rose with open pale pink flowers which can grow to about 5m (16ft). It was known as 'eglantine' in Elizabethan England. The flowers and fruit are beneficial to wildlife. The rose hips make a sweet wine and a syrup which is high in vitamin C. Use in the same way as cultivated roses: see ideas opposite.

Elderflower (*Sambucus nigra*) – fragrant, heady and floral

In early summer, elder trees are covered with creamy highly scented bunches of tiny ivory flowers. Gather by picking whole perfect heads (leave any which have turned a bit brown to grow on into elderberries) on a dry sunny day. Shake gently to dislodge insects. Strip the flowers from the stalks gently using your fingertips. Use to make syrup, cordial, wine, champagne, cider. Add to spirits for a summery tipple. Sprinkle into fritter batter, use to make sorbets and ice cream, make jelly, infused sugar, pickle or a chutney with gooseberries. Fresh and dried flowers make a refreshing herbal tea. Dried and fresh elderflowers make wonderful oils and salves for your skin and hair (see Chapter 6).

Hawthorn blossom (*Crateagus*) – light, floral vanilla taste

The hawthorn can live for hundreds of years. According to legend in Glastonbury, a town close to where we live, a hawthorn more than a thousand years old was cut down by Cromwell's army. In the countryside it is known as 'bread and cheese' and when in flower, 'Queen of the May'. There are many ancient links between hawthorns and fairies in folklore. The flowers make a delicious syrup, liqueur (steeped in brandy, although you can use gin or vodka) and wine. Dry both the flowers and leaves together to make hawthorn tea.

Herb Robert (*Geranium robertianum*) – light flavour

This delicate looking widespread wildflower was according to folklore named after a French monk living 1000 years ago, who used this plant to heal people from many diseases. Its benefits as a healing herb are widely documented. Herb Robert smells unpleasant, and the crushed leaves are an effective insect repellent, but the leaves are beneficial medically as an infusion, poultice and gargle. A handful of the chopped leaves and flowers in a bowl of hot water (as hot as is comfortable for you) make a beneficial foot bath. Soak the feet for 15 minutes. Sprinkle the small pink flowers on salad or use fresh or dried to make a refreshing herbal tea. Mix into salad dressings and sauces; use to decorate savoury dishes.

Jack by the hedge (*Alliaria petiolata*) – spicy garlic flavour

Jack by the hedge is a widespread, invasive weed which tastes of garlic. It is also called garlic mustard and poor man's mustard. It grows to around 1m (3ft) tall, flowering from April to July. The spicy leaves are tasty in sandwiches, salads or made into pesto. Use the roots like horseradish. Sprinkle the flowers on salad and into salad dressings, omelettes and rice dishes.

Meadowsweet (*Filipendula ulmaria*) – intense fragrant sweetness

Meadowsweet, one of the three herbs most sacred to the Druids, is a perennial wild flower of around 5ft (1.5m) which produces highly scented creamy flowers between May and August (in a mild autumn they can last right up until November). It grows prolifically in meadows, alongside rivers, verges and beside ditches. Meadowsweet has medicinal qualities and was used as one of the strewing herbs in Elizabethan times. It makes a delicious wine and in the past was used to flavour mead. Meadowsweet tea is beneficial for relieving the symptoms of colds and is an anti-inflammatory. Fresh and dried flowers make delicious flower syrups and alcohol infusions.

Red clover (*Trifolium pratense*) – sweet aniseed flavour

Red clover is a widespread wild plant which is also grown agriculturally as a fodder crop and green manure. The flower provides a wonderful forage for bees and other beneficial insects. In traditional medicine it is used widely for its medicinal properties. The tea is delicious hot and cold. Use the flower fresh and dried to make syrups, wine, infuse in spirits, jellies and jams. A vodka infusion makes a healing tincture (see page 187). Infuse in oil to make a soothing salve.

Wild garlic (*Allium ursinum*) – strong garlic taste

Wild garlic, also called ransoms, comes into season in the British countryside from April to June. The edible leaves make delicious pestos, risottos and salads. The pretty star shaped white flowers are a beautiful addition to salads or sprinkled on top of savoury dishes. They make a strongly scented vinegar and oil, useful for salad dressings. Pickled flower buds can be used in place of capers in recipes.

Drying edible flowers

Edible flowers that dry well include roses, dandelion, elder-flowers, lavender, violet, calendula, violas, chamomile, corn-flowers, hibiscus and marigolds. As I only preserve flowers that I have grown myself I usually give them a good shake to dis-lodge any hiding insects, but it is recommended that you rinse the flowers under cold water and dry thoroughly before pre-serving. Some flowers are dried whole, others only the petals.

Bamboo steamers make excellent small, stacking drying containers. I also use large circular Thai bamboo dishes. Those blue plastic mushroom crates which are discarded by greengrocers make ideal drying racks as the holes let plenty of air circulate and they can stack. Line them with muslin, a clean cloth or kitchen paper, spread the flowers or petals carefully, then leave to dry somewhere dark and airy. I use the cupboard which also houses our boiler. It is dark and well ventilated. The flowers take a week or so to dry; check regularly. They will feel dry, light and rustle when ready. You can also pop in some of those silica packets which come free with some bought goods to help keep the air dry whilst drying.

Alternatively use a dehydrator on the lowest setting (this method usually takes several hours) or tie the flowers whole in bunches and hang somewhere airy to dry away from direct sunlight (which will fade the colours) – hanging them inside a paper bag works well as this not only protects from dust but also catches any petals which may drop off.

Once thoroughly dry, store until needed in labelled glass jars in a cool, dry cupboard. They keep well for at least a year. They can be used as they are.

Some uses of dried flowers

- Add to baking mixtures (bread, cakes, other baked goods) for colour
- Add to fruit based desserts – crumbles, trifle, pie, summer pudding
- Add to chocolate based puddings
- Decorate the top of cakes, desserts and savoury dishes
- Mix with couscous or rice for extra colour (blue corn-flowers and deep red rose petals are great for this)
- Add to scrambled eggs or omelettes (including vegan versions)
- Use instead of fresh flowers in recipes (you'll need half the quantity, so ½ cup if the recipe requires 1 cup fresh petals)
- Use to make teas
- To flavour and colour alcohol for cocktails and syrups and infusions for mocktails
- To make herbal remedies and nurturing body lotions
- As a natural confetti for weddings, celebrations, table decorations and as a scented surprise in cards and letters (much more sustainable than manufactured glitter or confetti)

To make a natural food colouring, grind dried edible flower petals in a spice or coffee grinder (or use a pestle and mortar). The colours look festive but won't have the same consequences of using a chemical food dye – blue cornflowers make an amazing blue colouring, rose petals a soft pink, calendula a bright yellowy orange. Mix in cake batter, in icing sugar for cake frosting, to colour sweets (marshmallows, peppermint creams), in buttercream, vegan coconut frostings, pancake batter, wherever your imagination takes you!

Other preserving suggestions

Most of the recipes here use American cups (236ml/8floz). This makes things simpler as the weights of edible flowers depend on the type of flower. You can use any container as a measure; at home we often use an old bone china tea cup, as long as the ratios remain the same for all ingredients.

FLOWER SYRUP

- 1 cup edible flowers (e.g. rose petals, borage, cowslip)
- 1 cup water
- 1 cup sugar or honey

Bring the water, sugar and petals to the boil in a saucepan, stirring to dissolve the sugar. Reduce heat and simmer for 5 minutes with the lid off. Remove from heat and cool. Strain through muslin into a clean jar. This will keep refrigerated for a month or alternatively process in a water bath canner to store for longer.

If you want to use one of the intensely fragranced small flowers such as rosemary, lavender or sage, use 3tbsp rather than 1 cup.

Make a refreshing drink with still or sparkling water, or soda. Drizzle over cakes. Use as a 'simple syrup' in cocktails and mocktails.

FLOWER VINEGAR

- 1 cup of flowers/petals
- 4 cups vinegar (use white wine or cider vinegar)

Put the flowers in a large glass jar and pour on the vinegar. Leave on a sunny windowsill for about a week to infuse. Strain and bottle. Store at room temperature – it will last for about 6 months.

FLOWER LIQUEUR

- 1 cup flowers/petals
- 4 cups vodka (or brandy, gin, whisky)

Put the flowers in a large, lidded glass container and add the spirit. Leave for 2 or 3 days, shaking gently every day. Strain and bottle. Make some flower ice cubes at the same time to use in flower cocktails.

FLOWER SUGAR

In a large glass container, gently mix 2 cups unbleached granulated sugar with one cup of strongly scented flowers (best to use only flowers or petals that can be eaten whole for this) and leave for a week. The moisture and flavours will be absorbed by the sugar. Use in baking or drinks.

FLOWER ICE CUBES

Half fill the ice cube tray with water. Add the flowers and position carefully. Freeze for several hours then top up with more water and freeze until solid.

This method stops the flowers floating to the top when freezing.

PICKLED PETALS FOR SAVOURY DISHES

1 cup petals (e.g. rose) to make either:

Sugar-free pickle
Warm 1 cup of cider or white wine vinegar

Honeyed pickle
Combine 1 cup cider or white wine vinegar with 3 tablespoons of honey and gently heat in a pan.

Carefully mix in the petals and leave for at least two hours. Strain and reserve the vinegar to make salad dressings.

HOW TO MAKE A SUGAR SHAKER

For a quick, temporary one you will need:

- A glass jar
- Strong elastic bands
- Greaseproof/parchment paper
- A toothpick or similar thin pointed implement

Remove the metal disc from the lid and put in a safe place (somewhere you'll remember!).

Put the superfine sugar in the jar – you can make your own by grinding in a food processor

Spread a piece of greaseproof over the top and fix using a couple of elastic bands.

Poke holes in the paper using the toothpick.

Turn upside down and shake.

For a more permanent one you'll need:

- A glass jar with a metal lid
- A nail and hammer

Put the lid on the jar and very carefully hammer holes through the metal lid, avoiding the edges so you don't shatter the glass. For safety you may prefer to do this with the lid removed on a wooden board.

Rinse and wash the lid and jar thoroughly and allow to dry.

Pour the sugar in the jar and shake.

CRYSTALLISED EDIBLE FLOWERS

(Egg-white free version)

- 100 edible flowers, rinsed and dried if necessary
- 1 cup light coloured sugar (I use unbleached organic sugar)
- 1tbsp rose water (this is optional)
- ½ cup water
- Additional ½ cup superfine sugar
- Tweezers to hold the flowers
- Greaseproof/wax paper on trays
- Sieve or sugar shaker (see left how to make your own)

Make the sugar syrup by placing 1 cup sugar with ½ cup water in a pan and gently bring to the boil, Reduce the heat and simmer, stirring all of the time, until the sugar is dissolved then remove from heat and allow to cool to about 20°C (68°F). Using the tweezers to hold them, dip the flowers in the syrup and place on the greaseproof paper to dry.

Whilst the flowers are still damp, sprinkle with the superfine sugar. Leave to dry for at least 3-4 hours or overnight. You can use them slightly sticky in recipes that day, but they should feel quite dry before storing.

Store in glass jars in a cool, dark place.

FLOWER BUTTER – EITHER SWEET OR SAVOURY

- 1 packet (250g or US double stick) organic butter
- Around 12 nasturtium flowers or 10 chive flower heads or 1tbsp of rosemary flowers or about a cup of fresh rose petals – you can work this out by eye, depending on which petals you are using

Soften the butter and gently mix with the petals. Shape as you choose (you can be as fanciful as you like here), perhaps adding some whole flowers to the top, and refrigerate for about 2 hours before serving.

This freezes well.

Making flower vinegar

Flower ice cubes

STUFFED FLOWERS, TEMPURA FLOWERS

Courgette, squash and daylily flowers are delicious stuffed, dipped in a light batter and deep fried. This recipe uses homegrown and home stored Czar beans and garlic mixed with seasonal courgettes and spring onions.

- If you don't have Czar beans, use borlotti, chickpeas or broadbeans
- Substitute the courgette with summer squash
- To get 300g/10oz of cooked beans, soak 115g/4oz/½ cup dried beans

20-24 flowers (depends on the size) checked for insects
Batter
200g/7oz plain unbleached flour
85g/3oz cornflour
400ml/14oz very cold fresh water
2tsp bicarbonate of soda

Filling
300g/10oz (cooked weight) Czar beans, mashed
300g/10oz grated courgette
2 or 3 cloves of garlic, finely chopped
8oz/1 cup spring onions, finely chopped
1tbsp finely chopped fresh seasonal herbs of your choice
 e.g. basil, parsley, dill, marjoram, chives
2 or 3tbsp olive or sunflower oil for frying
Sunflower or other light oil for deep frying the flowers
Deep pan or wok for frying (the oil should not come to
 more than 1/3 of the pan's depth)
A few cubes of bread to check the oil is hot enough
A dish lined with kitchen paper or clean tea towels for
 draining

Fry the onions and garlic in the oil until soft. Add the courgette and cook on a low heat for 2 minutes. Stir in the mashed beans and herbs, and add salt and pepper if wanted. Leave to cool.

Stuff each flower with 3-4tsp of mixture and twist the petals closed.

Now make the batter by sifting the dry ingredients into a large bowl and pour in the cold water slowly, mixing carefully until it resembles single (light) cream.

Pour the cooking oil into the pan until it is 6cm/2.5in deep and heat. Carefully add a cube of bread: if it rises to the top and cooks to a golden brown in a few seconds, the oil is hot enough for the flowers.

Dip the flowers in the batter one at a time and carefully place in the hot oil using tongs or slotted spoon, frying 3 or 4 at a time until golden brown. Remove using tongs or slotted spoon and drain. Repeat until all of the flowers have been cooked.

Decorate with other fresh seasonal edible flowers.

DANDELION WINE

4.5l/8 pints/1 gallon dandelion heads (remove the stalks, they are bitter)
4.5l/8 pints/1 gallon water
1.6kg/3.5lb sugar
Peel and juice of 1 lemon
Peel and juice of 1 orange
Wine yeast

You will need a large pan, fermentation bucket, and a demijohn.

Pour the cold water into the large pan, add the dandelions and bring to the boil. Simmer for 10 minutes. Meanwhile, pour the sugar into the fermentation bucket along with the citrus peels. Strain the dandelion liquid into the bucket and stir well. When lukewarm, add the citrus juice and wine yeast (following the instructions on your yeast; some have to be previously activated). Cover and leave in a warm place. After 2 days, strain and pour into the demijohn and leave to ferment.

When fermentation has finished, siphon into bottles. It is best kept for at least a year before drinking.

Alternatives: replace the 1 gallon of dandelion heads with the same quantity of marigolds or cowslips.

FLOWER VINEGAR SALAD DRESSING

Use flower vinegar to make a salad dressing:

Mix together:

20 flower petals (optional)
½ cup olive oil
½ cup flower vinegar (see above)
Pickled flower buds (enough flower buds to loosely fill
 your clean, sterilised jars)
For each standard 454g/1lb jar you will need:
400ml/13.5floz/1 ¾ cups) cider vinegar
1tsp salt
1tsp peppercorns
1tsp pickling spice seeds (optional) – dill, fennel, mustard

Put the jars in the oven to get hot.

Bring the vinegar, salt, peppercorns and spices to the boil, simmer for a minute and remove from the heat. Carefully put the flower buds in the jar and pour the hot vinegar over the top. Seal immediately and leave to cool.

Label and leave for 2 weeks before using. Unopened, they should keep for 6 months. Once opened, store in the fridge and use within 2 weeks.

See page 94 for preserving tips and methods.

Chapter 19
Some Different Plants to Grow

Tubers, medicine and a sweetener

Apart from stevia, these are tubers of varied flavour and colour. Like potato they come from the Andes, but unlike potato they are not solanums. Therefore their tubers do not create poisonous solanine when exposed to light, and they have edible leaves and flowers. See Chapter 12 for recipe ideas.

Oca, yacon, tomatillo growing together, September

Growing and Harvesting

Vegetable	Sow	Plant	Space	Height of growth	Tubers initiate	Harvest	Yield/plant
Mashua	Early spring, in pots of compost undercover	Late spring after risk of frost	60cm/24in	3m/10ft	After the autumn equinox, oca and ulluco even in late autumn	Late autumn	1-2kg/2-4.5lb
Oca			45cm/18in	45cm/18in		Early winter	0.5-1kg/1-2lb
Ulluco			30cm/12in	30cm/12in		Early winter	100-400g/0.2-0.5lb
Yacon			45-60cm/18-24in	1.2-1.8m/4-6ft		Mid to late autumn	3-6kg/6-13lb

Some of the harvests have unusual amounts of protein and calories. The lowest calorie count is of stevia, not included in the table as it is used only for sweetening.

Vegetable 100g/3.5oz	Calories	Carbohydrate	Protein	Other
Mashua	60-70	23-27	2.0-2.5	high vit C
Oca	30-70	10-17	0.5-1.1	high vit C*
Potato	75-100	17-26	1.8-2.5	high vit C, iron
Ulluco	70-80	14-17	2.0-2.5	med vit C
Yacon**	15-20	9-13	0.3-0.5	potassium and vit C rich

* 60% of recommended daily need from 100g serving
** Yacon data from http://cipotato.org/library/pdfdocs/RTA58114.pdf

For comparison, here are the equivalent values per 100g of other root vegetables.

Vegetable 100g/3.5oz	Calories	Carbohydrate	Protein	Other
Beetroot	35-45	7-10	1.3-1.6	7% sugar
Carrot	28-42	6-10	0.9-1.0	high vit A
Jerusalem artichoke, sunchoke	60-75	15-20	1.8-2.0	high iron
Onion	30-40	6-9	1.0-1.1	160 cal fried onion
Parsnip	65-75	12-18	1.0-1.2	high vit C

Figures from www.weightlossresources.co.uk/calories-in-food/veg/potatoes.htm and Wikipedia

Mashua (añu) (*Tropaeolum tuberosum*)

Mashua, a tuber-forming relative of the nasturtium, is a food crop in the Andes, but I wonder if it's an acquired taste, and we are still searching for preparation methods that leave you wanting more. This is a shame because it is easy to grow and gives a reasonable yield of oval shaped white tubers, each around 60g (2oz) in weight.

Opposite, clockwise from top left:

Mashua harvest in December, washed tubers, 2kg altogether from one plant

2kg oca harvest from two plants, the best yield at Homeacres

Ulluco: small harvest, great colours!

Yacon tubers uncovered for harvest, November

Flavour and eating

Eaten raw, tubers have a brassica pungency, and a texture slightly firmer than turnips. Cooked, there is a hint of ginger, and an Andean trick is to freeze them after cooking, as they are reckoned to taste better frozen!

Growing

Mashua plants climb any support offered, or crawl, and with a few together, you could grow them as ground cover – they send out new roots where stems touch the soil. If growing just one or two plants, a sturdy wigwam

Mashua in October: one plant fully grown from spring planting, not yet flowering

support keeps them compact, and is good for showing off the late autumn display of small orange flowers, which are the tastiest part to eat. The leaves are also good in salads through summer and autumn until, as with nasturtium, all surface growth is killed by frost.

Harvesting, storing

Tubers continue to swell after a slight first frost, then want harvesting before it's below -2°C (28°F). Store them, washed or unwashed, dry and cool; in any warmth and dampness the tubers are quick to send out long shoots.

At harvest time you find small, shooting buds, similar in style and placement to yacon, best kept cool, even in the fridge. At Homeacres in early winter, buds grew straight after harvest in temperatures around 10-12°C (50-54°F) with 60cm (2ft) stems by Christmas.

Growing again

The simplest method is to set aside the largest tubers, to plant direct in the spring, 5-7cm (2-3in) deep and just before last frost. Alternatively plant tubers or buds, in pots undercover in early spring, to have plants ready after spring's last frost.

Oca (*Oxalis tuberosa*)

Oxalidaceae, wood sorrel family (garden sorrel is *Polygonaceae*, *rumex*)

Oca is edible at all stages, starting in summer with the lemon-tasting leaves, and the yellow flowers are delicious too. However oxalic acid in the leaves means you cannot eat many at a time: best add them in small quantities to salad mixes and to smoothies.

The tubers have great colour, crunchy when eaten raw, tender after being cooked, with a zesty lemon flavour. Most varieties grow bright red tubers, but there are also yellow and white varieties, even bi-coloured ones. At Homeacres the red varieties give bigger harvests.

Flavour and eating

Oca is rich in zinc and potassium, and the oxalic acid is reduced by exposing tubers to sunlight after harvest. After a week on a sunny windowsill they taste noticeably sweeter. Most of the acid is in the skins, then during cooking it migrates into the flesh, so best peel before cooking if you are worried about it. Tubers are the size of an egg at best, so peeling is fiddly, and older tubers sometimes develop black patches on the surface.

Growing

First shoots appear in late winter, the best time to chit tubers in the same way as potatoes, in a mild, bright and frost free place. Keep them chitting until planting after last frost, at a depth of 7-10cm (3-4in). Or you can pot sprouting oca into small pots in a frost free place, to gain some growing time while there is still a frost risk outside.

The spreading plants need 40-52cm (15-20in) of space. Tubers develop in or just below the mulch and during late autumn many small tubers also develop along the sprawling stems, at surface level.

Harvesting, storing

Tubers develop when there is less than nine hours between sunrise and sunset, so the timing depends on your latitude. At 51°N, mid November is the earliest time for a worthwhile yield, say 450g (1lb) per plant, and this can double by early December, especially if there has been a frost, which somehow helps translocate the plants' resources into their tubers.

A drawback however is that early winter sees hungry rodents looking for food, and they like oca. Steph had similar problems with sweet potato (which swell less late but are not harvestable until mid autumn) and this emphasises the value of potatoes, which are harvested by late summer, when rodents are less interested.

You can harvest most oca tubers without any tools as they are within the surface 10cm (4in), mostly in a cluster around the central stems. Use a trowel to find the few deeper ones, often a cold job. You can save a lot of preparation time in the kitchen by rinsing tubers in a bucket of water, straight after harvest, when the soil and compost comes off most easily.

Next, spread them out on a sunny windowsill, as light as possible, to develop their sweetness. It's fascinating how the flavour improves. After a week or two they can be stored anywhere dry and frost free, preferably cool, for use until mid spring, when they sprout and are ready to grow again. For seed, set the largest and most even tubers on one side, after harvest.

Oca tubers at harvest, early December

Oca seedlings, grown from tubers planted six weeks earlier

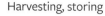

Ulluco (*Ullucus tuberosus*)

After potatoes, ulluco is the most grown root crop in Andean South America. Tubers boast a range of bright colours, taste a little like beetroot and are high in carotene, and vitamin B. The crisp flesh turns soft after roasting or boiling, and the leaves are edible.

Growing

Plants need a long growing season and prefer steady warmth without great heat, and regular moisture. Plant tubers are about the size of a small plum, which is big for ulluco! Tubers grow more numerous than large, such that a tuber-length of 5cm (2in) is unusual, and yields in our climate are far less than oca.

Plant tubers 2-5cm (1-2in) deep in 7cm (3in) pots filled with compost, and grow frost free until all risk of frost has passed. Leaves are pretty; plants are more compact than oca and grow well in containers. In autumn they do not need earthing up, even when you see tubers above ground, where they turn green but without the solanine poison of green potatoes.

Harvesting, storing

As with oca, wait as long as possible until moderate frost. Plants keep growing through autumn, so any early frosts lead to lower yields, by preventing the final phase of tuber growth. Harvest as late as you can before the first frost of say -4°C (25°F).

Ulluco total harvest from 8 plants of 0.73kg, just before frost of -7°C (19.4°F)

Homeacre's first ulluco harvest was disappointingly small, just 0.73kg (1.6lb) from 20sq.ft (1.85sq.m) of bed, after growing for the whole season. In comparison, the same area of oca yielded 2.2kg (4.85lb) and the same area of beetroot yielded 20.9kg (46lb). Furthermore, the beetroot took only a half season to give all that, from being planted after early summer cauliflowers.

Ulluco plants raised from tubers, ready to go out in late spring

Yacon (*Smallanthus sonchifolius*)
(formerly *Polymnia sonchifolia*)

Yacon, related to sunflower, has small, yellow flowers by the end of a warm summer, on its 1.5m (4-5ft) stems. The flowers set seeds only if they are not rained on, but it's straightforward to grow next year's crop from either tubers or buds.

By mid autumn the pale, oval tubers are large, and a zone 8/9 harvest can be 3-6kg (6-13lb) per plant, even higher if they have more space.

Flavour and eating

Nicknames such as 'Peruvian ground apple' refer to the refreshing sweetness: the tubers' brix of 9-13 compares favourably with Sungold tomatoes' 9-10. See below for the curing process to increase this sweet taste.

The sweetness does not come from the usual glucose or fructose, but from fructo-oligosaccharides (FOS), almost the same molecule as inulin which is present in Jerusalem artichokes, and both are difficult to digest, although yacon causes little flatulence after it is cured in sunlight.

Instead of raising blood sugar, this sweetness has beneficial effects such as decreasing the liver's production of glucose, and lowering glucose-fasting levels in the blood. Yacon's high content of potassium is linked to reductions in blood pressure; it generally aids digestion and may lead to loss of weight, when eaten regularly.

Slice tubers into salads, or roast them, or cook in a stir fry, where yacon absorbs flavours but keeps a crunchy texture. Leaves are good as a wrap.

Growing

Plants grow either from buds kept alive through winter, or from tubers potted into compost in a frost free place. You can start them on windowsills but they easily grow large in the warmth of a house, then need potting on. Set out after the last ground frost, following which there is no special care except for staking in late summer, if your garden is exposed to wind.

Harvesting

Tubers develop strongly after the equinox and continue to grow after any slight frost blackens the leaves. Hence the harvest window is as late as possible after the first slight frost, and before any moderate frost.

Gently wash tubers at harvest and then treat as oca, placing them in light for a week. This brings out the sweetness, caused by compositional changes to the FOS. In appearance tubers change from a pale, creamy colour to reddish brown, always with white flesh.

Store in paper bags or sacks in a cool, dry place. Tubers shrink a little but their flesh stays crisp all winter, and contributes to a lovely fresh-tasting salad when that is a rare commodity, or extra sweetness in a tray of roasted vegetables.

New plants – plan ahead

Growing new plants for spring starts way back at harvest time, when you notice new shoots (buds) on the main stem, just above the tubers. Some of these conveniently snap off; others need cutting. Aim to keep any buds the size a small plum or bigger, on which you can see a pointy end with even a shoot already developing. One plant may give as many as 15 buds.

Put the buds together in a large pot, covered by damp but not soggy compost, to keep over winter, frost and rodent free. Tip the pot out in early spring when the buds should be growing bright shoots. Each one can have its own pot of compost, to grow into a plant for setting out after frost.

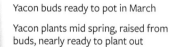

Yacon buds ready to pot in March

Yacon plants mid spring, raised from buds, nearly ready to plant out

Yacon plants (and little yellow flower) after slight frost; oca is bottom left

yacon

Stevia (*Stevia rebaudiana*)

A homegrown, no-calorie sweetener. Stevia is in the huge family of Asteraceae, distantly related to lettuce and dandelion. Most of the plant is leaf, on stems 1.2-1.5m (4-5ft) high, and yields can be impressive in hot summers. In Japan, stevia accounts for 40% of all sweeteners used.

Growth is best undercover in zones 8/9 or less.

Flavour, eating

One or two teaspoons of green stevia powder, made from dried leaves, gives the sweetness of a whole cup of sugar. The sweet glycosides contain no carbohydrates. You can use the leaves fresh too, for example just three or four in a smoothie. Larger amounts mean more aftertaste of liquorice and other flavours, which are not to everybody's liking.

The stevia you buy is refined (usually a white powder) and has little or none of the bitterness found in leaves. Studies into the health benefits and possible problems of stevia use the extracts, so if you consume stevia as green leaf, its effects on your body may be different.

Growing and preserving stevia

Sow in late winter in warmth of 18-27°C (65-80°F), and always frost free. Aim to have plants 7-10cm (3-4in) high by May, then plant at 45cm (18in) apart. By July you should have plants of a fair size, whose stems may need to be loosely tied around a stake.

Harvest leaves from mid summer onwards, little and often, and/or make a main harvest in early autumn, before flowering is too prevalent. Strip all leaves off the stems and dry for four hours at around 50°C (120°F) in a dehydrator, or slow oven. Sun drying is possible undercover, such as on a sunny windowsill over a few days.

Once leaves are completely dry, they easily crumble into a powder to store in jars. To make a very fine stevia powder, grind in a nut or coffee grinder. Our best harvest from two-year-old plants in a polytunnel gave three honey jars of 80g dry powder each. Multiplying by 300 gives an equivalent of 24kg (53lb) sugar, or 8kg (18lb) per plant!

Growing again

Stevia plants tolerate slight frost and are perennial. In areas of frosty winter you can dig them out in mid autumn, trim off most branches and side roots, to place the main root cluster and length of main stem in a pot of compost, undercover and frost free. At Homeacres they survive winter on the windowsill of a conservatory, next to chilli plants, to transplant outside in late spring.

Two-year-old stevia plant, about to be planted

Stevia harvest: three plants from the polytunnel

Overwintered stevia plant (sown previous spring) in the conservatory

Further ideas

There are other unusual crops you can attempt. Before trying, check this:

- Are there enough indications that I shall enjoy eating this food?
- Is the climate right to give a reasonable yield for the time and space needed?

Dahlia for tubers (*Dahlia* hybrid)

While the flowers are widely esteemed, some varieties are also recommended for eating their tubers. Even in Europe they were commonly eaten in the sixteenth century.

We have eaten dahlia tubers several times and are yet to be impressed: the flavour is faint and they can be fibrous to stringy. However varieties such as 'Black Jack' are reckoned to be more tender and tasty. Sow seeds undercover in early spring, or plant tubers in late spring after frost, for harvest in autumn to early winter, before moderate frost.

Sweet potato (*Ipomoea batatas*)

These plants need heat, there are no two ways about it. In a temperate zone 7-9 climate, summers are too cool for a worthwhile yield. Even in a hotter than average summer, we struggle to harvest more than 1lb (0.5kg) per plant, from a whole season's growth. And unlike potatoes you need cooler weather for tubers to swell, pushing the harvest window to mid autumn, and at risk of rodents.

Tomatillo (*Physalis philadelphica*)

Native to Mexico, great for salsa and easy to grow; however to eat on their own, they are rather acidic and pungent: although related to cape gooseberries, they are less sweet. Harvests in temperate climates are late summer to early autumn when it is often damp, and slugs enjoy fruits at ground level.

To discover which tomatilloes are ripe, you need to feel them from underneath to check that the paper-like husks are filled out and the flesh is softening, sometimes colouring a pale yellow or purple too, depending on the variety.

Tomatilloes, many ready, in early autumn

Flowers of edible dahlia; this plant yielded 1.35kg tubers in late summer

One plant of dahlia tubers yielded 1.35kg

Chapter 20
Selling, Trading

When you enjoy growing vegetables, fruit and flowers, and sell them for a living, you are living the dream. Or are you?

The relative price of food keeps slipping downwards compared to other commodities one needs, such as housing, travel, insurance, water and almost any financial interaction with the outside world.

Food is cheap now, not always in stores, but in prices paid to growers and relative to other prices. By comparison in the 1950s, a local farmer bought a car from his profits of selling the eggs of just 20 hens during one year.*

However there are ways and means to sell and trade for some profit.

Harvests of early summer
sell easily

* www.tradingeconomics.com/united-kingdom/housing-index

Is it worthwhile?

Count or weigh how many vegetables you harvest in an hour, multiply by your selling price and see your hourly wage. Simple, but it's not true earnings, because you need to factor in all the costs of growing.

Calculate true earnings

It's a sobering calculation when you add the cost of time and materials spent in growing, including charges for rent, packaging, water, and so forth. Also the costs of delivering, and of time spent selling at market.

To allow for these expenses, growers use a rule of three: divide gross earnings by three to discover your true wage. To pay yourself £10 for an hour for harvesting carrots, you need to pick £30 of saleable carrots in one hour. That includes time spent grading out any rejects, and at average British wholesale prices of 66p/kg (30p/lb) for washed carrots, you need to pick and clean 45kg (100lb) saleable carrots per hour. That is more carrots than most gardeners grow in a whole year.

Or to increase earnings you could sell them as bunched carrots, say at a roadside stall, perhaps for £1.50 each with 0.4kg (1lb) in a bunch. At this price, you could earn the net £10 by harvesting 'only' 20 bunches in an hour, which is possible, allowing for time to wash and pack them. However this is retail price so it involves maintenance of an outlet.

When selling to a shop or restaurant, you receive wholesale prices, around two thirds of the retail price. This means picking 30 bunches per hour for a wholesale price of £1.

Continuity of cropping

Selling is often more difficult because your glut probably coincides with everyone else's. You have a surplus to shift and need to find a buyer, who almost certainly has regular suppliers already, and in periods of glut, the price is falling even while you are picking. Produce is perishable and cannot be stored to sell later, except for what you can preserve; see Chapter 10.

To earn more than occasional pocket money, and to sell reliably without hassle, you need commitments at both ends:

- A regular supply of any product that customers need all the time. Find out what vegetables fit this description, then check that they are profitable to grow.
- Regular buyers who 'buy into' a trading relationship because they know that you offer produce of a consistent quality, reliably and regularly.

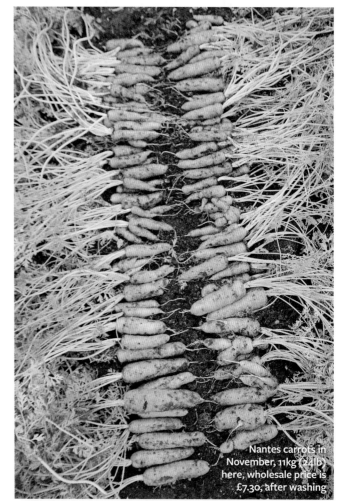

Nantes carrots in November, 11kg (24lb) here, wholesale price is £7.30, after washing

Purple Haze and Rainbow carrots, five bunches for £7.50

Harvesting speed is helped by good growing. For example when carrots are reasonably even, from consistent spacing, and sowing in good conditions, are mostly unblemished by pests, and are a decent size from good soil fertility, you can make a small profit.

Salad mix for sale in October,
washed and ready to bag, £45
value per crate

Early autumn, greenhouse
seedlings to plant for
winter salad leaves

Which crops

In much of the UK, almost the only garden output to pay a wage is salad leaves, thanks to customers' perception of them as a ready meal. By weight, washed and mixed leaves in a bag sell for 10-20 times the price of carrots. Furthermore salad plants grow again after harvesting, unlike carrots, so growing costs are lower. And they store for a limited time, so customers need a regular supply. Plenty to like there and your wage is respectable when everything goes well, although it's still at a level where you won't pay the mortgage.

Other vegetables in the economically worthwhile category are almost all leaves, thanks to their continuous cropping of the same plants. Spinach, chard, kale and herbs are good, when you have local buyers.

Fruiting vegetables offer many harvests but tend to sell at lower prices. Should you find high paying buyers, then it's just worth growing courgettes (zucchinis), tomatoes and runner (pole) beans. Cucumbers are often a profitable crop, but French beans less so in Europe due to African imports. They sell at a low price because the growers pay relatively little, in European terms, to their pickers and packers, which is the main cost of beans and many other vegetables.

Jupiter tree full of apples, may be saleable for £30 locally, with careful picking

Price problems

Some crops are lamentably unprofitable for selling at wholesale prices – apples for example have barely increased in price for 30 years. Large growers have become incredibly efficient, and use a precise amount of pesticides, fungicides and herbicides to produce apples with a visual quality that customers have come to expect. The price of apples is now incredibly low compared to other products and services.

Organic growers then find that their sale price of many fruits is brought down, because in the customer's mind there is a comparison to the perfect-looking, cheap, chemical apples. Even the most organically minded customer baulks at paying more than a particular level of premium, and when the base level price is as low as it is, even a 50% premium is 50% added to not much. You need to be a really good orchardist to make a profit selling organic fruit.

Pricing

It's difficult to put a value on what you have grown, but it's worth working out along the lines of the carrot example above. For a comparison, supermarkets usually sell fresh produce at the high end of a price range, so use their prices as a baseline and go up to 50% higher; this should keep customers happy. Sometimes this price approaches the cost of growing.

Freshness is worth emphasising because you can do that better than wholesalers and importers. Fresh-pulled carrots have a unique flavour and justify a 50% price increase over other supplies, and you need to persuade the buyer of that. Other vegetables in this category include tomatoes ripened on the vine, soft skinned tomato varieties that don't travel, all salad leaves, green garlic and bunches of beetroot in early summer.

Selling professionally

Strive to be first with whatever vegetable or fruit you want to sell plenty of. Having produce early in its season establishes your presence to the customer, and makes it easier to sell than produce in the main part of a season when others are offering the same.

Always maintain an ongoing and uninterrupted supply. Any week of sudden dearth can see you lose customers fast. It's far better to have small unsaleable surpluses, even for the compost heap, than to have a week with no offering.

Selling a small surplus

For domestic gardeners in the UK, selling your excess vegetables to the neighbourhood – via a small stall at the end of your drive with an 'honesty box', for example – is not considered running a business by tax authorities. Spare produce, cut flowers, plants, seedlings, bundles of pea sticks and homemade preserves sold from your garden or occasionally via a car boot sale, local country markets, etc. can boost your budget, and pay for seeds, compost and other gardening needs.

Charles stacking shelves with his fresh veg in the local wholefood store

May harvest of spring onions sell for 80p per bunch, small surplus to sell/trade

Charles showing Homeacres garden to a visiting permaculture group

Trading

This is an opportunity for fair exchange without money changing hands. It's an informal cashless system; trade with friends, local businesses and the wider community for resources, services or skills you need. Many communities are opening up skill sharing facilities which enable local people to offer their surpluses, skills and time, in return for commodities and services they need.

Another word for it is bartering, one of the earliest forms of trade. It's an empowering, creative opportunity to exchange with others outside of the monetary system, enabling a human-scale interaction which promotes community and equality.

Collaborating in this way not only helps to survive economically, it creates a circle of giving and closer, more inclusive communities. It can be the opportunity to learn new skills, extend friendships and find greater happiness and wellbeing.

Look out for Local Exchange Trading systems (LETs). In a similar vein, some allotments and community gardens have a trading area where people can leave excess produce, seeds, books and gardening equipment. This can be 'help yourself' or with an arrangement.

TRADING EXAMPLES

Trade surplus with a local pub/ restaurant for meals/drinks

Gardening advice for firewood

Box of seasonal vegetables for a yoga class or massage

Selling or swapping homegrown seeds with other gardeners

Gift economy

This is the opportunity to share your bounty with others, either by offering excess produce free at your garden gate, or for example by donating it to a 'community larder' project, whence it goes to those in need.

There are various initiatives online, some with apps, which connect people and businesses who offer surpluses with those who have a need, for example Olio.

Finances

During the more abundant months, it is a good idea to get into a rhythm of putting some of your income aside in a savings account each week, to help with the lower wintertime income, as well as saving towards NI and tax payments.

Stacking by teaching

There are teachers and writers who base their output on the teachings and writings of others, akin to Chinese whispers. Assumptions and mistakes creep in and increase with telling. To be a good garden writer and teacher, you need a garden.

Homeacres garden does not earn a living from sales of produce, but it helps to sell the more profitable courses and writing. It demonstrates an ever changing plot of seasonal food and flowers, responding to weather and markets, plus the trials of different growing methods.

The garden's success is testament to the wonderful results of Charles' no dig techniques. Plus it shows the value of many other skills which make it easier and quicker to grow and sell vegetables, such as picking the outer leaves of lettuce.

There are many other ways of adding value to growing. They include designing and creating edible gardens for clients, making and selling arts and crafts, blogging, photography and making food to sell – preserves, bread, cakes. At open days, Steph's parsnip cake is always the first to disappear...

Bibliography

Around the World in 80 Plants: An edible perennial vegetable adventure for temperate climates
Stephen Barstow, Permanent Publications, 2014.
A guide across the world's edible perennial vegetables with a sprinkling of recipes.

The Art of Fermentation
Sandor Ellis Katz, Chelsea Green Publishing, 2012.
A huge amount of information with recipes covering all aspects of fermentation.

Back Garden Seed Saving: Keeping our vegetable heritage alive
Sue Stickland, eco-logic books, 2008.
Concise advice on how to save seeds in the garden from many common vegetables.

Ball Complete Book of Home Preserving
Judi Kingry and Lauren Devine, Robert Rose Inc, 2006.
An American preserving book, a good introduction to a wide range of preserving techniques and recipes.

Charles Dowding's Vegetable Course
Charles Dowding, Frances Lincoln, 2012, eBook only.
Covers all aspects of growing with an emphasis on starting out, chapters on weed identification too.

Charles Dowding's Gardening Calendar
www.charlesdowding.co.uk/product/charles-dowding-gardening-calendar-2018
A veg growing summary for each month, plus Charles' favourite sowing dates for each vegetable, based on decades of fine tuning. A4 opening to A3, with 29 pages of both advice and photos from his beautiful vegetable garden.

Creating a Forest Garden: Working with Nature to Grow Edible Crops
Martin Crawford, Green Books, 2010.
A huge range of useful information, looking at the principles of forest gardening as well as a wealth of detail, stunning photos.

Edible Perennial Gardening: Growing Successful Polycultures in Small Spaces
Anni Kelsey, Permanent Publications, 2014.
How to create a low maintenance edible perennial garden in whatever space you have.

Forest Gardening in Practice: An Illustrated Practical Guide for Homes, Communities and Enterprises
Tomas Remiarz, Permanent Publications, 2017.
A guide to creating your own forest garden, with in-depth case studies from around the world.

Gardening and Planting by the Moon
Nick Kollerstrom, Quantum, published annually.
Plenty of useful advice in the introduction and advice on many aspects of moon gardening.

Gardening Myths and Misconceptions
Charles Dowding, Green Books, 2014.
Aimed at saving the reader's time and money, explaining the labour- and resource-demanding misunderstandings which are still common.

Homemade Country Wines, Beer, Mead and Metheglin
Compiled by Dorothy Wise, Hamlyn, 1976.
The first home brew book Steph owned and still the one she refer to the most.

Homemade Wines, Syrups and Cordials
ed. F. W. Beech, Women's Institute, 1954.
An interesting collection of recipes.

Hot Beds: How to Grow Early Crops Using an Age-old Technique
Jack First, Green Books, 2013.
How to make and sow hotbeds for early crops, lots of practical advice based on long experience.

How to Grow Perennial Vegetables: Low-maintenance, Low-Impact Vegetable Gardening
Martin Crawford, Green Books, 2012.
Wide ranging subject matter, lots of good ideas and plenty of information on lesser-known, edible perennials.

How to Grow Winter Vegetables
Charles Dowding, Green Books, 2011.
For food all year round, this book actually covers much of the year, from sowing in spring to harvesting in the hungry gap of spring!

How to Make a Forest Garden
Patrick Whitefield, Permanent Publications, 1996, 3rd edition 2012.
A step-by-step guide to creating a 'maximum output for minimum labour' food producing garden, designed using the ecological principles of a natural woodland.

Jekka's Complete Herb Book
Jekka McVicar, Sino Publishing, 1997.
A well illustrated reference book for growing and using herbs.

The Maria Thun Biodynamic Calendar
Matthias Thun, Floris Books, published annually.
One of many calendars, this one concentrates on moon-constellation relationships.

Organic Gardening: The Natural, No-dig Way
Charles Dowding, Green Books, 2007, 3rd edition, 2013.
Bestseller in its third edition, covers most vegetables and some fruit too, with a first part that many readers say is like reading a novel, a bedtime book!

The Polytunnel Book: Fruit and Vegetables all Year Round
Joyce and Ben Russell, Frances Lincoln, 2011.
Advice on growing undercover, from an experienced couple.

The RHS Encyclopedia of Herbs and their Uses
Deni Brown, Dorling Kindersley, 1995.
Growing and using herbs including varieties from all over the world.

Salad Leaves for All Seasons: Organic Growing from Pot to Plot
Charles Dowding, Green Books, 2008.
A wealth of salad leaves explained, showing how you can grow more successfully when adapting your sowings to each season.

Teaming with Microbes: The Organic Gardener's Guide to the Soil Food Web
Jeff Lowenfels and Wayne Lewis, Timber Press, 2006, revised edition 2010.
An excellent explanation of soil life; in fact this book brings the subject matter alive too and will enthuse you.

Which Gardening? magazine
www.which.co.uk/magazine/gardening
Information and research into latest trends and proprietary products such as composts, tools and seeds.

Wild Fruits, Berries, Nuts and Flowers: 101 Good Recipes for Using Them
B. James, M.C.A. Medici, 1942.
More of a pamphlet than a book, I found this fascinating collection of recipes in a jumble sale.

Winter Harvest Handbook: Year-round Vegetable Production Using Deep-organic Techniques and Unheated Greenhouses
Eliot Coleman, Chelsea Green, 2009
The genuinely practicable, tried and tested concepts described are brilliantly simple, but the results and glorious colour photos are utterly inspiring.

Websites

www.nodighome.com
Stephanie's blog, including posts about gardening, making potions, recipes and small scale homesteading in her garden and allotment.

www.stephaniehafferty.co.uk
Information on Stephanie's workshops, courses and talks.

www.charlesdowding.co.uk
Information on no dig, seasonal updates on vegetable growing, dates of and booking on courses at Homeacres, dates of open days, purchase of books by Charles.

Suppliers

Delfland Nurseries Ltd
Benwich Road, Doddington, March, Cambridgeshire
PE15 0TU
Tel. 01354 740 553
www.organicplants.co.uk
A range of organic plants available at all seasons.

Ferryman Polytunnels Ltd
Westleigh, Morchard Road, near Crediton, Devon EX17 5LS
01363 84948
www.ferrymanpolytunnels.co.uk
A range of polytunnels for sale, with installation on request.

Franchi Seeds
Available in the UK from: Seeds of Italy, D2 Phoenix Business
Centre, Rosslyn Crescent, Harrow, Middlesex HA1 2SP
Tel. 020 8427 5020
www.seedsofitaly.com
Italian specialities such as tomato, chicory, endive and
Florence fennel, and good-sized packets of most other
vegetable seeds.

Implementations
PO Box 2568, Nuneaton CV10 9YR
Tel. 0845 330 3148
www.implementations.co.uk
Copper tools of quality and durability.

LBS Horticulture Ltd
Standroyd Mill, Cottontree, Colne, Lancashire BB8 7BW
Tel. 01282 873 370
www.lbsbuyersguide.co.uk
A good-value range of useful accessories, including netting,
mesh, fleece, plug/module trays and polytunnels.

Naturally Balmy
www.naturallybalmy.co.uk
For a wide range of vegan waxes, beeswax, butters, oils and
other ingredients for making natural skincare.

The Organic Gardening Catalogue
Riverdene, Molesey Road, Hersham, Surrey KT12 4RG
Tel. 01932 253 666
www.organiccatalogue.com
An extensive range of seeds and sundries.

REMIN (Scotland) Ltd
Burnhead, Raemoir, Banchory, Aberdeenshire AB31 4EB
T. 01330 820 914 and 07715 707 009
jennifer@reminscotland.com
www.reminscotland.com
Basalt rockdust in sacks or by the tonne.

The Real Seed Catalogue
PO Box 18, Newport, near Fishguard, Pembrokeshire
SA65 0AA
Tel. 01239 821 107
www.realseeds.co.uk
A range of good, homegrown seeds and also advice on seed
saving.

West Riding Organics Ltd
Halifax Road, Littleborough, Lancashire OL15 0LF
Tel. 01706 379 944
www.westridingorganics.co.uk
Potting composts based on peat sieved out of reservoirs.

Wiggly Wigglers, Lower Blakemere Farm, Blakemere,
Herefordshire HR2 9PX
Tel: 01981 500 391
www.wigglywigglers.co.uk
Suppliers of worms, other farm-sourced products and
diatomaceous earth.

Appendix

Month naming, numbering, descriptions

Month	Number	Season
January	1	Midwinter
February	2	Late winter
March	3	Early spring
April	4	Mid spring
May	5	Late spring
June	6	Early summer
July	7	Midsummer*
August	8	Late summer
September	9	Early autumn
October	10	Mid autumn
November	11	Late autumn
December	12	Early winter

* In contrast, 'midsummer's day' is 24th June

Quarter days

Spring equinox, March 20
Summer solstice, June 20-21
Autumn equinox, September 22-23
Winter solstice, December 21-22

Preserving weights

Preserving weights make sure that herbs, flowers and other ingredients remain submerged in the liquid. You can buy special glass weights – homemade alternatives are glass lids from smaller preserving jars or, my favourite, carefully chosen and washed flattish stones from the garden.

How to make a light reflector for indoor growing

A reflector made from card and foil helps to increase the available light and reduces legginess. Mirrors or other glass reflectors are not a good idea as strong reflected light can frazzle the young plants and if it is particularly sunny, can pose a fire risk.

You need sturdy cardboard (from a packing box or similar), aluminium foil and glue, or sticky tape. Cardboard is excellent because it is free and can be cut to whatever size you need (and the scraps can be composted or recycled). Cover one side of the cardboard with the foil, smoothing it out for maximum shininess, fold the foil over onto the back neatly and tape or glue to fix. You may need several of these for your window growing space, depending how large your pieces of cardboard are. Either use one long piece, with either end folded in 15-20cm so that it can stand upright, or two shorter pieces, each with one end folded and then overlapped in the middle, fastening with paper clips or tape if you want greater stability. These will last for many years (don't get them wet!) – any tears in the foil can be fixed with clear tape to extend the life.

Tip: You can make reflectors for your radiators to reflect heat back into your room, reducing bills, in the same way – cut the card to size to fit between the wall fastening of the radiator, cover with foil and slide into place.

Index